Contents

But you, who are wise, must know that different nations have different conceptions of things and will therefore not take it amiss, if our ideas of this kind of education happen not to be the same as yours. We have had some experience of it. Several of our young people were formerly brought up at the colleges of the northern provinces: they were instructed in all your sciences; but, when they came back to us, they were bad runners, ignorant of every means of living in the woods ... neither fit for hunters, warriors, nor councillors, they were totally good for nothing.

We are, however, not the less obliged by your kind offer, though we decline accepting it; and, to show our grateful sense of it, if the gentlemen of Virginia will send us a dozen of their sons we will take care of their education, instruct them in all we know, and make men of them.

— Response of the Indians of the Six Nations to a suggestion that they send boys to an American college, Pennsylvania, 1744.

Part One
Thinking about Majority/Minority Issues

1 Beginning to Map the Issues

Who this resource book is for

This resource book is intended for the use of teachers in secondary education, further education and teacher education. It provides ideas, materials and support for a wide range of situations: these range from specific subject areas such as Social Studies, Geography, Modern History, English, Moral Education, Sociology and General Studies to the wider fields of multi-ethnic education, development education, social education and political education.

What this resource book is about

The central theme of this book is the crucial role of majority/minority issues in the world today and the need for students to understand the nature of such issues. It is thus about discrimination against ethnic, cultural and religious minorities and the perspectives that the minority experience engenders. It is also about the mechanisms by which dominant groups attempt to keep particular minority groups on the periphery of society. The view explored here is that minorities are not in themselves a problem, but rather that the problem often lies in the way in which the minority is perceived by the dominant group in society. It is thus more appropriate to talk about majority/minority issues rather than 'minority problems' for the focus of attention then becomes the attitudes and values of the dominant group and the way in which the society is structured. Accordingly the book explores issues

of culture, of rights and the distribution of power, all of which are generally embodied in majority/minority issues whether overtly or hidden beneath the surface.

Most societies today are multi-ethnic in nature — that is to say they are made up of diverse groups with differing, although sometimes overlapping, cultural backgrounds and expectations. In the United States for example one needs to consider, amongst several other groups, the role of Native Americans (Indians), Chicanos (Mexican Americans) and Asian Americans in society. Similarly in the UK diverse cultural backgrounds are manifested in the presence of Indian, Chinese, Cypriot and Black communities to name only a few.

Although the book does not focus directly on the multi-ethnic classroom as such, teachers involved in multi-ethnic education will find much of use here since the book attempts to relate some of the dilemmas of such classrooms to the broader context of majority/minority issues in the world today. Equally teachers working in areas where the plural nature of society is not readily apparent will also find much of use as the need for a multi-ethnic curriculum at all levels of education is increasingly being recognized.

The resources offered here range from theoretical considerations of the nature of majority/minority issues to practical examples of materials for classroom use. Part One explores the nature and scope of majority/minority issues and considers why and how they fit into the school curriculum. In Part Two will be found case studies of particular majority/ minority issues together with suggestions on how they might be used in the classroom. Examples are given from different schools of particular curriculum developments in this field. Part Three includes a detailed resource section, ideas on evaluating teaching materials and describes some current projects relevant to a consideration of majority/ minority themes.

Why teach about minority rights?

Why teach in school or teacher education about the problems facing minority groups when they are often complicated and seem, almost by definition, peripheral to the interests of most students? The study of majority/minority issues is already part of many existing curricula and could make an important contribution to many more. A variety of reasons can be given for the inclusion of such studies, some of which are set out below.[1] They are not intended to be in any order of importance neither are they mutually exclusive.

(a) *The importance of rights*

The concept of human rights and freedoms is increasingly recognized as fundamental to the functioning of a just world. Civil, political, social, economic and cultural rights need constantly to be fought for and guarded. Many minority groups, as well as other groups, will find that their rights are restricted and circumscribed in indirect as well as direct ways. The ways in which this can happen need to be studied and analysed.

(b) *Living in a plural society*

The history of a country like Britain records the arrival of many groups from the Romans, Saxons, Danes and Normans to the Irish, Chinese, West Indian and Asian. There are thus many minority groups within most societies and the consequent cultural diversity is something that students need to be aware of and can themselves benefit from. Whether in an area where minorities live or not, the school or college curriculum needs to reflect the plural nature of society. If it does not then it fails to reflect reality.

(c) *Understanding majority attitudes*

As soon as one begins to look at the nature of majority/minority issues it becomes clear that, whilst many minorities are far from faultless, it may be more appropriate to look at the problems presented by entrenched attitudes amongst the majority, rather than looking upon the minority itself as the problem. We are all aware of the need to identify with a particular group, but often less aware of the ways in which intergroup perception leads to prejudice, stereotyping, scapegoating and discrimination. An exploration of these themes in the classroom context can enable students to understand more fully not only situations that they may find themselves in, but also situations in other parts of the world.

(d) *Countering racism*

Racist attitudes which deny a group access to its full potential are not only damaging to the identity and self-image of members of that group, they are damaging to all concerned. The activities of the National Front may only affect directly a relatively small number of schools, but the crude perspective of that and similar bodies is all too easily available in times of stress. Attitudes and assumptions engendered in Britain's colonial past are very much with us today and provide easy explanations. Nor is it merely a question of attitudes, for discrimination against minority groups in housing, employment and education is still widespread today as many reports have shown.

(e) *Making sense of the news*

One task of education must be to help students make sense of the news. An informed adult needs to be able to interpret the events that are constantly happening, whether in one's own society or, equally important, elsewhere in the world. This must include knowledge about one's own culture, history, social structure and political institutions, as well as those of other groups and societies. The Middle East, Namibia, Cyprus, Northern Ireland, 'race relations' in the UK – majority/minority issues are always in, or not far from, the headlines.

(f) *Coping with change and conflict*

Since one of the few constants in the latter part of the twentieth century is change itself, learning to

MINORITIES

A Teacher's Resource Book for the Multi-ethnic Curriculum

David W. Hicks

Coláiste Oideachais Mhuire Gan Smal

Luimneach

HEB

Heinemann Educational Books

Acknowledgements

Heinemann Educational Books Ltd
Halley Court, Jordan Hill, Oxford OX2 8EJ

OXFORD   LONDON   EDINBURGH   MELBOURNE
SYDNEY   AUCKLAND   SINGAPORE   MADRID
IBADAN   NAIROBI   GABORONE   HARARE
KINGSTON   PORTSMOUTH (NH)

First published 1981
Reprinted with amendments 1982
Reprinted 1988

British Library Cataloguing in Publication Data

Hicks, David W.
  Minorities.
  1. Minorities – Study and teaching (Secondary)
  I. Title
  301.45′07′12   HM131
  ISBN 0-435-80416-2

Many people have aided in the gestation of this resource book. Thanks must go first to the Leverhulme Trust Fund who financed my initial work as Education Officer for the Minority Rights Group when all the groundwork was done. Thanks must also go to Ben Whitaker, Director at the Minority Rights Group, for giving me the freedom to write the book in my own way and to Georgina Ashworth, until recently Assistant Director, for all her thoughtful encouragement. Several educational publishers were kind enough to supply me with books on minority groups, and many people from the various organizations listed in chapter 11 were enormously helpful. My thanks go to Chris Power, David Selby, Scilla Alvarado and Steve Harrison for the important contributions to chapter 7. Last, but by no means least, I must warmly thank Rob Aspeslagh, Annie Hedge, Andrew Hutchinson and Robin Richardson for their sound advice and unfailing support.

The author and publishers wish to thank all those who have given permission to reproduce extracts, both those who are acknowledged in the sources and in the notes and references. Acknowledgement must also be made to the following:
British Library Newspaper Library for Extracts 4.1, 7.1 and 10.1. International Development Action for Fig. 5.1.

Printed in Great Britain by J. W. Arrowsmith Ltd, Bristol

cope with change is a necessary requirement for survival in society. Since minority claims often upset the *status quo* as set by the dominant group, they produce change and therefore often anxiety on both sides. A study of such situations can shed light on the mechanisms of both peace and conflict. Learning to share power in such situations may well be a prerequisite for the future survival of society.

(g) *Acting to change society*

If there is to be more justice for religious, ethnic and cultural minorities then students need to see that this is desirable and have the knowledge and skills relevant to the creation of a more just society. Changing attitudes and providing a multi-ethnic curriculum will not, on their own, change the position of a minority that is exploited and oppressed by the very structures of that society. It may be necessary therefore to consider what a vision of the just society involves and engage in action for change towards that goal.

(h) *Acting to change oneself*

A major aspect of the self-development and fulfilment of students lies in learning, through personal change, to respect the right of others to equal fulfilment. This must take place not only in the classroom context but in the local, national and global communities as well. A vital part of such an understanding will be making the behaviour and beliefs of other groups, including minority groups, understandable from the perspectives of those involved. Gaining the ability to empathize with others provides an important reason for teaching about majority/minority issues, for only out of real empathy can understanding come and thereby a commitment to social justice.

What might one teach?

Of the many types of minority grouping found in societies this handbook is largely concerned with ethnic, religious and cultural minorities. Amongst these one might therefore include groups such as gypsies and other travelling people, the Basques, the Untouchables of India, Native Americans, migrant workers, the Palestinians and Black Australians. In some cases a group may not actually form a numerical minority in a particular situation, but nevertheless have all the characteristics of a marginalized minority because of its powerlessness. The black populations of Namibia and South Africa would be a case in point. In a different context, although not statistically a minority, women often share many of the characteristics of a minority group in the discrimination that they have to face in male dominated societies.

Most students will probably instinctively look at issues from a majority viewpoint which identifies the minority as *being* the problem. This, of course, is only to blame the victims for their own oppression. The view explored here is that it is not generally the disadvantaged minorities in a society that constitute, say, a 'race problem', but rather that it is the perception of the dominant group that is nearer to the real problem. Thus already existing deficiencies in a society — for example in housing, employment and education — are highlighted by the presence of marginalized minority groups. We must remember, too, that minority groups are made up of individual human beings like ourselves.

A course of study about majority/minority issues, or even a few lessons, could appropriately be based around four questions. What are the problems faced by minority groups? What is the background to these problems? What is being done about these problems? How does this relate to the sort of society that we might want to move towards? These questions could be used to draw a 'map' of the issues as in Fig. 1.1. It is in no way intended to be definitive and should be redrawn in the light of experience.[2]

A map of the issues

As Fig. 1.1 indicates, all four questions are closely interrelated. They can be summarized by the key words — Problems, Background, Values, Action — all of which influence, and are in turn influenced by, each other.

Problems

The particular problems that minority groups face may vary in detail according to circumstances but broad patterns can be discerned. First one might identify the general climate of *prejudice* that surrounds majority/minority relationships, a climate

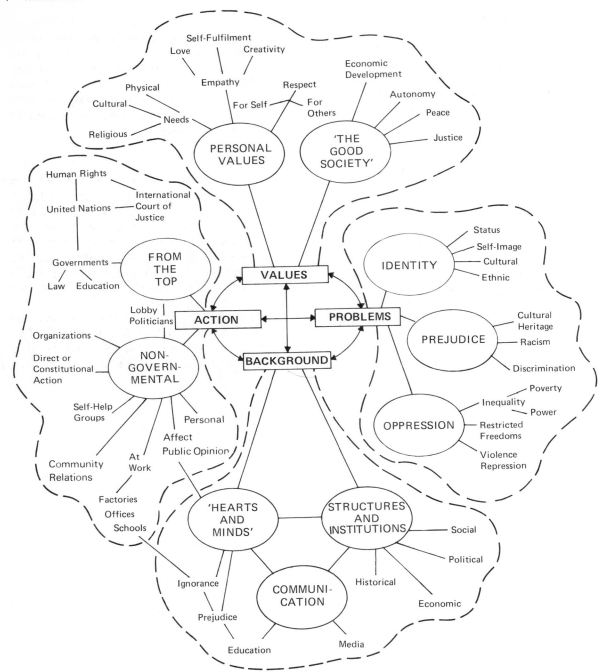

Fig. 1.1   Majority/minority relationships: a map of the issues

NOTE: I am greatly indebted to Robin Richardson, until recently Director of the World Studies Project, who first developed this matrix. He describes this and other approaches to course design in 'Studying World Society', *New Era*, 58 (6), 1977, pp. 175–84.

in which discrimination may flourish as a result of racist attitudes that arise out of the cultural patterns of the dominant group. On an objective level this may encourage various forms of *oppression* ranging from inequalities over access to resources and political power to restricted freedoms, violence and overt repression. On a subjective level this often threatens the *identity* of the minority group and the identity of its members through loss of status, undermining of cultural and ethnic identity, and a lowering of self-image.

Background

No problem can be understood without reference to, and study of, its background. This will relate particularly to the *structures and institutions* of a society, both historical and economic as well as social and political. It will also relate to the *'hearts and minds'* of the people, that is the way in which individuals are kept in ignorance and succumb to prejudice. Linking the structures and people together is the whole field of *communication* in its broadest sense, involving both formal and informal education and the various channels of the media.

Values

Values have potentially three aspects: they affect how people see a problem in the first place; how they analyse the causes; and what action for change they may consider. This will involve both *personal values* and whatever images of *'the good society'* one may have, which in turn will have been influenced by cultural and ethnic background.

Action

Action to solve problems, whether short-term or long-term, can be initiated either *from the top* or from below at *non-governmental* level. The former will relate to international action on human rights and government directives nationally for example. The latter relates to community relations, self-help groups, organizations such as the Minority Rights Group or Amnesty International, as well as initiatives at work and in school.

The map in Fig. 1.1 by no means exhausts the possibilities. It is a rough draft of how some of the issues may be seen and how they may be inter-related. Like all maps it needs to be redrawn as the ground is further explored.

2 The Minority Experience

Minorities: some definitions

An understanding of what has been called the 'minority experience' necessitates some prior consideration of definitions. What exactly *is* a minority group? Is it merely a question of statistics – a group that is numerically in the minority – or does it involve other characteristics? Wirth has suggested that:

> We may define a minority group as a group of people who, because of their physical or cultural characteristics, are singled out from others in the society in which they live for differential and unequal treatment, and who therefore regard themselves as objects of collective discrimination. The existence of a minority in a society implies the existence of a corresponding dominant group enjoying higher social status and greater privileges. Minority status carries with it the exclusion from full participation in the life of the society. Though not necessarily an alien group the minority is treated and regards itself as a people apart.[1]

Most minority groups, then, share several characteristics: particular physical and/or cultural traits; unequal treatment; and a perception of their separateness. All these characteristics are related to a dominant group enjoying a more privileged position. Similar criteria have also been suggested by other writers:

> 1) Minorities are subordinate segments of complex state societies; 2) minorities have special physical or cultural traits which are held in low esteem by the dominant segments of the society; 3) minorities are self-conscious units bound together by the special traits which their members share and by the special disabilities which these bring; 4) membership in a minority is transmitted by a rule of descent which is capable of affiliating succeeding generations even in the absence of readily apparent special cultural or physical traits; 5) minority peoples, by choice or necessity, tend to marry within the group.[2]

Here the self-conscious nature of minority status is stressed as well as the way in which membership of a particular minority group may be self-perpetuating.

It is interesting to note that in neither of these definitions is there reference to numerical criteria. Certainly the size of a group may have some effect upon its status, but it is lack of social, political and economic power that are the key elements here: in South Africa, under apartheid, most of the population suffers from minority status.

It is possible in very broad terms to identify different categories of minority group. Amongst indigenous minorities one would include Native Americans, Inuit, Amerindians, Maori, Aborigine and the Burakumin of Japan. Most of these are groups which have been forced into a subordinate position by invasion and conquest. Other minority groups are the consequence of forced colonial labour migration such as Blacks in Brazil, East African Asians and South African Indians, to name only a few. Western Europe's migrant workers are a contemporary case in point arising out of neo-colonial influences. Some groups are migratory by nature, such as the Roma (Europe's gypsies) or the nomads of the Sahel, others such as the Kurds or Armenians may seek, or have sought, a state of their own.[3]

Is it possible that amongst such diverse groups there could be any common experience? Investigation would seem to suggest that despite the magnitude of the differences, because of the shared minority status of these groups some common, or parallel, experiences may exist. It is these parallel circumstances that make up the minority experience.

Objective deprivation

Most, although not all, members of such minority groups will *objectively* occupy a disadvantaged socio-economic position in society. By comparison with the dominant group they will often be deprived of full social, economic and political equality. Such deprivations limit the individual's freedom of choice and add to the climate of insecurity that is thus created.

The main point about such objective deprivation is that it relates to a measurable situation that can be observed by outsiders. The minorities that we are concerned with here will occupy disadvantaged positions in society, positions which limit their access to the social, political and economic fields. Socio-economic disadvantage is thus a key part of the minority experience. Its effects are far reaching:

> These deprivations circumscribe the individual's freedom of choice and self-development. The members of minority groups are held in lower esteem and may even be objects of contempt, hatred, ridicule and violence. They are generally socially isolated and frequently spatially segregated. Their subordinate position becomes manifest in their unequal access to educational opportunities and in their restricted scope of occupational and professional advancement. They are not as free as other members of society to join the voluntary associations that express their interests. They suffer from more than the ordinary amount of social and economic insecurity. Even as concerns public policy they are frequently singled out for special treatment; their property rights may be restricted; they may not enjoy the equal protection of the laws; they may be deprived of the rights of suffrage and may be excluded from public office.[4]

It is thus possible for any minority group, given the availability of the data, to map out the features of objective deprivation. Clearly deprivation is a relative thing but in the context of majority/minority issues it is the status of the minority group vis-à-vis the dominant group that must be examined. For example the average per capita income for Native Americans in the USA is substantially lower than that for Blacks and Chicanos and less than half that for the whites. Per capita income on reservations, where most Native Americans live, is even lower. Here unemployment may be around forty per cent, approximately ninety per cent of housing may be substandard and communicable disease a major problem. Native people are eight times more likely to contract TB and forty-two times more likely to suffer from dysentery than other Americans.[5]

In the UK the objective disadvantage suffered by minority groups was researched by PEP (Political and Economic Planning) between 1972 and 1975 and published as *Racial Disadvantage in Britain*. In this David Smith sets out quite clearly the extent of racial discrimination in employment, housing and education.[6] With this it is possible to gain a picture of both the extent and geographical location of disadvantage.

Subjective deprivation: image and identity

The objective characteristics of the minority experience that have been outlined above are closely related to *subjective* characteristics associated with the feelings that members of a minority group may have about their own status. This subjective deprivation is the key to minority group attitudes and behaviour: the fact that it is subjective makes it no less important. It begins to answer the question 'How does it feel?' It is about how the minority group members themselves perceive their own situation.

> One cannot long discriminate against people without generating in them a sense of isolation and of persecution and without giving them a conception of themselves as more different from others than in fact they are. Whether, as a result of this differential treatment, the minority comes to suffer from a sense of its own inferiority or develops a feeling that it is unjustly treated — which may lead to a rebellious attitude — depends in part upon the length of time that its status has existed and in part upon the total social setting in which the differential treatment operates. Where a caste system has existed over many generations and is sanctioned by religious and other sentiments, the attitude of resignation is likely to be dominant over the spirit of rebellion. But in a secular society where class rather than caste pervades the stratification of people, and where the tradition of minority status is of recent origin, minorities, driven by a sense of frustration and unjustified subordination, are likely to refuse to accept their status and their deprivation without some effort to improve their lot.[7]

One of the extracts in the case study on Native Americans (chapter 5) illustrates graphically the identity problems that may be associated with the minority experience. As Wilfred Pelletier says there: 'Being surrounded by an aggressive and confident majority has made me somewhat defensive: I have spent a lot of years trying to convince myself, after being told all my life that I was no good, because I was an Indian, that I am really all right.' Such experiences may be very common to some members of minority groups. In large part it is a question of imposed identity — not only does the dominant group impose directly or indirectly a particular status on the minority, it also defines the identity that members of that group are supposed to have. Thus Pelletier had internalized an image of his own worthlessness in society.

'Internalization of the image of the oppressor', as Freire has called it, is of course not only limited to the experience of minority groups but can be applied equally to many colonial situations.[8] Wren has also explored these issues and their educational implications with great clarity in his *Education for Justice*.[9] One of the most important characteristics of subjective deprivation in the context of majority/minority issues is the sense of powerlessness. There is not only powerlessness to define your own identity in the face of majority prejudice but also powerlessness in defining socio-economic status and in acting to change these things. In *The Social Psychology of Minorities* Tajfel has very usefully explored many of these dilemmas, including the need for many minorities to 'achieve a new group distinctiveness' in the face of hostility and prejudice.[10]

The climate of prejudice

The minority experience is very much shaped by the climate of prejudice and discrimination itself which surrounds any majority/minority situation. Simpson and Yinger have suggested that there are at least three factors involved in the creation of this climate. One thus needs to consider the prejudiced people and the way they are socialized, together with their own image of themselves and how they perceive their needs as individuals. Secondly one needs to look at the structure of society and the power arrangements within it. Who makes the important political, educational, economic and religious decisions? What beliefs are used to rationalize decisions which are at the expense of minority groups? Thirdly, culture itself teaches attitudes towards other groups. Ethnocentric responses are part of the cultural heritage that each new generation acquires to some degree or other. Thus a person 'does not have to have any individual experience with members of minority groups; he will often be equipped with ready-made responses in advance of any such experience, or even in the complete absence of contact'.[11]

Katznelson has highlighted the way in which culture feeds prejudice in the UK context:

'How is it possible', Cobbett inquired in 1808, 'for us to justify our conduct upon any principle of morality? Conquests in India are not at all necessary for our safety or comfort'. The imperialist response to this gnawing moral question was an affirmation of moral idealism — the backward races need civilizing. Exploitative racist and humanitarian impulses fused to produce an ennobling paternalist doctrine. The colonized were pictured as children, the offspring of the family of Empire, later the Commonwealth, headed by the benevolent matriarch Britain.

Contemporary racial attitudes have been shaped by the colonial experience, forged in the crucible of imperialism. A nation's culture, both social and political, is the outcome of a unique historical process. Though not all learning is culture, all culture is learned, and Britain in particular, is characterized by a hereditary culture. As a consequence of the heritage of imperialism, British feelings of racial superiority became part of the country's cultural baggage, not always consciously felt, but always potentially operative. Most Englishmen alive today have grown up nurtured by a press, literature and education that promoted the related notions of the civilizing mission and racial paternalism.[12]

The whole area of racial attitudes and the cultural bases of racism is looked at in the next chapter which examines the background to minority/majority issues. Suffice to say here that these are important determinants of the minority experience.

This chapter has attempted to answer, or to begin to answer, the questions 'What is it like?' 'How does it feel?' It has also begun to outline some of the problems commonly faced *by* minority groups. So often in traditional thinking about minorities it is a particular minority that is seen as *being* the problem. This is of course the dominant group's definition of the situation which does little to resolve the issue. By starting with the minority experience one starts with the perceptions of those who are discriminated against. Obviously generalizations have been made, it would be impossible to do otherwise. Distinct differences are to be found between different minority groups: the Basques and religious minorities in the USSR have little in common. However, similar sorts of processes are often at work in these situations. Their degree will vary from group to group as it will from person to person within one minority group.

Objective deprivation can be measured by the restricted freedoms that any group has. It will also manifest in inequality over both power to change things and access to resources. In some instances minority groups will be faced by violence and even repression. Subjective deprivation, the other side of the coin, reinforces all the outward signs of discrimination. Low status may be continually forced on one and one's culture, religion or ethnic identity consistently portrayed as inferior. To have the *mores* of the dominant group thus held up as the only desirable ones is to have one's whole identity and self-image called into question. One has only to consider the problems faced by Native Americans, migrant workers in Europe or Black British students in the classroom to begin to understand this. It is of course particularly difficult to persuade a dominant group that prides itself on being tolerant that it does nevertheless at the same time practice discrimination. Ethnocentric attitudes can thus prevent the minority experience from being seen as valid or even relevant.

3 Understanding the Background

Origins of minority groups

No problem or issue exists in a vacuum. Yet how often is the study of a particular problem *per se* seen as sufficient in itself? The nature of any issue is determined by the context within which it takes place and in its turn affects that context. Thus to identify a minority as the problem is to miss the point completely. It ignores the context and it blames the victims for their own oppression. Naturally the background to different majority/minority issues will vary: the partition of Cyprus can only be understood in the light of Greek and Turkish history; the Aborigine's struggle in Australia makes little sense outside the context of land rights. Yet despite such differences common questions still remain for helping us to understand the background. What are the origins of minority groups? What is the policy of the dominant group towards them? What part has socialization played in nurturing prejudice? What is the nature of racism? How do social, political and economic structures reinforce majority/minority inequality?

Concerning the origins of minorities one can say that:

> There are unique elements in the history of every minority, but a few general principles are involved. Since a minority is a group of people that can be distinguished by physical or social characteristics, it follows that anything which makes a population more heterogeneous may create a minority situation. The kind of heterogeneity that will be noticed, of course, depends upon national, cultural, religious, and racial ideologies – in other words, on the characteristics of the majority, those with the greatest power and highest status. Migration, cultural contact, conquering armies bring diverse peoples together. This process has doubtless been accelerated by modern technology and transportation. 'The genesis of minorities must therefore be sought in the fact that territory, political authority, people, and culture rarely coincide.' Whether or not a minority situation would develop in a stable, isolated society starting from an original homogeneity one can only guess. It is possible that the internal

struggle for the values of that society would result in some categorical system of rights and privileges. The evidence of anthropology, however, seems to show that homogeneous societies have little group prejudice. There are conflict and hostility but they are focused on individuals, not on supposed categories of people. It is the modern, mobile, heterogeneous society that is most likely to face a minority situation.

The development of the nation-state system has been the central fact in the origin of minorities. Both the spread of dominance over formerly separate groups and the common desire to create a homogeneous nation (leading to attempts to repress cultural variation) have created the minority-majority situation...dominant groups particularly 'have tended to act as if the state society to which they belong ideally ought to consist of their own physical and cultural type'.[1]

The following three examples will illustrate the diverse ways in which minorities may be formed; they also highlight the broad processes described above.

Aborigines

The first example takes an indigenous minority, the Australian Aborigines, and also touches on the way in which the dominant group will build up its own protective myths about the origins of a minority group. Aborigines had lived in Australia for something like 40–50 000 years before the arrival of Europeans. There were as many as 500 Australian nations each made up of a series of clans. Trade, settlements, farming and respect for the environment were the principal concerns of the population of about 300 000. European settlers decimated these peoples and as late as the 1920s they were still being hunted for sport. Deprived of their livelihood, Aborigines have been forced to the margins of white society and suffer all the marks of cultural oppression and objective deprivation.

To counteract the painful necessity of facing up to these facts many white Australians prefer to believe that Australia was empty when it was 'discovered' by Cook, that friendly approaches were rejected, that anyway Aborigines are lazy and unable to look after themselves because they are a 'primitive' people. The case study in chapter 5 elaborates on several of these themes.

Kurds

The Kurdish people form a minority in five different countries: Turkey, Iraq, Iran, Syria and the USSR. They have their own history, culture and language and are the fourth most numerous people in the Middle East. In these terms they form one of the largest nations in the world to have been denied an independent state. As a people they have inhabited the same area for at least three thousand years and have seen many empires – Persian, Greek, Roman, Arab, Turkish – come and go. Yet for much of this period they have had their homeland partitioned. When the Ottoman Empire was divided up after the First World War the Kurds were offered the possibility of independence in 1920 under the Treaty of Sèvres but this was never implemented. So the struggle continues with varying demands for autonomy and national rights depending on which state the Kurdish minority is in.[2]

Sahrawis

The third example arises in the context of de-colonization in north-west Africa. It was the colonial period in this area that forced the concept of nationality on the Sahara nomads such as the Sahrawi of Western Sahara. This territory was formerly ruled by Spain as the Spanish Sahara up until 1975. Spain's withdrawal came largely as the result of international anti-colonial opinion and the action of the Polisario guerrilla front. However, this was not to mean straightforward independence for the Sahrawis as Morocco in the north and Mauritania in the south both laid claim to parts of the territory. Although the UN had declared that the Sahrawis should have the right to self-determination, Spain signed a tripartite agreement with Morocco and Mauritania giving them control of the territory. Access to phosphate reserves played no small part in the agreement.

Currently, therefore, the Sahrawi are fighting a war of liberation in the desert backed by Algeria. Much of the population lives in the occupied territories whilst other Sahrawis are in refugee camps in Algeria.[3]

Majority aims

Within any majority/minority situation the policy of the dominant group plays a major part in determining the climate of negotiation. Although the policies explicitly or implicitly put forward by dominant groups will vary over time, broad patterns are discernible. Thus in many cases assimilation, or merging, of the minority group into the dominant culture will be expected to take place, the intention being that the minority become eventually absorbed into the majority. This is perhaps one of the most common expectations on the part of majority groups, especially with regard to indigenous minorities. It is the attitude held by many people in the UK towards ethnic minority groups in this country. Assimilation of course will only be successful when it is desired by both parties. Thus many European minority groups have been assimilated in the USA as in the UK. On the other hand assimilation may be the ultimate insult to a minority group that has learnt to have little respect for a hostile majority.

Theoretically a pluralist society in which majority and minority groups can live side by side offers the freedom and dignity necessary for non-oppressive relationships to flourish. However, what may be seen as pluralism by the majority may still be seen as an unequal and exploitative situation by the minority. This situation would be endorsed by many members of minority groups in the UK and the USA, for example. This in turn takes us back to the way in which dominant groups define what the problem is on behalf of oppressed groups. The latter's definition of reality is thus ignored or put on one side as being unreasonable.

Other majority policies may include deliberate population transfer, as with the Ugandan Asians or the Vietnamese boat-people. More extreme policies, although not necessarily official ones, may involve the deliberate extermination of groups as with the Amerindians in Brazil. Thus majority policies and majority attitudes form an important part of the background to these issues.

Socialization

The attitudes that any one social group may have towards another will often have been greatly influenced by the process of socialization in childhood. That is parents will interpret and pass on the norms and values of the dominant group in society and these will certainly involve particular attitudes towards other social, religious and racial groups. These may refer to other groups within that society or towards other countries. Enormous social pressures are thus brought to bear both at home and at school.

> The development of attitudes towards the child's own country and other countries is primarily a result of processes of social influence. The child is dealing with abstract entities – 'nations' – with which he has no direct contact (and whose members are not obviously distinguishable from one another by virtue of physical or other characteristics). His sources of both factual and evaluative information are therefore social sources – his parents, siblings, peers and teachers, together with some non-human equivalents like comics, books and television. Within this system the child acquires a preference for his own country and an enduring identification with it. At the same time he develops a pattern of preference for other countries in advance of some of the simplest items of factual knowledge about them. These preferences and dislikes derive from contemporary and historical national alignments; they mirror the portrayals in his own and other countries in his social world. The strength and pervasiveness of these mechanisms of attitude formation is best illustrated by those children who belong to national or other groups which in some sense have an inferior status. These children may not show the same preference for their own group, a direct reflection of its devalued portrayal in their social world. And this operates even in situations where no overt inter-group tension or strife is evident, and where the group is not substantially disparaged. The child is apparently sensitive to the most subtle nuances of social influence and incorporates them in his attitudes.[4]

Socialization itself must of course be seen in the context of culture and the way in which this may nurture prejudice has already been touched on in chapter 2. While this book is not the place for a detailed examination of the various theories relating to racial prejudice, it is important to identify some key ideas here as an essential part of the background to majority/minority issues.

Ethnocentrism and prejudice

Obviously to some degree or other all cultures are ethnocentric, i.e. each considers its own way of doing things, of looking at the world, to be normal.

In the most naive form of ethnocentrism a person unreflectively takes his own culture's values as objective reality and automatically uses them as the context within which he judges less familiar objects and events. As in Piaget's stage of egocentric thought, it does not occur to such a person that there is more than one point of view. At a more complex level is the ethnocentric attitude or outlook that takes account of multiple points of view but regards those of other cultures as incorrect, inferior or immoral.[5]

If this latter viewpoint is taken it is a short step to holding racist attitudes both in a global, national and local context. One useful definition of racism describes it as:

> ... the belief in, and practice of, the domination of one social group, identified as a 'race', over another social group, identified as another 'race'. Racism thus involves three basic components: i) the belief that humankind consists of well-defined 'races', ii) the belief that some 'races' are superior to others, and iii) the belief that the superior 'races' should rule over the inferior and the attempt to put this belief into practice. Racism is often looked upon as consisting only of the first two components. From this standpoint, racism is primarily a 'prejudice'. But to look at racism in this way is to belittle or overlook its most harmful aspect, which is its third component....The harm occurs when a group not only believes in its superiority but also believes that this superiority entitles it to rule and control.... (it is) the predication of decisions and policies on considerations of race for the purpose of *subordinating* a racial group and maintaining control over that group. The problem of racism, then, is not prejudice, but domination.[6]

The important sentence there is the last one for it makes a vital distinction. To the dominant group racism may seem merely a question of prejudice which, given time, appropriate education will remove. To the supposedly 'inferior' groups – and this may refer to whole nations as well as minority groups – it is more correctly seen as a worldview which tacitly assumes the need for control by those self-appointed as 'superiors'. That a dominant group cannot recognize its own racism merely illustrates the blinkering effect of ethnocentrism.

The cultural bases of racism

One very valuable exploration of this whole field is *Cultural Bases of Racism and Group Oppression* by Hodge, Struckmann and Trost, which examines the way in which traditional 'Western' concepts, values and institutional structures sustain racism:

> That Western nations have engaged in the oppression

of many non-Western peoples can be documented easily enough. It is generally thought, however, that this oppression occurs in spite of, and in conflict with, the basic ideas and values of the Western tradition. It is true that this oppression does conflict with some aspects of these traditional values, but it is also true... that this oppression occurs *because* of some basic features of these values. Overcoming this oppression will require changing many of these traditional ideas and values and changing the institutional structures corresponding to them.

A common Western notion, occasionally expressed, usually tacit, is that Western culture is superior to other cultures. In Western eyes, Western culture is generally considered to be identical with 'civilization', and the non-Western world is considered to be in varying stages of development, moving towards civilization. 'Primitive' and 'uncivilized' are terms frequently used by Westerners to refer to peoples and cultures which are unlike the West.

That the people of a culture should view themselves as culturally superior is certainly common. But not so common is the feature contained in Western cultural thinking, that the superior *should control* the inferior. It is this kind of thinking, which emphasizes the value placed on control, that produces a missionary imperialism. The notion of 'white man's burden' is also derived from this type of thinking. Western control over non-Western peoples is thereby often considered morally defensible...

One of the traditional components of Western thinking is the belief that human reason should dominate and control nature. Westerners identify themselves with reason; they identify non-Western peoples with nature. They therefore conclude that they are justified in dominating and controlling non-Western peoples...

Another component of Western dualism... is the habit of either-or thinking. It is a habit of thinking which results from the traditional Western tendency to see all elements of the universe in terms of conflicting forces of good versus evil, or of superior versus inferior. Any two things which differ, accordingly, are not seen just as two different things, but as a superior thing versus an inferior thing. A person is then faced with having to choose which of the two things is superior: *either* this one *or* that one...

Appeals to 'human nature' are often made, sometimes in the attempt to justify or excuse existing oppression, and sometimes in the attempt to refute those who argue for change ... (however) 'human nature' cannot be validly defined by what happens only in Western culture ... The Westerner too easily makes the mistake of assuming that the cultural norms of Western culture are those of humankind.[7]

This overall context is invaluable for an analysis of racism in the European and North American

contexts as well as in other situations where Western culture has been absorbed. It can be seen now why indigenous minorities such as Native Americans and Australian Aborigines may feel they have more in common with some 'third world' peoples than the majority group in their own country. From the minority perspective they can be said to be suffering from what has been termed 'internal colonialism'.

Obviously, oppressive treatment of indigenous minorities had to be rationalized and, as illustrated above, all the appropriate schemata were there. Thus in the case of Australian Aborigines one can trace a historical progression in which they 'grew up' in the mind of white Australian society.

> The Aborigine was:
> 1. *Non-human* – a totally evil servant of Satan, or a beast, a wild animal with no soul, a pest of the wilderness (like the kangaroo); therefore with no rights to land.
> 2. *Sub-human* – (a) stone-age man-ape, cunning and treacherous; (b) a very primitive version of ourselves (which we would prefer to forget, or idolize as 'uncorrupted noble savage').
> 3. *Young human* – a child-like human, needing paternal protection in order to survive or 'advance'.
> 4. *Adolescent* – Today our society has gone past viewing Aborigines as children. Rather, we see them as adolescents – we pretend to take their protesting seriously while agreeing among ourselves that they are not yet capable of managing their own lives.[8]

One could similarly apply these stages in perception by a dominant group to other minorities such as Inuit, Native Americans, and Amerindians.

To begin to understand the nature of, and reasons for, majority attitudes is to go a long way in understanding the backgrounds to majority/minority issues. Attention has particularly been drawn to Western perspectives on this because it helps to clarify not only attitudes towards ethnic minority groups in the UK but also attitudes towards 'third world' countries (a point further touched on in chapter 6). Perhaps Husband sums up the dilemma of majority/minority perspectives in his study of the media:

> Britain is a nation with a long history of parliamentary rule; we pride ourselves on our legal system and on the freedom enjoyed by citizens of this country. Much of what the British think and feel is pervaded by an appreciation of the long and glorious past. Nowhere is this more apparent than in the British self-perception of

Britain as a tolerant society with a particular tolerance of immigrants, which is seen as a marked feature of our history. Yet this view of Britain's long established tolerance has acquired mythical properties not borne out by a closer examination of reality.... And yet, such is the strength of this belief in our tolerance that it inhibits any objective perception of our actual behaviour. Not only does this pathological acceptance of our national tolerance create an exaggerated estimation of 'tolerant' behaviour when it does occur, but more than this it makes any consideration that we may be positively intolerant well-nigh impossible. Very often prejudice is not seen where it exists, and where it is acknowledged it is perceived as a freak deviation from society as a whole. Thus we find a willingness to accept interpretations of racial prejudice which suggest that such prejudices are the product of the abnormal psychology of a minority of individuals. In this way responsibility for such prejudice as is recognized can be detached from society as a whole and be attributed to a minority of social and psychological defectives who inevitably are found in every society....

Convinced of our tolerance and continuing to perceive Britain as a white society that has black immigrants, rather than as a multiracial society with black and white citizens, we as a nation have sought to defend the old rather than adapt to the new. We are a society with racist beliefs entrenched in our culture and racial discrimination evident in our laws and in our behaviour.[9]

4 Perspectives on Change

Several of the reasons given for teaching about majority/minority issues in chapter 1 relate to the need to cope with change or to engage in action for change. It was also suggested that four questions could usefully be asked about any majority/minority situation: What are the problems (the minority experience)? What is the background to these problems? What is being done about them? What sort of image of society/value positions does this involve? The first two questions have been further looked at in chapters 2 and 3 respectively. This chapter outlines some of the perspectives on change that relate to the last two questions.

These four questions are of course all closely interrelated. They have been summarized in Fig. 1.1 (page 4) by the key words: Problems, Background, Action and Values, all of which influence — and are in turn influenced by — each other. This is a useful reminder that action for change potentially has three aspects — tackling immediate problems now, tackling the longer term background, and realizing certain values. At the same time it is important to remember that values potentially have three aspects also — values affect how people perceive a problem in the first place, how they then analyse the underlying causes, and how (if at all) they involve themselves in action for change. One's view of each of these four areas is thus affected by one's view of the other three.[1]

Action to tackle the problems faced by minority groups and their causes need to be initiated not only 'from the top', by governments and international bodies, but also at the local level by community groups, pressure groups and individuals. Action at the macro level may thus take the form of interest in human rights by, for example, the United Nations and the International Court of Justice, or of initiatives by national governments in the fields of law and education. At the non-governmental level action may come from organizations such as Survival International, Amnesty International and the Minority Rights Group.[2]

Action at local levels may come in the form of supplementary schooling by self-help groups, working for improved community relations in the local neighbourhood and at work, initiatives to combat racism in the classroom and the personal struggle to face one's own racism.

Opinions as to the effectiveness of these different courses of action will vary but they all hinge on particular value positions and visions of the 'good society'. In terms of majority/minority issues it would certainly need to include the absence of any form of oppression and include social and economic justice for all. This would involve the right of cultural, religious and ethnic minorities to define their own needs and to participate fully in the social and political structures of society. In most cases achieving this requires more equitable distribution of both power and resources so that those at present on the periphery can fully share the resources of the centre.

This chapter therefore begins by looking at some of the aims of minority groups and then at some of the dimensions of change in the USA, Europe and the UK. In no way does it attempt to be comprehensive but only to offer some perspectives on change in particular majority/minority situations.

The aims of minority groups

The way in which a minority group perceives its position and the course of action it chooses to change that position are central to an understanding of majority/minority issues. Naturally there will be differing opinions and stances amongst individuals within a group, but nevertheless as Wirth illustrates broad categories relating to aims are identifiable. Thus:

Minorities may be conveniently typed into: i) pluralistic; ii) assimilationist; iii) secessionist; and iv) militant.
A *pluralistic minority* is one which seeks toleration for its differences on the part of the dominant group.

Implicit in the quest for toleration of one's group differences is the conception that variant cultures can flourish peacefully side by side in the same society. Indeed, cultural pluralism has been held out as one of the necessary preconditions of a rich and dynamic civilization under conditions of freedom. It has been said in jest that 'tolerance is the suspicion that the other fellow may be right'.

Toleration requires that the dominant group shall feel sufficiently secure in its position to allow dissenters a certain leeway. Those in control must be convinced either that the issues at stake are not too vital, or else they must be so thoroughly imbued with the ideal of freedom that they do not wish to deny to others some of the liberties which they themselves enjoy.... While on the one hand the pluralistic minority craves the toleration of one or more of its cultural idiosyncracies, on the other hand it resents and seeks protection against coerced absorption by the dominant group. Above all it wishes to maintain its cultural identity....

Although the pluralistic minority does not wish to merge its total life with the larger society, it does demand for its members a greater measure of economic and political freedom if not outright civic equality. Ever since the revolutionary epoch of the late eighteenth century the economic and political enfranchisement of minorities has been regarded not merely as inherent in the 'rights of man' but as the necessary instrument in the struggle for cultural emancipation.

....the first stages of minority movements have been characterized by cultural renaissances. The primary emphasis in this stage of development has been upon accentuating the religious, linguistic, and cultural heritage of the group and driving to obtain recognition and toleration for these differences. This movement goes hand in hand with the clamour for economic and political equality. In the course of such movements what at first are marks of inferiority – a homely folk tongue, an alien religion, an obscure law, and eccentric costume – are transformed into objects of pride and positive group values in which the intellectuals among the minority take an especially avid interest and the promotion of which becomes the road to their leadership and power.

....Unlike the pluralistic minority, which is content with toleration and the upper limit of whose aspiration is cultural autonomy, the *assimilationist minority* craves the fullest opportunity for participation in the life of the larger society with a view to uncoerced incorporation in that society. It seeks to lose itself in the larger whole by opening up to its members the greatest possibilities for their individual self-development. Rather than toleration and autonomy, which is the goal of the pluralistic minority, the assimilationist minority works towards complete acceptance by the dominant group and a merger with the larger society.

Whereas a pluralistic minority, in order to maintain its group integrity, will generally discourage intermarriage and intimate social intercourse with the dominant group, the assimilationist minority puts no such obstacles in the path of its members but looks upon the crossing of stocks as well as the blending of cultures as wholesome end products. Since assimilation is a two-way process, however, in which there is give and take, the mergence of an assimilationist minority rests upon a willingness of the dominant group to absorb and of the minority group to be absorbed...

The *secessionist minority* represents a third distinct type. It repudiates assimilation on the one hand, and is not content with mere toleration or cultural autonomy on the other. The principal and ultimate objective of such a minority is to achieve political as well as cultural independence from the dominant group. If such a group has had statehood at an earlier period in its career, the demand for recognition of its national sovereignty may be based upon the cultivation among its members of the romantic sentiments associated – even if only in the imagination – with its former freedom, power and glory. In such a case the minority's cultural monuments and survivals, its language, lore, literature, and ceremonial institutions, no matter how archaic or reminiscent of the epoch of the group's grandeur, are revivified and built up into moving symbols of national grandeur...

The protest against the dominant group, however, does not always take the form of separatism and secessionism. It may, under certain circumstances express itself in movements to get out from under the yoke of a dominant group in order to join a group with whom there exists a closer historical and cultural affinity. This is particularly true of minorities located near national frontiers. Wars, and the accompanying repeated redefinitions of international boundaries rarely fail to do violence to the traditions and wishes of some of the populations of border territories...

There is a fourth type of minority which may be designated as *militant*. Its goal reaches far beyond toleration, assimilation, and even cultural and political autonomy. The militant minority has set domination over others as its goal. Far from suffering from feelings of inferiority, it is convinced of its own superiority and inspired by the lust for conquest. While the initial claims of minority movements are generally modest, like all accessions of power, they feed upon their own success and often culminate in delusions of grandeur...

The justification for singling out the four types of minorities described above for special delineation lies in the fact that each of them exhibits a characteristic set of collective goals among historical and contemporary minority groups and a corresponding set of motives activating the conduct of its members. These four types point to significant differences between actual minority movements.[3]

Where majority policies and minority aims co-incide, that is, where both groups are working towards the same ends, conflict will naturally be minimal. In the vast majority of cases, however, majority and minority aims will not coincide. It is this disparity which lies at the heart of most majority/minority issues. Wirth's four categories are of course generalizations — aims are not necessarily so clear cut. Aims will often differ within a minority group depending on different interests. Some brief examples of these main categories will illustrate some of the tensions.

Up until about a decade ago the Mexican Americans, or Chicanos as they themselves prefer to be called, were often referred to as the 'forgotten people'. In the 1970s this all changed and the Chicanos are now recognized as the fastest growing minority in the United States, perhaps surpassing the Blacks in number within the next decade. From being a word of abuse Chicano has now come to designate 'the politically awakened Mexican American'. Inspired by the struggles of people like Cesar Chavez a re-awakened sense of identity emerged. Both language and culture have become new foci of concern. The Chicano movement thus seeks social equality, advancement and national rights in a plural society. Not only does this often appear threatening to many white Americans, it is also paradoxical in that the ancestors of Mexican Americans were founders of the nation long before Europeans 'discovered' North America. The wish for equal rights in a plural society will not be realized without a long, and perhaps bitter, struggle.[4]

Fifteen million or so migrants now live in Western Europe. They are workers and their families who have come to meet the growing demand for labour over the last twenty-five years. They have come from Greece, Turkey, Spain, Portugal, Italy and Yugoslavia as well as North Africa and the former French colonies of West Africa. Migrant workers and their families will be found in West Germany, France, Britain, Switzerland, Austria, Sweden, Belgium, the Netherlands and Luxembourg. Whether they have settled where there is work or intend to return home, all these groups might expect some recognition for their services to the host country. Foreign workers have become necessary for the economic well-being of most European countries. However, whilst pluralism would seem an appropriate stance, and the position most acceptable to migrant workers themselves, such families often find themselves facing severe discrimination.[5]

Minority groups which desire full assimilation into the dominant group may have migrated specifically to settle, e.g. European settlers to the USA in the nineteenth and twentieth centuries, or they may be groups which have been categorized as 'outcasts' in their own society. A case in point would be the Burakumin of Japan who form the largest minority in that country. In no way physically different from other Japanese, Burakumin can only be identified today by their place of residence. They are the descendants of people whose occupations were traditionally considered polluting, a role which put them clearly outside the traditional boundaries of society. The Burakumin have every wish to pass in mainstream society but are confronted with a racism motivated by myths of racial purity with no foundation in biological or historical fact whatsoever.[6]

A similar situation is found in India where, although 'untouchability' has been abolished on paper, over 80 million people are regarded as inherently inferior to the rest of society. The reasons for this do not lie in any racial differences but in the nature of their work: street sweeping, scavenging, cleaning gutters, skinning carcasses. It is probable that Brahmanical Hinduism originally supplied the hierarchical structures which brought about this situation. Untouchables continue to suffer discrimination including physical violence. As with the Burakumin most Untouchables would wish to live peacefully in a plural society. The fact that political interest has been shown in this issue for seventy years, with only minimal actual change in status, is testament to the difficulties of radical social change.[7]

In view of the problems of achieving pluralist or assimilationist aims in the face of majority hostility it is not surprising that several minority groups call for even greater degrees of autonomy. Neither should it be surprising that some members of some groups see armed struggle as the only way left to achieve such aims. Such struggles may range from the occasional attack on the property of the dominant group to a war of liberation. Between these two poles come, for example, the Basques, Corsicans, Nagas, Kurds, Palestinians, Tamils and Eritreans. Certainly most of these groups are fighting for a greater degree of autonomy if not outright secession. In as much as they no longer see any answer other than violence these groups, and others like them, tend to be more in the news than some other minority groups. From a majority viewpoint they are all too easily condemned, but their desperate response is again a reaction to the minority experience at its most extreme.[8]

Wirth's fourth category of militant minorities is perhaps somewhat misleading here. After all, several of the minority groups mentioned above are taking a militant stance. His use of the term, as explained in the extract, refers to minority groups that wish to move from a position of oppression to one of domination. In most majority/minority situations it is difficult to tell what stance a group would take if it achieved all of its aims. Most minorities would probably not wish actively to return hatred and discrimination: this often seems the case where indigenous groups are faced with white racism. However, in some contexts – for example, Northern Ireland and Burundi – minorities *have* shown a wish for violent domination of their opponents.[9]

Minority politics in the United States

Dominant and minority groups will often have quite different views of the political system that they are involved in and nowhere is this more true than in the United States. For the majority of people party politics are seen as the appropriate way in which to negotiate change according to a particular set of norms or rules. Throughout there is an emphasis on orderliness, on being law-abiding and on competition within set limits. As in most democratic systems of government this system is felt to be fair, just and proper, working efficiently in as much as people put their trust in it. From a minority perspective, however, things may appear different.

Makielski, in his *Beleaguered Minorities: Cultural Politics in America,* gives not only a clear picture of minority politics in the USA but also an excellent introduction to majority/minority issues generally. He points out that there are of course many minority views but that they share several elements in common. Amongst these are the fact that the political system is culturally biased and only 'works' for part of American society, that it abounds in myths about hoped-for conditions that never come

about, and that it stresses processes whilst ignoring the results of those processes.

Political, social and economic power are seen to be concentrated in the hands of the most powerful people within the dominant group. They can thus determine not only how issues will be resolved but also which issues will even be considered. People thus do not have equal access to power and meaningful participation in decision-making processes. Minority groups are of course not the only groups to lack this access; nevertheless, they occupy the lowest position in the overall structures. Because of their powerlessness minorities can conveniently be ignored most of the time although, as Makielski points out, the 1960s may in retrospect be seen as some sort of turning point:

> In the 1960s this country was plagued by the threat of domestic revolution, widespread rioting, individual acts of violence, bitterness, distrust, and alienation.
>
> The roots of the difficulty lie in unresolved conflicts of belief, behavior, and assumptions about our political order. Since the turn of the century, American scholars and public figures have rejoiced in the 'pluralism' of our society. Within the context of a universal acceptance of the nature of society, individuals, groups, and organizations were seen as free to struggle to attain their own special interests. In practice, however, there were unpleasant aspects of pluralism. Even in the early 1900s, the condition of the cities, the 'Negro Question' (as it was then called), and the persistence of urban and rural poverty indicated that the American system worked imperfectly. But it can be safely said that most Americans assumed that 'progress' was taking place: today's poor would be tomorrow's affluent; slums would be converted into garden cities; the family farm would once again become the sturdy backbone of society. Even the Negroes could hope to attain eventually the same economic and social status that others, such as the Jews and the Irish, had attained before them.
>
> The widespread belief was that the United States could solve its problems without having to change fundamentally its political processes or economic order. Even more, it was assumed that its political and economic institutions would solve the problems. There were, of course, doubters. The hardy band of socialists and progressives, the much smaller band of communists, a sprinkling of anarchists, and simply skeptical intellectuals dissented noisily, but these were, truly, a handful.
>
> In retrospect, what seems difficult to understand is how tenacious the dream was. The Depression of the 1930s shook many of the faithful badly; but surges of patriotism caused by war seemed to heal temporarily

most of the scars of the Depression years. Well into the 1960s, the number of doubters remained small. Those who struggled against 'the system' usually said, and quite evidently believed, that their goal was not to change it, but simply to make it work a little better by distributing its benefits to everyone.

It would be easy to say that the burning of the cities in the mid-1960s also burned out a great part of the faith in the American system. The war in Vietnam and the bitter confrontations on college campuses only underscored a disillusionment that had already set in. As the following chapters will show, however, the seeds of fundamental conflict were sown long before the 1960s; they have, in fact, been the history of America's beleaguered minorities.

The 1960s marked the arrival of a critical point of grievance, neglect, and, ironically, concern. America's Negroes, Indians, and Mexican-Americans had been groping toward a mode of self-expression for decades. In the 1950s they found their voices; in the 1960s they established new political vehicles. Moreover, two other segments of society also began to consider seriously their position in the American scheme. Women, although numerically more than a majority of the population, began to see their status as that of a minority (like the blacks of South Africa who have numerical superiority but minority status). Students in colleges and universities (and high schools) also began to think of themselves as a minority. Both women and students based their minority status on their inability to control the forces shaping their lives. Many felt that at best they were treated with indifference; at worst, as objects to be oppressed and exploited.

What occurred in the 1960s was akin to a revolution of rising expectations in underdeveloped nations. Self-consciousness arises; it is realized that nothing is immutable and change can be brought about by deliberate action. But, and the qualifier is important, often the hope for change outstrips the progress that actually occurs. The disparity between expectation and reality is painful enough if it is between economic capacity and human wants, as in so many developing nations; it is even more agonizing if it is between segments of a population, such as a minority and a dominant set of interests.[10]

Although the events of the 1960s focused attention on minority needs it did not, could not, remove the discrepancies involved in measuring minority gains. From the majority viewpoint progress was measured in how far minorities had come; from the minority perspective change was measured in how far one still had to go. Change also needs to be assessed of course in terms of minority aims or goals.

Makielski suggests that minority groups bring three sets of goals into politics which may generally be classified as group-survival goals, intermediate goals, and ultimate goals. Thus preserving and strengthening the group as a source of identification for its members is basic to group-survival. It is also a basis for further intermediate goals. These may involve fighting for the removal of legal barriers and for welfare goals consisting of concrete economic benefits for the group. For many minority groups in the United States – Blacks, Chicanos, Native Americans – these goals must take priority over all others for they involve basic issues of food, health and living conditions. Less tangible intermediate goals refer to status, an equal acceptance of minority members with 'the elimination of de-humanization', and integrity as part of the search for self-respect.

Ultimate goals involve the sort of society that minority groups need to live in for a self-respecting future. They are the same sort of goals as those explored by Wirth earlier in this chapter. Whilst assimilation was once perhaps the goal of most minority groups in the United States it is now increasingly resisted. The older minorities, for example, Polish-American, Italian-American, German-American, Greek-American, have found assimilation easier than other groups but even this has occurred to a lesser extent than many expected. Whilst pluralism is perhaps part of 'The Great American Dream' it is useful to distinguish between cultural and structural pluralism. The former involves sharing the opportunity structures of the dominant institutions, the latter means that the opportunity structures of a particular minority are largely confined to that group. Structural pluralism has increasingly become an attractive goal because it means that emphasis is on the minority grouping and working within it rather than trying to make it outside.

There are those who fear that this could merely become another form of colonial indirect rule and therefore prefer, even within the United States, to think in terms of separatism. Whatever the goals, fighting for social change and the creation of a more just society will continue to be a major factor in minority politics.

The fragmentation of Europe?

Over the last decade Europe has also been the focus of several majority/minority clashes and yet is still often portrayed as a collection of fairly homogeneous states. It is only when one begins to focus on the many various majority/minority issues within its borders that one begins to see just how fragmented Europe could become. The way in which dominant group assumptions are coming increasingly under question is well illustrated in the recent report from Brussels in Extract 4.1.

Extract 4.1

The politics of language may end by shaking up Europe

From John Palmer,
European Editor
in Brussels

Predictions that, by the end of the century, the European nation state will have practically disappeared, and that in its place we shall have a "Europe des regions," are now commonplace. There is hardly a state in Western Europe where the assumptions about its political and cultural integrity have not been severely shaken.

In Britain, Scottish Nationalism — and to a less extent Welsh nationalism — are forces in the land. In Spain, the Basques are only one of a number of regional and linguistic minorities determined to secure recognition of their status as nations.

The renaissance of ancient minority languages and cultures has in every country in Western Europe posed more or less serious political problems.

There are a great many more linguistic minorities alive and kicking in Western Europe than is generally realised in his book Linguistic Minorities in Western Europe (Gomer Press). Meic Stephens, a Welsh writer, has discovered more than 50. True, they range enormously in size and influence, but everywhere they display the same obstinate refusal to bow the head to a neighbouring "great culture" and accept assimilation.

In some countries, the minorities are having to fight for the very recognition of their language. Elsewhere, their linguistic identity is so developed that it poses a problem for the functioning of the state.

Nowhere is the power of linguistic politics seen more dramatically than in Belgium. Contrary to popular opinion, there are three, not two, language groups native to Belgium. Apart from the Dutch-speaking Flemings and the French-speaking Walloons, there is also a community of some 60,000 German speakers on the country's eastern borders. But it is the Walloon and Fleming conflict which has called into question the very existence of the Belgian state on occasions in the past.

Both sides have now agreed to divide the country into three regions: Flanders (Dutch-speaking), Wallonia (French-speaking), and Brussels (bilingual, with a French-speaking majority). The details of the new constitution have not all been agreed, and apparently minuscule issues can still pose political problems out of all proportion. Recent controversies include whether the offshore limits on Belgium's Dutch-speaking coast will be a federal resource or belong only to Flanders, and how to divide up the great forest of Soignes, on the outskirts of Brussels, which will overlap the borders of the three regions.

It is not generally appreciated that three other smaller European states have significant linguistic minorities. But in two of them — Holland and Denmark — there has been relatively generous recognition of the rights of the minorities, and consequently little political strife. In Holland, the Friesiens — whose language is thought to be very close to Old English and Lowland Scots — can be educated in their own language and have a thriving literature. But they do press for far greater television and broadcasting time.

In Denmark, the German speakers on the country's southern frontier, and the Faroese and Greenlanders, have few complaints about the treatment of their languages.

In Austria, there has been much more conflict between the German-speaking majority and the smaller Slav-speaking minorities on its eastern and southern borders. The Slovenes of Carinthia openly identify with their fellow Slovenes across the border in Yugoslavia, and have won sympathy there for their claim that they are in danger of losing their cultural identity. The Croat and Magyar minorities in Austria seem well on the path to total assimilation by the German-speakers.

Next to Britain, the political revival of national and linguistic minorities has had its most traumatic effect in France and Spain. Until recently, many French denied that Corsicans, Bretons, Catalans, Basques or Flemins — all ancient communities in France — had any separate cultural, let alone political identity. Even now, the claims of the Occitan-speakers of the south go unrecognised.

Yet about 10 million "Frenchmen" have knowledge of one or other of the dialects of the Langue d'Oc.

There are now slogans to be seen by tourists in the Midi proclaiming support for Occitan separatism. But such demands are held most tenaciously in Celtic Brittany and Corsica. While outright independence is unlikely to be a serious issue in any of these communities for the forseeable future, the agitation for greater devolution and recognition for the education and broadcasting rights of the minority languages is slowly but surely forcing changes in Paris. It is now possible to take a university course even in the Picard language.

In Spain, it is still an open question whether the Basques will be satisfied with much less than independence, though there, as elsewhere, the problem is complicated by a minority within a minority, since there are large numbers of Spanish-speakers in the southern Basque province of Navarre. The Catalans and Galicians are also demanding a greater degree of "home rule,"

and could be followed by other, more dormant regional groups, who have begun to question their relationship with Madrid.

Portugal is the only Western European country without any indigenous linguistic minority. Even West and East Germany, normally thought to be culturally monolithic, have minorities. In the Federal Republic, there are Danes and Frisians, in East Germany are to be found the Slav-speaking Sorbs, an ancient community with a language and culture related to, but distinct from Polish or Czech.

Everyone knows that Switzerland contains French, Italian, and Romance speakers, as well as German. But on Meic Stephans's count, Italy can boast no fewer than 12—Ladino apart, that is, from Italian. German, French, and Ladino are spoken in the mountainous north, slovens of the Yugoslav border, while in the south, there are old communities of Greek, Croat, and Albanian speakers.

That leaves Sard, Occitan, Romagno, Friulian, and Piedmontese, which many Italians deny are languages at all but

merely patois of Italian. However, a growing band of enthusiasts is championing the cause of their recognition and encouragement.

So far, linguistic minorities have made few attempts to unite. The speakers of Irish, Scots, Gaelic, Welsh, Breton, Manx, and Cornish are associated in the Pan-Celtic Congress. There is a Bureau of Unrepresented Nations in Brussels, which is supported mainly by the Bretons, the Alsatians, the Welsh, and the Basques. But they have been cold-shouldered by the Scots, who seem to be confident that they can make their own claims to nationhood in the EEC without help.

The revival of the small nationalities has provided encouragement for supporters of European federalism, but there is as yet no consensus about the social, economic, or political profile of a "Europe of the regions." Without such a consensus, the movement of the smaller nations and the language minorities will have a more lasting effect on the cultural than the political climate of Europe.

Source: *Guardian,* 28 August 1978.

It would seem that for a variety of reasons many minority groups, in Europe, North America and elsewhere, have experienced a tide of rising expectations. Part of this has involved the realization that minority rights are as important as any other human rights, whilst together with this has often gone a cultural renaissance which calls into question the rights of the dominant group to rule over the minority. Notwithstanding the recent experience in Britain, since the nation state is a relatively recent invention might this not mark the beginning of a major trend towards devolutionist strategies? It certainly also relates to calls for greater participation, grass-roots control, and self-reliance in what is seen by many (and not just minority groups) as an already over-centralized world.

Only hindsight will show whether this turns out to be a continuing trend or a minor fluctuation:

However, Europe, which is considered the outstanding example of the modern nation-state system, and which,

as a result, has become a tacit model of political development for others, has a far from consistent record. Within the 150 year span between 1815 and 1965, Europe was the scene of twenty-seven state 'births' and twenty-three state 'deaths', an average of one every twenty-seven months. In brief, then, there is no reason to believe that alternatives are not possible... (and that) it is conceivable that more extensive devolutionary measures may come into existence in the near future in western Europe.[11]

Changing Britain

Several of the issues relating to curriculum change in Britain are explored in chapter 6 on the 'multi-ethnic curriculum' which must, of course, be seen in the wider context of race relations in Britain. A detailed analysis of many of the issues can be found in *Colonial Immigrants in a British City* by John Rex and Sally Tomlinson (Routledge and Kegan Paul, 1979). The first brief account below recalls the fact that the British educational system is often ill fitted to meet the needs of children from different minority groups. This has partly been as a result of a lack of clear directives and policy on multi-ethnic education, but also arises out of the assimilationist approach of many teachers – that all minority-group children need to do is to learn to fit into society and they have no special needs of their own. One consequence of this situation is that parents, community leaders and social workers have often set up 'supplementary' schools to try and rectify some of these omissions.

The need for supplementary schooling

In 1974 a worker from the North Lewisham Project spent some time observing in local schools, two of which had an intake of more than 50 per cent of children of West Indian or African origin. Observations confirmed the findings of a number of authorities on the issue of West Indian children under-achieving in schools. Some of the factors contributing to under-achievement in Deptford schools were considered to be:

(i) Low expectation towards black children on the part of some teachers.

(ii) The lack of liaison between the school and parents. As a result teachers seem very often to have little knowledge of the children they teach, their home circumstances, their cultural background, which in turn leads to the curriculum being unrelated to the children.

(iii) Negative self-image on the part of the black children, due to bias and inappropriate materials as well as the low expectation mentioned above. The school often reinforces the image which black children see portrayed of themselves and their parents by the media, and the roles ascribed to, or attitudes towards black people held by society at large.

The specific objectives of the supplementary school, held on Saturday mornings, were therefore:

(i) to improve the work performance of black children participating e.g. in reading, writing, arithmetic, general understanding and awareness.

(ii) to improve the self-image of the children, which in turn will lead to increased confidence and hence better work performance.

(iii) to raise the level of the child's awareness of her/himself as a black person, through positive emphasis on her/his culture and history and so to assist the child in finding an identity which is not alienating.

Arising out of this, activities were centred around Reading, Mathematics, Art, Music, Cookery, and the Caribbean Project.

The children attending the school, as is the case with most children living in Deptford, daily experience an environment which is invalidating to them as human beings. The lack of beauty and order in Deptford, a depressed area, twinned with the comparisons children draw between themselves and other children seen on the television reinforces a negative self-image. Black children have the double disadvantage of living in such an environment and having themselves further undermined by the materials used in schools. This self-invalidation is experienced either through the message portrayed in books, in which the accepted standards and norms are not only blatantly middle class but almost exclusively white as well. Alternatively, self-invalidation comes through the mis-information communicated by teachers whose level of awareness and sensitivity are low and who therefore in their desire to be 'multicultural' use unsuitable materials which are insulting to black children. For example the picture portrayed of Africa is often through slides of animals; little reference is made to its peoples, ancient kingdoms, modern capitals and rich culture.

Despite the brevity of this project – the school ran for a year – the children on the scheme were found to have benefited greatly from working in an environment where they and their work were appreciated, and where they were enabled to respect their own identity.[12]

Myths and facts

Much of the prejudice and discrimination faced by minority groups is based simply on misinformation. Disentangling myths from facts is an important way, although only one, of beginning to change attitudes. Here a series of commonly held opinions are compared unemotionally with the facts.

Extract 4.2

Myths and Facts

While my own view is that racialism is an evil, and these organisations (like the National Front and the National Party) are malicious and destructive, I think it would be harmful to repress them or prevent their existence. We must combat them in a more positive way, by pointing out the errors in what they say, and by showing that their message is sterile. — Brynmor John, Minister of State at the Home Office with special responsibility for race relations.

IMMIGRATION

MYTH: There is uncontrolled immigration into this country.

FACT: This is not so. Under the Immigration Act 1971, very few categories of people can come and settle in this country.
They are:-
* Commonwealth citizens, whose parents or grandparents were born here

* Spouses/fiancé(e)s and specified dependants of those already here

* Certain people with UK passports who have no other citizenship

    All EEC nationals have the right to work in any EEC country. The member States of the EEC are Britain, France, West Germany, Italy, Denmark, Belgium, Holland, Ireland and Luxembourg.

MYTH: Immigration is making us an overcrowded island.

FACT: * Since 1964 more people have left the UK each year than entered. In 1975 190,000 people came to live in Britain and 230,000 left, a net loss of 40,000. (Office of Population Censuses and Surveys)
* The population of the UK fell between mid-1974 and mid-1975. (OPCS)
* Holland, Belgium and West Germany, all prosperous industrial countries, have more people per square mile than the UK. (*Pan World Atlas*, 1973)

MYTH: White people are leaving this country and are being replaced by black immigrants.

FACT: * Only one in every three immigrants to this country was born in the New Commonwealth. (Census 1971)
* The countries of birth of people who came to the UK between 1971 and 1973 for at least a year and were not born here were as follows:-
    41% New Commonwealth
    15% Old Commonwealth
    44% Other

(OPCS)

MYTH: The black population of this country is many millions.

FACT: The latest estimate of the size of the black population is $1\frac{3}{4}$ million — 3.2% of the total population. In 1974 nearly 40% of the black people here were born in Great Britain. (OPCS)

MYTH: The numbers of births to black immigrants is increasing all the time.

FACT: The number of births to mothers born in the New Commonwealth fell from 46,100 in 1970 to 39,900 in 1975. (OPCS)

MYTH: There are large numbers of illegal immigrants entering the country.

FACT: It is impossible for *anyone* to know how many illegal immigrants there are, but some indications can be drawn from the figures below:-
* In 1975 only 188 people were detained and removed as illegal immigrants.
* In April 1974 the Home Secretary announced an amnesty for certain illegal immigrants; after two years only 1,990 people had applied. (Hansard, Commons, Col. 580, 24.6.76)

MYTH: The Home Office is concealing the facts.

FACT: Not so. The Government publishes the facts about immigrants in the following ways:-
* The Census (1971 is the latest)
* Home Office Immigration Statistics
* DES statistics on numbers of immigrant pupils (up to 1973)
* Department of Employment counts of unemployed people
* Registrar General's return of births and the International Passenger Survey

* The General Household Survey of the Office of Population Censuses and Surveys
* Answers to Parliamentary questions (Hansard)
(Her Majesty's Stationery Office)

SOCIAL SERVICES

MYTH: Blacks come here to sponge off the state.

FACTS: * Blacks as a group are younger than whites, so proportionately more blacks than whites are working and therefore paying income tax and national insurance. 91% of black men are working compared with 77% of white men. (*The Facts of Racial Disadvantage,* Political and Economic Planning, 1976)
  * Since there are proportionately fewer older people in the black community, they take much less from the state than the white population.
  * Black people are likely to receive only 80-90% as much as their fellow citizens from state funds for health, welfare, education, social services, and housing. (*The Economic Impact of Immigrants,* Cambridge University Press, 1970)

EMPLOYMENT

MYTH: They come here and take our jobs.

FACT: * During the 1950s and '60s when there was a shortage of labour, we, like many industrialised countries, looked to other countries to help us out. 11% of the total work forces in West Germany and France, and 28% of that in Switzerland, are migrants, compared with 7.5% of workers in Britain. (*Western Europe's Migrant Workers,* Minority Rights Group, 1976)
  * Today it is very hard for someone from the New Commonwealth to get a work permit, as they are not issued to overseas people if the job can be filled by a local person. In 1975 we admitted 2,074 12-month work permit holders from the New Commonwealth and Pakistan, compared with 7,986 from the other non-EEC countries, including the Old Commonwealth. (Home Office Immigration Statistics, 1975)
  * Racial discrimination makes it harder for a black man than for a white man to get a job.

(*The Extent of Racial Discrimination,* PEP, 1974)

EDUCATION

MYTH: Because they don't speak English they hold back our children at school.

FACT: * Many children of immigrant parents were born here and English is their first language.
  * Most local education authorities make arrangements to teach English to non-English speaking children in special classes with special teachers so that they do not impede the progress of the rest of the children. (*Immigrant Pupils in England,* National Foundation for Educational Research, 1971)
  * There is no evidence to say that the proportion of black children in a class has any significant influence on the attainment of white pupils. (*Language Proficiency in the Multi-Racial Junior School: A Comparative Study,* NFER, 1975; *Race and Education across Cultures,* Heinemann, 1975)

HOUSING

MYTH: They get priority in housing.

FACT: 4% of Asians and 26% of West Indians live in council house accommodation, compared with about 30% of the population as a whole. (*The Facts of Racial Disadvantage,* PEP, 1976)

MYTH: Immigrants are running down our inner-city areas.

FACT: Urban decay has existed in this country since the Industrial Revolution. Bad housing conditions were here long before black immigrants. In the areas where 70% of black people live, eight out of ten people are white. (Census 1971)

THE BRITISH

MYTH: The British race was a pure one until these people came.

FACT: There is no such thing as *the British race.* The British are made up of many different groups who have come here at different times.

PEOPLE SAY . . .

there is nothing wrong in being prejudiced in favour of Britain.

Of course not — provided that one is proud of all that is good about Britain: British tolerance, the British sense of fair play, British hospitality, British democracy and British freedoms. There is no virtue in being proud of intolerance, irrationality, ignorance, fear and bigotry just because they are labelled *Made in Britain.*

PEOPLE SAY . . .

the immigrants don't want to integrate.

It depends what you mean by integration. If we ask immigrants to give up their religious, their cultural traditions, their food, dress and music and their strong belief in the family, we are asking much more than the British who settled overseas were prepared to give up. If, by integration, we mean equal opportunities in education, jobs and housing and in making a positive contribution to society, this is certainly what immigrants do want, and are being denied it at present by racial discrimination.

I define integration not as a flattening process of assimilation but as equal opportunity, accompanied by cultural diversity, in an atmosphere of mutual tolerance.

Roy Jenkins

The Community Relations Commission was established under the Race Relations Act 1968. Under the Act it has the broad duties:

[a] *to encourage the establishment of, and assist others to take steps to secure the establishment of, harmonious community relations and to co-ordinate on a national basis the measures adopted for that purpose by others; and*

[b] *to advise the Secretary of State for the Home Department on any matter referred to the Commission by him and to make recommendations to him, on any matter which the Commission considers should be brought to his attention.*

SOURCE: *Some People Will Believe Anything* (Commission for Racial Equality, 2nd ed., 1979).

Conquest and migration

The presence of different minority groups in Britain, and their situation in society today, can only be understood in the light of British history. Until recently this was a history of conquest and colonization (see page 13) which had a profound impact on large parts of the world. Domination by a once powerful nation has long-term effects — effects which continue well after decolonization. Thus Britain, having underdeveloped its colonies, then looked to its former territories to supplement its own work force. The corollary of conquest for several European countries turned out to be migration back to the metropolitan centres.

Extract 4.3

MY PEOPLE are showing great interest in reports from England of the immigration debate at present taking place. Many of them react sympathetically to the determination of Mrs Thatcher not to let her own tribe lose its cultural values in a tidal wave of immigrants, although they seem surprised that the British should feel that less than 5 per cent of the population is a cause for concern.

Perhaps it would comfort the British to know that we Maoris

KEEP BRITAIN FOR THE BRITISH
Only 200m to absorb

NGATA TE KOROU

Maori teacher in New Zealand

have managed to keep our lan-

guage and some of our traditions alive in spite of being overwhelmed 10 to one by British immigrants over the last 150 years—and that in spite of a determined attack upon our culture by the immigrant majority which lasted for over a century.

We also notice that elements of British political life wish to send back the immigrants from Asia and the Caribbean. This has given great heart to our own radical young. They claim that, thanks to the British passion for fair play, we can now expect concern for the cultural threat posed by immigrants to Britain to be matched by an equal concern for the threat posed by British immigrants to other cultures, such as our own.

Should any future Conservative, Powellite, or National Front government succeed in repatriating immigrants, we will hope to return your emigrants to take up the vacancies. It so happens that we have almost exactly the same number of "cultural aliens" as Britain has "coloured immigrants"—about 2½ million whites of predominantly British extraction. There seems to be no reason why the indigenous populations of other old Commonwealth countries should not expect likewise.

This would mean that for every West Indian or Indian deported, we could send you, on a fair statistical basis, as replacements, one "pakeha" New Zealander, four Australians, four Canadians, half a South African white, part of a white Rhodesian, and no fewer than 50 American WASPs. It would take some time for you to absorb the extra 200 million people involved, but there is no reason why, if phased over a decent period (say a century) and with sensible birth control measures being taken, England should not be the exclusive home of those who speak English and live in the English manner.

Others among us would prefer more moderate solutions to our immigrant problem—which is the problem of your emigrants. Such people would wish us to absorb what is good in other cultures, while preserving the good in our own. They say that the world is now too small for anyone to claim rights of ethnic homelands, as Hitler did. This, you must agree, shows great tolerance from those whose parents and grandparents were tricked by treaties, robbed by land grabs, ravaged by wars fought for even more land then evicted from what was left as a punishment for resisting the attacks, their children forced into schools in which their own language and cultural values were proscribed. In spite of that our moderates still dream of a world where any man can live wherever he likes.

Our radicals on the other hand say that this is ridiculous and sentimental, and that we should accept that racism exists everywhere, and that everyone should go back to his own ancestral homeland as soon as possible.

They too have a dream, a dream of the forest returning to cover the land which has been almost ruined by intensive and destructive methods of pastoral farming, a dream of the return to a proper balance with nature. Perhaps the day may come again when we can dig kumara, and harvest the fruits of forests, rivers, and the sea. They dream of the warm comradeship of family group and sub-tribe; of telling of ancient stories around the cooking fires, as the long Pacific waves thunder up on empty beaches. And never a single greedy, grasping, calculating, tricky white face to be seen anywhere.

They are depending upon the success of Britain's ultra Right wing.

SOURCE: *Sunday Times,* 19 March 1978.

Part Two
Teaching about Majority/Minority Issues

5 Three Case Studies

The case studies in this chapter begin to answer the question 'How?' That is, 'How might one begin to tackle a particular majority/minority issue?' In the three examples that are given, attention is paid to the minority experience, and the extracts include the voices of the participants themselves. Attention is drawn to some of the key issues in each situation as well as appropriate resources. Comparison with some of the descriptions in chapter 9 will show just how big the gap often is between what is needed and available stereotyped resources. It is hoped that the general approaches indicated in this chapter can, and will, be transferred to other case studies chosen by the teacher to meet the needs of particular situations.

The three case studies dealt with are:
1. *The Aboriginal struggle* over land rights in the face of multinational mining companies and government inertia.
2. *The Sahel nomads* and problems of defining 'development', together with reflections on how 'disasters' in the Third World are often misrepresented.
3. *Native Americans* and their fight for justice in the richest country of the world.

They are not intended to be self-contained studies but to show the sort of materials that are available and the kind of discussion points they could be used to provoke. Some would be suitable for older students as they stand, others would need adaptation.

1 The Aboriginal struggle

Most materials on the Aborigine people concentrate exclusively on the past to the detriment of the present. This study focuses on the situation of black Australians today and in particular the role of multinational mining companies in the destruction of Aboriginal culture. It also gives an Aboriginal perspective on their land and towards colonization.

Key themes:

(a) Culture and traditions with particular reference to the land.
(b) Invasion and oppression.
(c) The Aborigine's white problem.
(d) The multinational mining companies.

Extract 5.1

The Life of the Natural People

(as told by the Mapoon peoples of Northern Queensland)

'Living with the Land – The Land and the People are of one Mind'

Long before Europeans came to live **on it**, Mapoon peoples lived **with** their land. The people acted so that all the things they consumed might be renewed. Land was not viewed as a **resource** to be exploited for private profit but as the **source** of the group's very being. 'Everything is done in its proper time and kept and used in its proper time – not this just going round killing and wasting things', said Jerry Hudson at Mapoon, 1975.

Through the land people came to be and remain alive. The land is the core experience of their lives. It is personalized in the image of their grandfather – that term being the same as that for Totem. It is the source of their personhood and the means through which they relate to one another as groups. For Mapoon peoples the land was not only soil and rocks but wells, streams, swamps, lagoons, animals and vegetables and, above all, rivers.

At Mapoon the clans of the Tjungundji tribe took their names from the territories they occupied. Only the land had a name. It was the land and the position it occupied relative to other clan lands that gave the group its identity. The clans of the Tjungundji tribe, for example, married into each other according to their geographical position, they became a member of one of four groups, named after the cardinal points of the compass. Amongst the Tjungundji, people also inherited a relationship with their land through their grandfather. The term 'for the father's father' is the same as that for Totem. The grandfather shares in the timeless quality of being that Totems possess. This sharing of being is of the class 'kangaroo' as against 'a kangaroo', (in the 'kangarooness' of the kangaroo species) thus while the kangaroo might be killed, it might not be eaten, being 'Too much like father belong we'. The tribe was a group who spoke a common language.

As members of their land, Mapoon people had rights to receive its foods. These foods took the form of fish and marine life, birds, animals and plant vegetables. As in most clans strict laws and routines govern the hunting and gathering of these foods. The elders ensuring that everything was done **'at its proper time and in its proper way'**. In turn the elders perform certain rights at specific times and in doing so participated in nature's renewal of the food supply. Harry Toeboy and Jerry Hudson tell it this way.

Harry Toeboy: 'The yams have bosses to look after them. There is a man or a woman who has to look after them. If it's not time to dig then nobody can dig. They have to wait until the boss says the time has come. He tells his people or he tells his wife, 'Yam very good, nice and soft'. So everybody is told and everybody claps their hands and they dance. Oh, they are glad to dig the yam!'

Jerry Hudson: 'They bury again what they cannot eat, and then after a two or three weeks they move on to another patch. When the dry season comes and the ground is too hard to dig, they go back and dig up the ones they buried and they have enough to keep them going.'

As Lawrence says: 'Aboriginals understood very well the habits of the animals they hunted, and capitalized on the peculiarities of the local area.'

When water became scarce, the people sunk wells and tapped certain water-bearing trees. Different cooking methods were developed for the various foods along with specialized processes for leaching out toxins. Occasionally tribes sent out invitations to one another to participate in a hunting drive. In this way all peoples could share in a variety and abundance of food to their different areas. Jerry Hudson tells it this way.

'When they all get together, the boss of the land gives them the time to begin burning. Every person right down to the youngest takes spears in their hands, and the women take their dilly bags to go and pick up the catch. So they go and form a big circle with a narrow neck. Everything has to come through the neck and that's where the people are with their fighting sticks.'

Harry Toeboy laughed, 'You chase kangaroos, you kill wallabies or anything you want to kill — and a lot of snakes come out too!' Jerry continued, 'You would be surprised to see how much they can catch in that day. They stop there and cook. They never waste. They don't just go there for the fun of killing. They can keep the meat there for nearly a week underground (e.g. in earth ovens), they heat it up every day and when the last bit is finished, they all say goodbye to each other and travel back to their own territory.'

SOURCE: Abridged from J. P. Roberts (ed.), *The Mapoon Story by the Mapoon People* (Victoria, Aust.: International Development Action, 1975)

Discussion points

1. How many things can you list that the Aborigines were skilled in? How would they have learnt these? (Explore the nature of 'skills' and the fact that school is only one place where education occurs.)
2. Do *you* possess any of these skills? Do you think that they would be easy to learn? Could you survive on your own in Mapoon territory? (Explore definitions of culture: urban-industrial culture is only one sort of culture; also discuss individual versus group perspectives on survival.)
3. Why is their land vital to the survival of an Aboriginal group? (i.e., not just for physical survival but as part of the group's spiritual and cultural roots.)
4. Many people feel we have lost the ability to live with the land in our urban-industrial culture. If

anything went wrong with our highly technological support system do you think we could survive? Why do you think that many groups of people in industrialized countries are moving back to the land, growing as much of their own food as possible and re-learning rural crafts?

Extract 5.2

Invasions and Massacres

One-hundred-and-sixty-four years before Aborigines defended themselves against Cook at Botany Bay, Europeans trespassed on Australian land for the first time at Mapoon. 'The French, the Portuguese and the Spanish usually professed to religious motives, the English often gave scientific reasons. Only the Dutch told us quite frankly why Australia was discovered' (O. R. Scott – *The Discoverers*).

In 1606 the Dutch ship *Duyfken,* financed by the Dutch East India Company, set out under Willem Janz to tour New Guinea waters and discover new areas to trade and plunder. Its previous voyage ended in the establishment of the first Dutch territory in Indonesia. Thinking it New Guinea, the *Duyfken* sailed into Mapoon territorial waters but – 'Every attempt at a landing was opposed by native hostile Aborigines with spears in their hands'. Eventually a landing party set out to investigate the Batavia River, where the Mapoon people today are now living and struggling to keep their land. The Australians quickly organized armed resistance to the Dutch, spearing and killing one man. Nine others, nearly half the crew, were killed before the *Duyfken* finally left the Australian coast despite it being armed with eight cannons.

On May 12th 1623, the Dutch sailed another three ships to Mapoon and were confronted by – '200 natives making a violent noise and with their spears ready to throw, and evidently very distrustful, for though pieces of iron and other things were thrown to them, they would not stop to parley, but tried every trick with the object of wounding and capturing one of our men'. Carstenz, the Dutch captain, had offered his crew a reward of ten pieces of eight for each Australian captured. Only one Australian was captured, and one other fatally wounded. The Dutch searched the Australians' huts along the beach for valuable loot but to no avail.

The cattlemen Lachlan Kennedy and Frank Jardine were the first Europeans to settle the area (in the 1890s).

'Jardine and Kennedy came through Batavia River (now called the Wenlock on Government maps). Jardine wanted to put his station 50 miles up – you can still see the stone walls he made for his footpath. They were killing people all the way up. At Dingle Dingle Creek they killed most of a tribe. That's the Batavia River people. Billy Miller and Andrew Archie are of that tribe. Only 50 left out of 300,' said Jerry Hudson. But the Aboriginal people were a fighting people and not easily cowed. 'About this Moreton Station. Well, we people took spears, people from Mapoon and Weipa and all them places. They came together from Coen Creek to go to Moreton. They were fighting there with the spears. They killed one bloke. He fell down. He was out of the mission, but they were very strong in the mission,' said Harry Toeboy.

Jerry Hudson continues, 'They were chased out by the Mapoon people and had to go up to Somerset' (on the tip of Cape York).

On the way up they passed through the territory known as the Seven Rivers, which extends from Mapoon up to Somerset. The massacring continued. 'You see,' says Mrs Jimmy, 'from all the Seven Rivers, that was all wiped out. Mr Jardine took over from up at Catfish Creek (on the Ducie River due east of Mapoon) right up to Somerset. They were wiped out completely. The only child he saved, he grew up as his son, but the rest were wiped out. They had no chance because Mr Jardine had his armour on. That's how they could not spear him. The spears were broken on his armour.'

Frank Don tells how 'The time when we were cutting timber for fence rails at the old mission, the story was told to me that they climbed up into the ti-tree, anything that had leaves, bushy you know. When they see them, they shoot them down. They fall like birds on the ground – and that's how the Seven River Men got killed. If they run away, they caught them for a tracker go with these men to find them so they can be shot. They had rifles too.' That is how today there are no Aboriginal people living along the rivers North of Mapoon, even though this region is as yet Aboriginal Reserve as it is mostly unwanted by the mining companies.

Mrs Jimmy tells about her uncle: 'What my Mother told me was that people got killed at the time when Rev. Hey and Rev. Ward – James Gibson Ward – was here (around 1893). The first child they picked up was my uncle. My Grandmother had to hide him inside a waterhole and cover him with a skin bark, but Lachlan Kennedy heard the little baby crying. I think the baby was about two years old. They took the child into the mission and gave him to Mrs Ward and she grew my Uncle Barkly, and that's how he was one of the young chaps that built up the Church that is burnt down here today at Old Mapoon.'

Up at Cowal Creek, at the other end of Seven River territory, they remember how Jardine used to kill black children by knocking their heads against trees, and how he and Kennedy together exterminated hundreds of Aboriginals.

Lachlan Kennedy, according to the Mapoon people, eventually mended his ways and started helping the people. Mrs Jimmy said, 'About the cattle now, it was given by Lachlan Kennedy in exchange for the lives of our Aboriginal people.' He married a local Aborigine. They say he asked to be buried in a vertical position as a sign of his disgrace as a murderer. He had some 20 notches on his gun for the Blacks he had killed.

Source: Abridged from J. Roberts, M. Parsons and B. Russell (eds.), *The Mapoon Story According to the Invaders: Church Mission, Queensland Government and Mining Company*, and J. P. Roberts (ed.), *The Mapoon Story by the Mapoon People* (both Victoria, Aust.: International Development Action, 1975).

Extract 5.3.

Unrecorded Bloodshed

by Mrs. Jean Jimmy

In our early history Aboriginals were shot and poisoned.
Therefore the voices of our generations cry from the ground.

This is regarded as a threatening story
Throughout every State of Australia
Also across each island that is near here,
Including Tasmania and her islands.

We deeply sympathize for the loss of our brothers and sisters.
We'll fight with voices and not by weapons
Because this was once Aboriginal land
Before any explorers ever explored.

This big island where black feet have trodden these golden shores
Long before any white settlers ever came.
Aboriginals have lived with their tribal laws and cultures
That were inherited by birth.
As our Lord spoke unto Moses,
'And ye shall divide the land by lot
For an inheritance among your families
And to the more ye shall give the more inheritance
And to the fewer ye shall give the less inheritance
Every man's inheritance shall be in the place where his lots falleth
According to the tribes of your Fathers ye shall inherit.'

Source: J. P. Roberts (ed.), *The Mapoon Story by the Mapoon People,* op. cit.

Discussion points

1. Recreate the scene on the arrival of the *Duyfken* off the Mapoon coast. What would the various reactions have been as the ship sent sailors ashore? As a Mapoon would your initial fears about the invaders have been proved right?
2. What right did the cattlemen have in the 1890s to take Aboriginal territory for cattle stations?
3. Imagine what it would have been like to be part of a group being hunted down by white cattlemen. Write a description of how you would have felt and what you would have done.
4. Write your own poem about the suffering of your people over the years.

Extract 5.4

The Aborigines White Problem

The native Australians have faced many problems since the original Cook's tour of 1770. An increasing amount of their country has been taken away from them by the settlers, the mining companies and the government. But recently the newly-installed Liberal-Country administration of Mr Fraser has produced yet another problem. It chose as a scandalous example of the former government's financial mismanagement, a project of the Department of Aborigine Affairs. Predictably enough it hit the headlines. And it was

quickly followed up with a swingeing cutback in the Aborigines Affairs budget. This satisfied the election promise to reduce government expenditure. But it contradicted the promise to the Aborigines that there would be no financial cuts at their expense.
CAMERON FORBES, a leading writer on the Melbourne Age, looks more closely at the Aborigine's white problem.

In the cemetery at Alice Springs — the town in the red heart of Australia — there is a growing grove of small headstones.

This is a region of haunting beauty: brown and purple hills, granite monoliths and, when the rare rain falls, a delicate carpet of lime-green grass.

It is elemental country, worn down to the bare bones, harsh and demanding. In the past those who survived it, let alone lived by it, had to walk lightly in a fragile ecosystem.

But the bodies under the headstones are not victims of the desert fringe regions. They have been/are being/will be killed by the struggle to subsist on the fringes of white Australian society.

In some seasons the Aboriginal infant mortality rate in the Alice Springs area exceeds that of rural India or Africa. In general an Aboriginal infant is four to eight times more likely to die before his first birthday than a white baby is.

This is only one of the indices of Aboriginal underprivilege and deprivation. Yet in this year's budget [1976], the conservative Liberal-Country Party government cut the spending programme on Aborigines by £25 million.

Only after intense lobbying by Aborigines and their supporters and a vigorous campaign by the media was £17 million of this restored. This leaves the allocation £5 million below the previous year's total — and the shortfall is more in real terms when Australia's double-figure inflation is taken into account.

The government which had before it a report showing that 4500 Aboriginal families live in humpies, shanties and abandoned cars slashed about £11 million off housing programmes.

The Treasurer, Mr Lynch, proffered as an explanation for cuts in expenditure on the neediest Australians the dazzling insight that injection of ever-increasing amounts of money would not solve the complex problems of Aboriginal welfare.

The only heartening thing about the Government's parsimony is the angry reaction from the Australian public, a pleasant change from the general apathy.

It is not an unusual pattern. A decade ago, in response to a referendum question, the nation gave an overwhelming 'yes' to the proposition that the government should have the over-riding responsibility for Aborigines and the power to discriminate in their favour.

But after this outbreak of public sympathy — an emotional payback for two centuries of destruction and degradation — little was done by the conservative government of the day and the public nestled into apathy again.

The rise of black consciousness and the election of Gough Whitlam's Labor Government saw burgeoning expenditure and a flurry of activity. It also led to some disappointment and frustration, though this was nothing compared to the reaction to the attitudes and actions of the conservative government on its return to power last year.

Public apathy is understandable. Most whites never see an Aborigine. The blacks are mostly tucked away in urban slums, segregated on the outskirts of country towns or gathered into artificial groups on government settlements or church missions.

Wrong or misguided policies, particularly by the Liberal-Country Party government, are understandable too. The Liberal Party is the party of capital and Aboriginal demand for control of their reserves makes it awkward for the giant multinational mining companies who want the mineral resources they contain.

The Country Party represents the graziers and farmers, the people who were historically in the vanguard of the European dispossessers and who at present have most to lose if traditional land is returned to the tribal and semi-tribal Aborigines.

The white problem

Land rights are the key issue in the Aboriginal problem — or the white problem, to put it more correctly. They are vital both to the rural and the urban Aborigines; practically and psychologically to rural Aborigines, psychologically to the urban Aborigines. There is also the question of compensation to those who do not live on or who have lost links with traditional land.

Before the white invasion, Aborigines had a physical and spiritual link with certain tracts of land, its flora and fauna.

It was their book of creation, marked by their ancestor figures on their Dreamtime tasks and journeys. Here Malu the Kangaroo rested. There he entered the ground.

They performed increase ceremonies to regenerate the animals and plants. They passed sacred objects round ceremonial routes which stretched thousands of miles.

The descent of the Aborigines

In the 1971 census, 106,000 Australians identified themselves as Aborigines out of a population of about 14 million.

Government experts estimate that by the end of the century the Aboriginal population will have doubled – restoring it almost to the estimated total of around the time Captain Cook sailed up the East Coast of Australia in 1770.

The Aborigines were decimated by disease, hunted down in so-called punitive expeditions, poisoned inadvertently by alcohol and sometimes deliberately by strychnine in flour.

Today they are at the bottom of the socio-economic ladder. The relative difference in white and Aboriginal mortality rates is even more unfavourable than the difference in infant mortality rates.

Those who survive are likely to be crippled mentally and physically by malnutrition. Life expectancy is considerably shorter than that of whites. They are educationally disadvantaged and there is still only a handful of black university graduates.

Whereas about 5% of the national workforce is unemployed, 27% of Aborigines are without jobs.

Aborigines form a disproportionate proportion of the prison population because of – according to experts such as sociologist Lorna Lippman – their higher visibility as well as police antipathy.

And some of them still do.

This link with the land and the continuance, in some areas of ritual life, is ignored, unknown or only partly understood.

Consider the comment of Mr Justice Blackburn when he gave his decision during a court battle by Yirrkala Aborigines against a mining company.

Dismissing the Aborigines' claim for control over their traditional land, the judge said evidence showed the Aborigines belonged to the land but not that the land belonged to the Aborigines.

To generalize about the Aboriginal situation is dangerous. In central Australia, there are about forty different dialects.

But there are areas which present problems at their strongest – Indulkena, for instance.

Indulkena is in the north of the state of South Australia. If you want to be more accurate, it is within the boundaries of one of the large cattle runs, Granite Downs, 3680 square miles in area.

Granite Downs, part of a chain owned by a rich and powerful family, provides income for a handful of people. Indulkena, 12 square miles of the most barren part of Granite Downs, is home for 200 people of the Yankuntjatjara tribe.

Round its boundaries runs a dog fence built to special specifications... it cuts across country and even down the perpendicular side of gorges.

The building of the fence was a condition of the sale to the South Australian government, because, it was claimed by the white graziers, sheep were coming and the Aborigines' dogs would be a danger.

When I was there several years later, the sheep had not come. Old hands said they never would. But the Aborigines were fenced in and also fenced out from something vital to them.

Listen:

'Do they think we are animals in a cage?' Whisky asks in the Yankuntjatjara language while Jim Lester, blind Aboriginal social worker translates. Whisky is talking to a meeting of Indulkena men. *'We are not dogs to sit behind a fence,'* he says, *'It makes us cranky.'*

'Uwa, uwa,' the men grunt. *'Yes, yes.'*

'Our sacred sites are outside the fence. We want our land,' Whisky says.

With even more vigor the men answer *'Uw, Uw'.* (That's just so. That's just so.)

The people feel cut off from spiritual sustenance ... and more.

They have written to the government saying: *'Now, before we used to eat kangaroo, emu, euro, rabbits, pirenti, goanna and porcupine also, and these meats of ours have disappeared and we can hardly think how to get meat.*

'We are shut in here and left like dogs. And our kangaroo, emu, euro, and so on have gone far away, because this fence is too close.'

There seems little chance that the Indulkena people will get their land and with it the sacred sites and the dignity which comes from being able to hunt instead of relying on hand-outs.

But the Labor Government did, in the northern territory, which it controls, begin a process of giving tribal and semi-tribal Aborigines control of traditional land. The conservative government may be less than half-hearted about this.

The urban blacks, with their search for what they call *'Aboriginality',* regard land rights as crucial for their survival and strength as a people.

'More than any foreign aid programme more than any international obligation which we meet or forfeit, more than any part we may play in any treaty or alliance, Australia's treatment of her Aborigine people will be the thing upon which the rest of the world will judge Australia and Australians.'

(*Gough Whitlam,*
Leader of the Australian Labor Party.)

A fragmented leadership

There has been militancy in the cities, cries of black power and a raising of black consciousness. There has also been bitter in-fighting and the leadership is fragmented — which may not be a bad thing on a couple of counts.

One is that the rural Aborigines, though they often regard themselves as fount and guardians of the culture, can be dominated by urban blacks in white-type meetings.

The other, black activist Bobbi Sykes points out, is that if the Government cannot easily identify a tame or tameable black leadership or define the authority structures the communities will have more chance of going their chosen ways.

That was the rule of thumb policy laid down by the Labor Government: the basis for Aboriginal development should be communities making their own decisions about the pace and nature of progress.

Making decisions involves the possibility of making mistakes which may mean the loss of money. But decision-making is another path to dignity and it is to be hoped that the Liberal-Country Party government realizes that the views of cost-efficiency experts on Aboriginal spending programmes must be off-set by assessments of social and psychological benefits.

After all, what the Aborigines have lost at the hands, guns, cattle and sheep of the whitemen is a little difficult to handle in an accounting ledger.

SOURCE: *The New Internationalist,* No. 46, December 1976.

Discussion points

1. List as many ways as you can in which Aborigines are an underprivileged group in Australia today. Is it a long list or a short one?
2. Who have most to lose if traditional land is returned to Aborginal tribes? Look back to the readings on culture and remind yourself of why the land is so important to Aborigines.
3. How do you think you might react to this continual attack on your culture? (Explore the reasons for apathy and indifference, also for increasing militancy.)
4. Can you find out about any other minority groups which have been exploited and oppressed in similar ways to the Aborigines? Was their history in any way similar?

Extract 5.5

The Burning of Mapoon

Mrs Jimmy:
'When we left the houses were burnt down, I think it was because they didn't want us to return back to Old Mapoon. We got witnesses who have seen the burning down of our homes. The witnesses are Rachel, Jessie and Harry. Is it true Jessie, Rachel and Harry? ('Yes, they reply.) Well, can you say something on that, Mr or Mrs Don?
Frank Don:
'Yes I can say something on it. Well, the irons that we bought (for the houses) with work from six to six to get money, sell crocodile hide to get money to buy iron to build our homes, then somebody come along and burnt it down. That's why today Mr Killoran wouldn't come and show his face towards us. I hate him for that. If he come, me and Maggie tell him what we want to tell him.'
Mrs Jimmy:
'Mr and Mrs Don Gilbert, Harry, Jessie and Rachel you know our custom is different, that when you burning down a home it means you burn the whole body of our Aboriginal custom and they die so fast. This is the custom, we believe in it.

'Armed police walked us along the beach — their revolvers or even their shining handcuffs and clubs they didn't use, though we all seen them hanging on their belts. Police O'Shea helped by taking my suitcase, also our short gun, so I carried our rifle and my hand bag. Mr and Mrs Archie and son rejoined us on the beach; we walked straight along the beach and turn up where the Mission house was, and to our surprise we all seen Mr R. Reid and family standing at the foot of the steps under a Saibai police guard. Orders were given by Mr Turner to police that they take us to the Mission cottage where we will leave our suitcases and swags then return back to the Mission house.

'Mr Turner took our names down on a book; Mr Turner had the two white police standing on his right and his Saibai police servant on his left, and four Saibai police stood guard at the foot of the step. Mr Turner asked us if we had our tea. We told him most of us didn't have our tea because we came home from duck shooting and was taken by surprise and had to leave our tea hot on our stoves. Most of us didn't eat, just had a cup of tea. After tea we all were taken across to the Mission cottage to spend the night under police guard. Four families slept with white police above our heads and below our feets. Saibai police sat guard all night until dawn.

'Next day was Saturday, 16th November, 1963. Orders were given to us to roll up our swags and to take everything we had down to the beach. While they were unloading the Gelam there was no respect of any kind to let women to have a bath or even use toilet. We sat all day after five before all four families were given orders to go on board the Gelam.'
Rachel Peter:
'I know that my father and mother were forced out, because the police they went out to Janie Creek to take them off me and my husband – we were camping out there too.

'My parent's home was burnt down. I went to my mother's place to get her belongings out of the house. She told me what to get and send it out to her in Bamaga but by the time I got there I saw Aunty Jean's home going up in flames.

'I saw the D.N.A. carpenters coming over and I saw them going to the coconut trees getting dry coconut branches, put it under the homes and into the homes and strike a match and up goes the flames and down comes the house with everything that they left in it. Even stoves, new stoves that were expensive, but they were burnt down we didn't have the chance to get anything out.'
Harry Toeboy described how he discovered what had happened:
'I was working for Alcan at the time. When we flew back over Mapoon, I saw that only a few houses were left standing. What was wrong? I didn't know. We landed at the airstrip and met Mr Stephen Mark and some others and they told me, "Mapoon is shifted," I said, "I could see that from the air."

Simon Peter had to say: 'Yes, I saw them go up in flames. I was here with my wife and six children when the whole place went up in flames. We have seen it with our bare eyes. From my Mother-in-Law's place down they burnt everything.'

Norman Wheeler added: 'It upset me a lot. Even when I went back to get some irons (corrugated iron sheets), they were all burnt and bent.'

Rachel Peter asked them why they were doing it. They replied: 'We are just carrying out orders.'
Simon Peter: 'The Church, cookhouse, school, work-shop, butcher shop, store all burnt down. They left the medical store but they took away all the medicines.'

The final group of about 48 stayed on for months after the burning. But eventually they were forced to leave early in 1964.

Norman Wheeler: 'We were all forced from this place because ... they took everything from us – food, medical equipment – everything.'

Rachel Peter: 'I had to leave because I had no medical treatment for my boy who was sick.'

SOURCE: Abridged from J. P. Roberts (ed.), *The Mapoon Story by the Mapoon People*, op. cit.

Extract 5.6

The People Get in the Way of the Mining Companies

By the 1950s, Government circles knew there were deposits of bauxite, the raw material of the aluminium industry at Weipa, Mapoon and Aurukun. A government geologist had reported in 1947 that the deposits at Aurukun were of good grade. The Australian Aluminium Production Commission, a body authorized to take up bauxite leases in the name of the nation, had requested samples from Aurukun, Weipa and Mapoon. The existence of large scale, easily accessible, mineral deposits in this region had been known since 1902.

However these deposits did not fall into the hands of private interests until after government and mining industry representatives quit the government commission to form a bauxite mining company to be known as COMALCO....

The Australian Mining and Smelting Company, Comalco's predecessor, took initally 3045 square

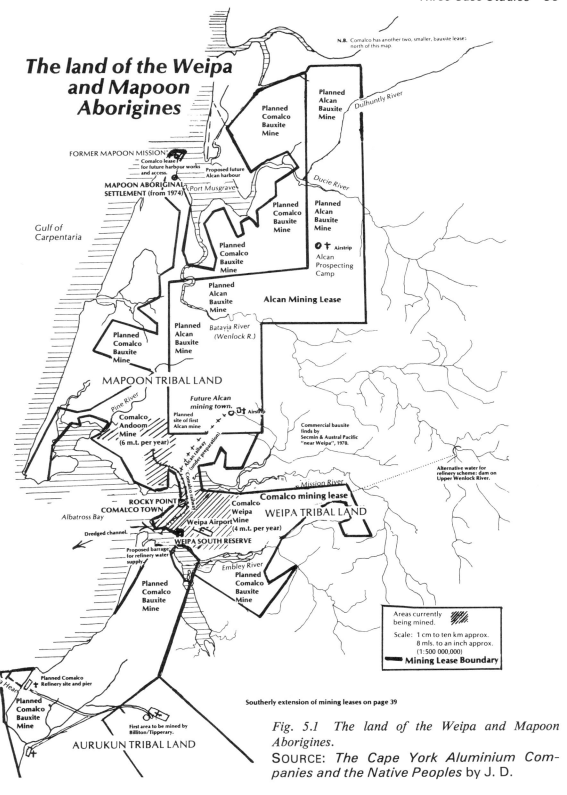

The land of the Weipa and Mapoon Aborigines

N.B. Comalco has another two, smaller, bauxite leases north of this map.

Planned Comalco Bauxite Mine

Planned Alcan Bauxite Mine

Dulhunty River

FORMER MAPOON MISSION
Comalco lease for future harbour works and access.

Proposed future Alcan harbour

MAPOON ABORIGINAL SETTLEMENT (from 1974)

Port Musgrave

Ducie River

Planned Comalco Bauxite Mine

Planned Alcan Bauxite Mine

Gulf of Carpentaria

Planned Comalco Bauxite Mine

Airstrip
Alcan Prospecting Camp

Planned Alcan Bauxite Mine

Alcan Mining Lease

Planned Comalco Bauxite Mine

Planned Alcan Bauxite Mine

Batavia River (Wenlock R.)

MAPOON TRIBAL LAND

Future Alcan mining town.
Airstrip

Planned site of first Alcan mine

Commercial bauxite finds by Secmin & Austral Pacific "near Weipa", 1970.

Pine River

Comalco Andoom Mine (6 m.t. per year)

Alcan railway (under preparation)

Comalco railway

Alternative water for refinery scheme: dam on Upper Wenlock River.

Mission River

Comalco mining lease

WEIPA TRIBAL LAND

ROCKY POINT COMALCO TOWN

Albatross Bay

Dredged channel.

Comalco Weipa Mine (4 m.t. per year)

Weipa Airport

WEIPA SOUTH RESERVE

Proposed barrage for refinery water supply.

Embley River

Planned Comalco Bauxite Mine

Planned Comalco Bauxite Mine

Areas currently being mined.

Scale: 1 cm to ten km approx.
8 mls. to an inch approx.
(1:500 000,000)
Mining Lease Boundary

Pera Head

Planned Comalco Refinery site and pier

Planned Comalco Bauxite Mine

First area to be mined by Billiton/Tipperary.

AURUKUN TRIBAL LAND

Southerly extension of mining leases on page 39

Fig. 5.1 The land of the Weipa and Mapoon Aborigines.

SOURCE: *The Cape York Aluminium Companies and the Native Peoples* by J. D.

miles, and Alcan 5675 square miles, as prospecting leases – most of this being Aboriginal Reserve. It was found that this land contained the largest, most accessible, purest and most easily mined deposit in the world, with at least 2700 million tons of commercial grade bauxite worth, at 1975 prices, at least $23 thousand million.

The eager desire of the Queensland Government to 'develop' the state by establishing industries (whether foreign owned or not) and to get white people to colonize the North as a protection against communist invasion, made the Government put as few obstacles in the path of the mining company as they possibly could. The negotiations went like this:

Company: *'The Aboriginal Reserves are in the way.'*

Government: *'That's no worry. We'll give you the land. Comalco can have over 2000 square miles, Alcan over 500 as a mining lease, as they requested. The Aborigines don't need their land any more.'*

Company: *'Compensating the Aborigines would embarrass us — we don't have the money to spare.'*

Government: *'We'll explain to the Church that runs the Aborigines' affairs in the local missions that you are too poor to pay compensation.'*

Company: *'We might like to have a few extras. How about perpetual grazing and farming rights over the former Aboriginal Reserve — and timber and water rights too?'*

Government: *'That's easy. They are yours for the asking.'*

Company: *'Could you provide us with a harbour to our specifications—and port facilities—free?'*

Government: *'We will pay for them.'*

Company: *'We can't afford to pay much in royalties.'*

Government: *'Would 5c a ton be too much? Jamaica (1975) charges 12c.'*

Company: *'What about the Aboriginal settlements on the Bauxite field?'*

Government: *'We'll let them be moved elsewhere if they inconvenience you.'*

Company: *'Don't make any stipulations about Aboriginal rights. It's best to leave them to us. You can trust us.'*

Government: *'We won't reserve any rights for them. We know we can trust you to do the right thing by them because of your fine reputation for looking after native people elsewhere.'*

SOURCE: J. P. Roberts, M. Parsons and B. Russel (eds.), *The Mapoon Story According to the Invaders*, op cit.

Extract 5.7

Back at Home on our Tribal Land

Rachel Peter:

'I was born here, my father was born here, my mother, my great grandparents. This is our tribal land...I hope we will never leave the place.

'Here in our home, our Mapoon, there's plenty of everything for us to eat. Everything you can think of: pigs, wallabies, kangaroo, oysters and crabs, fish, prawns, arrowroot, wild yams and a lot of other things that we were taught to eat by our grandparents and our fathers and mothers. We like all that because we grew up with it and when we were sent away we missed it a lot, because we can't get these things like this at Bamaga or Weipa.

'We feel happy to be now back home. We wish other people could do the same, if they think they want to come back home. But we're not asking anybody to come if they don't want to.

'However I feel that I'm so happy to be back home that I think I'll be here for the rest of my life now with my children. I went out and I travelled around a bit but I found that there is no other place like home. NO other place like Mapoon, so now I'm here I don't think I'll ever leave Mapoon again. I think I have the right to stay in my own tribal land like any other people in other places do.

'We love this place because there are a lot of hunting grounds. We like what our grandparents and our great grandparents taught us to eat such as wild yams and the fruits from the swamp that we call panja (water lily bulb) – and wild geese and ducks, kangaroos and pigs. We also get fishes from the salt water and oysters, crabs and prawns.

'In our home here, Mapoon, we just get these things freely. We don't have to buy them like if we living somewhere else, where we get these things if we got the money, but if we haven't got the money we can't get them even if we want them. Right here in our home we can get anything that we wish to eat — what we are taught by our grandparents and our parents to eat.

'Also, here we are free to go anywhere and everywhere we wish. There is no block to us moving around, no obstacles or anything at all. We just go everywhere we wish to go. Nobody is here to say: "You can't go over there. That's not your place to go", something like that. That's why I like to be at home because it's so free. We don't have to spend money on anything — just only if we need any tablets or stores from town we go in and get it. That's all we spend money on.

'I want you all to understand our feelings towards our birth land Mapoon.

'We want the land because the land is most important to we Aborigines. It is sacred to us, in our customs. We still carry our sacred customs. I think most white people don't understand us very much, but there comes a time they must understand our Aboriginal ways which we think are sacred. Looking now, we live by nature because God has made our ancestors civilized in our own way—BY NATURE, AND REALLY AND TRULY, WE LIVE BY NATURE.

'You cannot ask for anything better than the old place, Mapoon.'

SOURCE: J. P. Roberts (ed.), *The Mapoon Story by the Mapoon People,* op. cit.

Discussion points

1. In how many ways were Aborigine rights disregarded by the government and the mining companies?
2. How many different sorts of development are planned on Aborigine territory? (See the map.)
3. Write a letter to a relative describing your reactions on learning that your land has been taken over by a mining company.
4. Recreate the police eviction from Mapoon. How would *you* have felt about this?
5. In 1974 several people insisted on returning to live at Mapoon. After reading about how they felt (Extract 5.7) do you think they were right?
6. In what ways do you think Aborigines can fight the government and the mining companies? Do you think there are any ways in which you could help?

Key references

The best source of up-to-date information on Aboriginal issues is undoubtedly *CIMRA* (Colonialism and Indigenous Minorities Research and Action) founded in 1976. The organization's main aim is to raise international support for Aborigines and similarly colonized peoples by publicizing the way in which they are being dispossessed by 'Western' interests such as the multi-national mining corporations. Most of the books and papers referred to below are available from them at 92 Plimsoll Road, London, N.4.

Roberts, J. P. (ed.), *The Mapoon Story by the Mapoon People* (Victoria, Aust.: International Development Action (IDA), 1975).

Roberts, J. P., Parsons, M. and Russell, B. (eds.), *The Mapoon Story According to the Invaders: Church Mission, Queensland Government and Mining Company* (Victoria, Aust.: IDA, 1975).

Roberts, J. P. and McLean, D., *The Cape York Aluminium Companies and the Native Peoples* (Victoria, Aust.: IDA, 1976).

The address of IDA is 73, Little George Street., Fitzroy, Victoria 3065, Australia. In the UK the three books are available from CIMRA.

Roberts, J., *From Massacres to Mining: The Colonization of Aboriginal Australia* (War on Want and CIMRA, 1978).

Natural People's News, available from CIMRA. Excellent resource materials often taken from local newspapers. Issue number 1 included items on land rights in Australia, threats to Indians in Brazil, uranium mining in northern Canada and a letter from Rio Tinto Zinc's solicitors to CIMRA!

Australia's Policy Towards Aborigines 1967–1977, Minority Rights Group Report No. 35.

Gibbs, R. M. *The Aborigines* (Longman, 1974).

'Australia's Shame: The Undermining of Aborigines' *New Internationalist* No. 77, July 1979.

2 The Sahel nomads

The Sahel nomads were one of the groups very much in the news during the drought in 1973 which affected all the countries south of the Sahara. This study highlights the fact that whilst the traditional economy of the nomads acknowledges the need for recognizing ecological restraints, current development programmes by 'experts' do not. It also recalls the way in which press and officialdom often react to, and report on, Third World 'disasters'. It could form the basis of useful work on rich world perspectives of the Third World, on aid and development programmes, and could prompt a reconsideration of an often stereotyped minority.

Key themes

(a) Living in ecological balance with the environment.

(b) Models of development.
(c) The nature and reporting of Third World 'disasters'.

Extract 5.8

Disaster and Development

In 1973 an international disaster was declared in the main Sahelian countries of West Africa (Mauritania, Senegal, Mali, Upper Volta, Niger and Chad). It was reported that since 1968 there had been six years of drought, that most of the livestock were dead, and that the Sahelian population – numbering six million people – were in danger of starving to death. This crisis was identified and publicized by the Sahelian governments and by the Food and Agriculture Organization of the United Nations (FAO). As the year went by they were joined by various international charities and relief organizations.

The news of this famine threatening the lives of six million people caused worldwide alarm. In response various nations sent enormous quantities of food. By August, twenty countries had despatched 230,000 tons of relief supplies, and by September the total value of aid provided was $13 m. But the crisis continued. The amounts of food received did not equal the amounts requested by FAO and in November an international mission reported that, after the failure of the rains for a sixth year, the Sahel would need 662,000 tons of food in 1974.

This time the amounts of food exceeded the FAO demands and a total of 750,000 tons of food was donated to the Sahelian countries. But despite the fact that 1974 saw both massive food donations and 'the end of the drought', with the heaviest rains for thirty years, the situation had apparently deteriorated to such an extent that FAO considered that food aid would have to continue in 1975 and 1976.

To summarize, the picture presented to the world at the time was of a natural disaster of the first order, affecting six very poor nations. A prolonged drought

had led to the disappearance of almost all their livestock, destroyed their way of life, and resulted in mass famine. This had been caused by a change in climate which might continue. The traditionally self-sufficient nomadic peoples of West Africa were permanently weakened. The situation described amounted to no less than a sudden and complete collapse of living conditions in a vast area of the world. But was this an accurate description of the complexity of the reality there?

The traditional economy

The extent to which the recent drought, and the previous and subsequent development programmes, have affected the Sahelian nomads varies considerably. The Fulani, for instance, who practise transhumance are not pure nomads. And the purer nomads range from those who rely more on cattle and those who rely more on camels. None of these minorities is equally threatened by particular schemes to alter the use of grazing land or to favour the majority of settled agriculturalists. But all the nomads of the Sahel, both those who tend towards the desert on one side and those who favour the savanna on the other, share a culture and an economy which depend to a crucial extent on nomadic pastoralism. And it is the failure of current development programmes to respect this way of life which causes their common disadvantage.

Nomadic pastoralism was the basis of all traditional land-use in the Sahel. 'Herd numbers (and so the number of people who could live off the pastoral economy) were limited by the quantities of dry season pasture within reach of the herdsman's base well. The animals would eat out all the vegetation in a circle of up to 30 kms radius, and only a certain number would survive the dry season.' The wells were widely spaced. At the end of the dry season the Sahel grasses would start to grow and the herds would move away from the wells, allowing the pasture surrounding them to recover for the next dry season. Pasture and herd size would fluctuate. Animal disease and shortage of pasture kept human population and grazing pressure within bounds.

The peculiar achievement of nomadic pastoralism in the Sahel was to make human occupation a possibility at all. A delicate ecological equilibrium had to be maintained (based on the distribution of water, the use of pasture and the preservation of soil structure) to which the concepts of commercial cropping, stock marketing and taxation were generally alien and destructive.

By the pursuit of high herd numbers and herd variety, the nomads ensured a flexible, living reserve, which, in times of need, could be supplemented by an extended system of loans and sharing throughout an enormous area in which they enjoyed unrestricted movement. At such times the nomads moved into the southern savanna, and reclaimed animals they had loaned to farmers in the previous good years when their own herd numbers had swollen. The whole point of this economy was that it could and should be able to withstand drought and avoid or minimize famine.

However, Dr. A. H. Boerma, Director-General of FAO in 1973, described the Sahelian way of life as 'a form of intolerable suffering'.

Various blue-prints for development

All current plans for the Sahel start from the point of view adopted by Dr. Boerma in the above quotation, which is the classic opinion of the outsider. High-growth development and intensified agriculture were the solutions instantly advocated. 'To "develop" the Sahel, the rural economy must be monetized. And to begin with, the most reluctant of the nomad population must be forced to enter into the market economy. They must be obliged to sell their livestock, and, to do this, the entire animal production of the countries concerned must be reorganized by supervising the nomads' animal husbandry. It is in this light that the series of conventions which have been signed between the countries of the Sahel and the aid organizations must be understood. These conventions are all concerned with the financing of ranches and fattening centres for slaughter-houses...'

Nomadic stock-rearing is to be linked with the manufacture of agricultural by-products. The whole Sahelian region is to be divided into 'managed' and 'unmanaged' zones. Stock will be taken from Sahelian pastures to fattening stations where 'ill-advised' nomadic feeding techniques will be replaced by intensive feeding and mineral supplementation. The goat will be generally discouraged because of its 'fatal effect on supplies of wood' which would be needed for fuel in the new urban centres. And transhumance is to be replaced wherever possible, thereby safeguarding pastures and wells from its degrading effects. The plan reveals obvious contradictions between the demands of the high-consumption economy envisaged and the existing catastrophic damage to the Sahel caused by the mild increase in urbanization and intensive agriculture which has already taken place. It also displays a complete disregard for the values and advantages of transhumance in a harsh environment.

The effects of development on the Sahel

It is widely agreed that a crucial cause of the events in the Sahel in 1972 and 1973 were the inappropriate and destructive development programmes which had taken place in the preceding ten years. The governing simplification of that period was well-summarized in a famine appeal advertisement which appeared in 1973. 'Drought sets up a vicious circle. Without water vegetation dies. Without vegetation cattle die. Without food people die.' The obvious solution therefore was to tackle the problem at the root and provide more water, usually by the provision of wells. Sure enough the same relief agency stated that it was 'building dams and installing pumps and tanks'. It was also 'restoring cattle herds and transporting vets' and providing 'fertilizer, tools, and training on how to farm successfully against terrible odds'. But the real vicious circle was that the provision of wells and vaccination programmes had led to seriously over-stocked Sahelian pastures and the training provided amounted to little more than an ignorant interference with a subtle local economy. In the words of one experienced observer of francophone West Africa, the Sahel 'is not a "disaster" with all the unpredictability and chance that this term suggests. It is the logical outcome of the policies of colonization and development in the Sahel. The drought exposed and further precipitated the worsening crisis of the Sahel: over-exploitation and decreasing productivity of the land, the dismantling of rural social systems under the ruthless pressures of the money economy... An over-cultivated, over-grazed Sahel will always have droughts... The pastoral and agricultural economies of this semi-arid zone were traditionally geared to survival throughout long periods of drought, as is testified by their livestock accumulation and grain-storage customs. However "modernization" and the money economy have, in conjunction with the deterioration of the land, largely nullified these survival techniques.'

What was so little understood in 1973 was that the governing simplification was a formula for a repetition of the very disaster which it was supposed to prevent. The dams and pumps and cattle schemes and expensive inorganic fertilizer were indeed 'terrible odds' for the pastoralists to face: and it is these same schemes, with one or two nods in the direction of range management to obviate overgrazing, which are now underway in the Sahel. All the current blueprints foresee increased industrialization and urbanization in countries where there is not even enough firewood to provide domestic fuel for the local needs of the relatively small urban settlements which have recently been established. Ouagadougou's firewood reserves have been exhausted within forty miles of the city, forcing most people to spend up to twenty-five per cent of their income on buying firewood from further away. And this loss of wood-cover has seriously diminished the Sahel's ability to produce food, as the classic dust-bowl pattern emerges. In the Sahel there is the additional effect that a firewood shortage leads to people using dried dung as a fuel, thereby preventing its prime use as an organic fertilizer. The firewood shortage which follows on urbanization is directly linked to a consequent food shortage, and, in the fairly short term, it could lead to large areas of the Sahel which have been used by pastoralists and agriculturalists for centuries, being abandoned altogether by food producers (that is, being abandoned as areas of habitation by six million people).

Viewed from the planner's desk the development programmes may seem fragmented, grandiose and lacking any prospect of ordered fulfillment. But viewed from the Sahel even a partial programme has all the necessary capacity to destroy transhumance completely.

Summary

Minorities which occupy more than one country present a special problem. The great international conventions on human rights take no account of people outside nations. The people of a nation which has been dispossessed or overrun are within these conventions, but people who prefer not to align with any nation are not. Despite this, nomads possess the right to exercise some choice over their own future, and the right not to die as a side-effect of official development policies. The current development programme in the Sahel is likely to violate both these rights.

The risk to the continuation of transhumance in the Sahel which is posed by these projects far exceeds that posed by the familiar climatic stress. The exact extent to which this is the result of misunderstanding, as opposed to deliberate but covert policy of enclosure and resettlement, is still unclear. What is clear is that modern aid programmes to countries which have no unavoidable food shortage are used by the developed countries as a deliberate strategy: 'Food is a weapon'. USAID's grain shipments bolster the price of American wheat and introduce artificial levels of consumption into the Sahel which can only be supplied from outside it. They sap the Sahelian capacity to produce its own food, and increase the Sahelian need for foreign exchange to purchase imported food, consumer goods and technological components.

SOURCE: *Nomads of the Sahel,* MRG Report No. 33, July 1977.

Extract 5.9

Interviews with Farmers and Livestock Owners in the Sahel

Q: Why did you leave the Abala region?
A: Because of the poverty.

Q: Were you using the same grazing grounds as your elder brother?
A: Yes. We grazed the stock separately but we often met.

Q: So you each tended your cattle separately?
A: Yes.

Q: Who was the first to come here?
A: I came here before my brother on account of the *torra* (many problems, difficulties). He joined me when he was also experiencing difficulties.

Q: How many of your own head of cattle perished?
A: A hundred and forty.

Q: Where? Under what circumstances?
A: They died in the vicinity of water points; some of them died in the vicinity of a bore hole at Doumana in the Abala region. In fact, they began dying during the dry season by groups of three to four. Then came the time when on leaving a camping ground we had to leave behind ten or twenty head of cattle which could not stand up: those which we forced to stand staggered and then stopped. So we only took away those which could walk and those too were exhausted a little further on. These are the circumstances under which they died one by one.

Q: Was there no grass?
A: Not at that time.

Q: What were the cattle feeding on?
A: On branches of trees known as jiigaaje; we cut these branches until there were no cattle left: it was only after this that it began raining.

Q: How many cattle do you have left?
A: Ten: heifers and young calves.

Q: Who is now tending the calves?
A: A younger brother in the Ménaka region: we have the same father.

Q: What in your opinion destroyed a large proportion of the cattle last year?
A: The lack of fodder, for it did not rain. It is true that we lost a large number of cattle but this year's catastrophe has been the greatest of our lives.

Q: Have you known any period when as many cattle were lost as this year?
A: I have never witnessed such distress since my birth. I suffered so much that I wondered what would become of me. I remembered that I had 50,000 francs and this enabled me to feed my family until the rain came. Then, I found myself in a difficult situation: I left for Abala where I was not given anything, even if supplies were sent there. From Abala, I came to Filingué where I found people could buy sacks of millet. I spent the rainy season there until the millet was ripe...The President asked us to return to Abala where he told us we could be provided with food: we went back to Abala and we were given some provisions which were highly appreciated. But when the provisions stopped we had no money: nevertheless, we stayed in the hope of getting food. When we were on the point of death we returned by truck to Filingué where nothing was distributed to us. My brother and I went to our relatives living in Niamey: they gave us two sacks of millet and truck fare to Filingué...

Q: Who gave you the two sacks?
A: Our mother's elder sister...She gave us some money also...We distributed the contents of the two bags and then we came back to Niamey hungry: our aunt took us to those responsible for the distribution of foods and they gave us a sack of sorghum...Then we were settled here. Among the ten cows I left at home, there are five animals on loan. The others which are all three years old are my personal property. How can I sell them in order to support my family? During the dry season, while I was taking cattle to the market, they died of exhaustion on the way. I lost ten of them under such conditions. These are the reasons why I am now in Niamey.

Q: When do you propose to go back?
A: If the President orders me to go back, I will go, but I do not propose to go back because I do not see why I should.

Q: Did you not do any farming?
A: I have never farmed! I always bought millet from farmers. We used to come to Abala only to buy millet or to pay taxes...I did not know Filinqué or Niamey. It is because of the famine this year that I have got to know my relatives living here.

Q: Are your children attending school?
A: We do not attend school (it is not our custom). We were never told anything about schools.

SOURCE: 'Interviews with Farmers and Livestock Owners in the Sahel,' *African Environment* (Dakar, Senegal). 1(2), April 1975.

Extract 5.10

Disaster: how the helpers make things worse

This was the title of an article that appeared in the *Sunday Times* in June 1978. Some of the main points made about disasters were as follows:

(a) A famine that is only *about* to happen is not newsworthy.

(b) In order to raise money photos of a famine that is *happening* need to be seen by people.

(c) Most of the stereotypes about disasters in Third World countries are untrue, for example:
Survivors do not normally panic and medical needs (except in the case of earthquakes) are generally exaggerated.
Epidemics are not a common sequal to disasters.
Victims are not always starving, naked or in need of blankets.
The local government is not always corrupt, inefficient and in need of outside agencies to tell it what to do.

(d) The medical aid that is sent is often unrequested and inappropriate.

(e) Large imports of food aid will force local market prices of foodstuffs down.

(f) After the Guatemala earthquake in 1976 agencies were told, 'We know we're poor but please don't give us things. It causes a lot of dissension in our community'.

(g) If a permanent house can be built in a day sending emergency housing can be pointless.

(h) Disaster aid thus needs radical rethinking based on an appreciation of the *real* needs of survivors.

Discussion points

1. What sort of reasons were presented to the world for the Sahel disaster in 1973 and 1974?

2. In what way is the traditional nomadic economy in balance with the environment?

3. What does the short quotation in Extract 5.8 tell you about the way that 'experts' view the traditional way of life?

4. How do the 'experts' think that the Sahel should 'develop'?

5. Who do you think will benefit from this sort of development and who do you think will suffer?

6. What effects would this sort of development have on the traditional nomadic way of life?

7. Write a description of the sorts of things that might happen to you if you were a nomad in this situation and how you feel about it.

8. In what way does the sort of development described in Extract 5.8 lead to disaster in this area?

9. If you were a nomad whose traditional grazing lands were in more than one country how would you react to national borders? Recreate a scene where you are stopped by border guards who wish to turn you back from your destination. What would you say to them?

10. The latest thinking about development argues that it should be about satisfying people's basic needs. What might this involve for the nomads?

11. Any or all of the points from Extract 5.10 could be used as a basis for discussion. In particular they could be applied to any disaster situation currently being reported in the news. A scene could be role-played where officials from aid agencies bent on helping, local government officials and 'victims', each try to explain their needs.

Key references

Nomads of the Sahel, Minority Rights Group Report No. 33.

Laya, D., 'Interviews with farmers and livestock owners in the Sahel', *African Environment*, (1), 2, 1975.

Disasters: How the helpers make things worse', *Sunday Times*, 25 June 1978.

Oxby, C., *Pastoral Nomads and Development*, International African Institute, 210 High Holborn, London WC1V 7BW, 1975.

The Sahel: Drought and Development, a set of slides with teachers' notes available from the Centre for World Development Education.

3   Native Americans

The American Indian nations are probably one of the best known but most consistently misrepresented and stereotyped minorities. This stereotyping has played a large part in the creation of the 'myth of America' in the public (i.e. white) mind. This study explores a Native American view of the nineteenth century and also emphasizes the need for studies of minority issues to be about the present, not just the past.

Key themes

(a) A Native American perspective on the 'West'.
(b) Culture clash in education
(c) Discrimination and oppression today.

Extract 5.11

Native American Voices

(a) No white person or persons shall be permitted to settle upon or occupy any portion of the territory, or without the consent of the Indians to pass through the same.

— Treaty of 1868

(b) Where today are the Pequot? Where are the Narragansett, the Mohican, the Pokanoket, and many other once powerful tribes of our people? They have vanished before the avarice and the oppression of the White Man, as snow before a summer sun.

Will we let ourselves be destroyed in our turn without a struggle, give up our homes, our country bequeathed to us by the Great Spirit, the graves of our dead and everything that is dear and sacred to us? I know you will cry with me, 'Never! Never!'

— Tecumseh of the Shawnees

(c) The whites were always trying to make the Indians give up their life and live like white men — go to farming, work hard and do as they did — and the Indians did not know how to do that, and did not want to anyway... If the Indians had tried to make the whites live like them, the whites would have resisted, and it was the same way with many Indians.

— Wamditanka (Big Eagle) of the Santee Sioux

(d) Robert Bent's description of the soldiers' atrocities was corroborated by Lieutenant James Connor: 'In going over the battleground the next day I did not see a body of man, woman, or child but was scalped, and in many instances their bodies were mutilated in the most horrible manner... according to the best of my beliefs these atrocities that were commited were with the knowledge of (Colonel) J. M. Chivington, and I don't know of his taking any measures to prevent them'.

— Description of the Sand Creek massacre, 1864

(e) I have heard that you intend to settle us on a reservation near the mountains. I don't want to settle. I love to roam over the prairies. There I feel free and happy, but when we settle down we grow pale and die. I have laid aside my lance, bow, and shield, and yet I feel safe in your presence. I have told you the truth. I have no little lies hid about me, but I don't know how it is with the commissioners. Are they as clear as I am? A long time ago this land belonged to our fathers; but when I go up to the river I see camps of soldiers on its banks. These soldiers cut down my timber; they kill my buffalo; and when I see that, my heart feels like bursting; I feel sorry... Has the white man become a child that he should recklessly kill and not eat? When the red men slay game, they do so that they may live and not starve.

— Satanta, Chief of the Kiowas

(f) We have been south and suffered a great deal there. Many have died of diseases which we have no name for. Our hearts looked and longed for this country where we were born. There are only a few of us left, and we only wanted a little ground, where we could live. We left our lodges standing, and ran away in the night. The troops followed us. I rode out and told the troops that we did not want to fight; we only wanted to go north, and if they would let us alone we would kill no one. The only reply we got was a volley. After that we had to fight our way, but we killed no

one who did not fire at us first. My brother, Dull Knife, took one-half of the band and surrendered near Fort Robinson... They gave up their guns and then the whites killed them all.

— Ohcumgache (Little Wolf) of the Northern Cheyennes

Discussion points

1. Most of the treaties like the one of 1868 were later broken. What impression do you think Native Americans would therefore have gained of white people?
2. What reasons did Tecumseh give for fighting? Do you think that these were good reasons? (Explore the justification for Native Americans fighting to defend their territory.)
3. How willing would you be to give up your way of life if you were expected to do so by a majority group?
4. How often does one read about white atrocities on Native Americans in the last century? They were quite common but seldom mentioned in history books. Why do you think this should be the case? (Explore the way in which the dominant group defines history.)
5. What sort of relationship do Native Americans have with the land? Why did the Kiowas think that white people acted like children?
6. How would you have felt if you had been in Little Wolf's situation? What choices were open to you and what would you have done?
7. How do you think Native Americans today feel about the way they are portrayed on film and in books? What would you do about it?

Extract 5.12

How to Survive in an Alien Environment

The first step towards surviving in an alien environment is to feel proud of who you are. Being surrounded by an aggressive and confident majority has made me somewhat defensive: I have spent a lot of years trying to convince myself, after being told all my life that I was no good, because I was an Indian, that I am really all right. That I am a human being like everyone else and that maybe we Indians did have something to contribute to society, something that was sadly missing in the dominant culture.

In trying to do this, I have thought a lot about the Indian way of experiencing the world and the ways in which it is in conflict with white society. Every Indian kid is exposed to these contradictory ways as soon as he begins school. When he has to leave the reserve and go and look for work in the city, he can feel the tension between these cultures in his bones. He is caught in the middle, and often he finds the conflict just overwhelming. I don't know the statistics, but I know from talking to a lot of people that the number of Indian kids landing in mental hospitals is very high. Some avoid the hospitals by staying drunk a great deal of the time. And then there are those who find that nothing will take away their pain except doing away with themselves. We have the highest suicide rate of any ethnic group in the country.

White education for Indians

Being educated in white schools was a painful experience for me like for most Indian kids. I have therefore given a lot of thought to the Indian way of learning. I believe that it has a lot to do with our difficulties in your schools.

I grew up in a community where kids were allowed to discover everything for themselves, by personal observation rather than formal instruction. Nobody said to us 'this is a desk'. We learned that that was a desk by other people using the word, calling it 'a desk'. We began to use that word, too, but we related to that desk in our own way, not because somebody told us that was a desk and that's what you do with it, you write at it, or that is a table and you eat off a table, and this is a chair and you sit on a chair. We probably used chairs in many different ways, like most kids, but we also knew that you could sit on that chair. We made the same discoveries that other people had made centuries before us, but they belonged to us, they didn't belong to some despot or expert, someone who tells you, I've got the answers, so you quit being curious, quit exploring. That didn't happen to me until I went to school. From then on it was a matter of suppression.

I don't much like looking back at what happened to me at school. It seems to me that the only thing I enjoyed was playing hooky and running away from school. One of the difficult things I had to cope with at school was something called 'time'. The teacher would talk about wasting 'time'. I didn't know what that meant. I didn't know how you could waste 'time'. And then she would say you could make it up, you could

make up 'time'. She'd read us a story in school and then she'd say we've lost all that 'time', so now we have to hurry and make it up. I couldn't figure out what that meant, either. There were all kinds of things about time that really bewildered me. I did not understand what all this clock watching was about, because in our community we ate when we were hungry and slept when we felt tired. We did not do things on any kind of schedule, yet that never presented a problem. The things that were necessary always got done.

I discovered gradually that white people lived in two kinds of time, the past and the future. Indians, on the other hand, live in an eternal present. Our history only ran back to the oldest member of the community, so there was no way we could live in the past or in the future, we could only live in the here and now. When we become like you people, dealing with the past, trying to live some kind of a future that doesn't exist, then we'll have taken ourselves completely out of the present. That's what happens to me when I switch from our language to English. After I have been out in white society for a while, speaking English, I find myself having a really difficult time when I go back to an Indian community. I don't know how long it takes me to readjust, and I don't realize when it happens, I just find myself flowing in that community again, forgetting about that abstract time outside.

White educators always complain that Indian kids have difficulties with abstractions. I, too, had that problem. It is hard for us Indians to make sense of the segmented approach to learning taught in the schools to study 'chemistry' or 'math' or 'French' without relating them to each other and to some larger whole. We Indians approach things the opposite way. We start with the whole and examine every part in relationship to that whole. This is because our way of life was total, nothing was outside it, everything was within. So we didn't begin to explore in the same way you people began to explore: we looked for answers within ourselves, but always related it to the natural order that we saw ourselves part of.

This affected our politics as well as our education. I can remember as a boy, when we sat in council, we came to unanimous decisions. Everyone agreed, and if one person objected we didn't suppress that person. What we did was ask ourselves a question: 'Is it possible that we don't see this thing the same way as the other person? Let's explore ourselves.' I see white people attempting to use the same method, but they cannot make it work. For what they do, if one person disagrees, they begin jumping on that person trying to change that person's mind and to suppress him. They say, you're holding up the works, there is only one person who disagrees, so you must be wrong, because the majority cannot be wrong. I don't think that it works out that way, because it is quite possible for the majority to be wrong. I look around at the majority culture around me and at all the suffering it has caused both in this country and abroad, and I am very sure that something is wrong.

SOURCE: Pelletier, Wilfred, 'For Every North American Indian that Begins to Disappear I Also Begin to Disappear', Ch. 4 in J.S. Frideres, *Canada's Indians: Contemporary Conflicts* (Toronto: Prentice-Hall, 1974).

Discussion points

1. Why did the writer find it difficult to be proud of himself?
2. Why do many young Native Americans end up as alcoholics, in mental hospitals, or commit suicide?
3. What were some of the difficulties the writer found at school between the Indian and the white ways of looking at the world?
4. What are some of the advantages of the Native American way of decision making? (Quakers also prefer consensus decision making.)
5. How do you think you might have felt after several years of schooling if you were a Native American?

Extract 5.13

Native Americans

The immigrant view

Over the past five hundred years Europeans and their descendants in the Western Hemisphere have made the original American one of the most potent symbols in their culture, but the great majority of them still know virtually nothing about him. This is not a superficial paradox; it is crucial to the native situation today. Since Columbus first called them 'Indians' under the misapprehension that he had reached Asia, the original inhabitants of America have been consistently misinterpreted and misrepresented to make them fit the framework of a European world-picture and European aims. Generations of whites have revised the misconceptions of their fathers to suit the political and philosophical prejudices of their own day; and as the Indian himself has become a shadowy and elusive figure, pushed to the fringes of American life and increasingly obscured by a growing mass of fable and half-truth, he has been replaced in the popular imagination by a series of powerful but simplistic stereotypes: the Noble Savage exalted by eighteenth century philosophers; the bloodthirsty brute obstructing the path of Victorian Progress; the lazy drunk, squandering the taxpayers' money, who ought to be thrown off the reservation to fend for himself; the oil-rich Indian, just like everyone else except that he sometimes puts on a colourful costume and dances.

These caricatures represent far more than the white man's natural inability to understand diverse and complex cultures very different from his own; they are part of the mythology by which the United States, a predominantly decent country dedicated to the highest principles, has disguised the truth that it grew to greatness by dispossessing and very nearly exterminating a number of viable and flourishing human societies. This fact has determined, in a very practical way, the nature of Indian life today. From the earliest colonial days, the seizure of tribal land was justified by presenting the native as a scarcely-human creature lacking in finer feelings, moral sensibility and the capacity to own property, and when at the end of the nineteenth century the Indians were finally reduced to complete dependence on their conquerors it was for this grotesque figure that the government framed its native policy. The individual Indian, a child-like incompetent whose primitive race was doomed and whose feeble culture barely merited the name, was to be saved by becoming – under compulsion if necessary – a brown-skinned white man who could then be absorbed in the superior Anglo-Saxon civilization. A vigorous program was undertaken to bring about this transformation and – not surprisingly, given the unreality of its premise – it failed; but in the process of failing it created a political and economic system that has made Indians the poorest and most depressed ethnic group in the United States, and has kept them so physically and culturally hidden that the fantasies on which it is based have been perpetuated. In this report I shall try first to show how this system, by continuing to dominate and impoverish native people, constitutes the major factor in the 'Indian Problem' today, and then to consider how the present situation developed and how the past will affect the kind of solutions that may be possible in the future.

Who are they?

There is no overall legislative or judicidal definition of who an American Indian is – the criteria used differ both from one tribe to another and among the various government agencies concerned with Indians – but the US Census would suggest that there are probably more than a million people in the United States who identify themselves as Indians. They are all descended in some degree from the original inhabitants of North America, but – contrary to one of the most persistent illusions about them – they do not form a homogeneous population; they are scattered through most of the states, though with a heavy concentration in the west and south-west, and display enormous social, cultural, economic and linguistic differences that reflect both the huge diversity of the Pre-Columbian tribes and nations and their disparate experiences since the arrival of the white man. The great majority of the Indian population today is made up of members of the 266 tribes in the mainland US which are recognized by the Bureau of Indian Affairs and which receive, usually under the terms of nineteenth century treaties by which they ceded the bulk of their territory, special federal services and federal trusteeship for their remaining lands and assets. Recognized tribes range in size and character from the Navajo, with a reservation of 22,000 square miles and a population (many of whom are illiterate and cannot speak English) of more than 130,000 to tiny bands of less than a hundred individuals with a few acres on the Pacific coast and to groups such as the Osages in Oklahoma who in most outward respects are almost indistinguishable from their white neighbours. The BIA also recognizes some 216 Eskimo, Aleut and Indian communities in Alaska. In addition, there are a number of groups that regard themselves as Indian although they are not officially recognized: several tribes and bands, primarily in the far west, have had their special federal relationship terminated, while other communities, mainly in the east, have never enjoyed federal recognition at all. Almost half of all Indians now live in towns or cities, where they cease to be eligible for BIA services, but most of them have moved only to find work and many of them plan one day to leave what is to them an alien environment and return permanently to the reservation.

What gives these widely-differing groups some kind of common identity is the fact that most of them suffer, to a greater or lesser extent, from a series of problems stemming from their historical and current relationship with white America. To begin with, the majority of Indians are very poor. According to the Census for 1970, the average per capita income for Indians was $1573, substantially lower than the figures for Blacks and Chicanos and less than half that for whites, but this statistic by itself disguises the true nature and extent of the problem for most native people because urban Indians tend to do better financially than other racial minorities. The same census found that for all *rural* Indians the annual per capita income was $1140 and for those on the 115 largest reservations it was $974, so it is clear that the root of Indian poverty lies in the Indian homelands where the majority of native people still live. Other findings confirm the appalling conditions on most reservations: unemployment runs at around 40%, and 18% of those who are unemployed have only temporary or seasonal jobs; approximately 90% of the housing is substandard and sanitation is non-existent or so inadequate as to pose a serious health hazard. The incidence of almost every communicable disease is far greater among Indians than among the population as a whole; native people are, for example, eight times more likely to contract TB and forty-two times more likely to suffer from dysentery than other Americans, and such illnesses prove fatal far more often among Indians than non-Indians.

The poverty of the reservations is a direct result of the authorities' contempt for the tribal Indian and their consequent lack of faith in his ability to run his own life. Convinced that the tribes had no future, the government forced them, by bullying and legislative compulsion, to sell 64% of the land which they still retained at the end of the Indian Wars in the 1880s and on which they could have supported themselves while they found a place in American life. Today only about 53 million acres – excluding the 40 million acres recently awarded to the Alaskan Natives – remains, all of it eroded, much of it in areas where there is an acute shortage of water and most of it severely limited in economic potential. The BIA estimates that more than three-quarters of Indian land is suitable only for grazing, the least intensive and – on a per acre basis – least profitable form of agriculture, while less than a tenth has commercially viable reserves of oil, gas or minerals. Most Indians have acquired neither the skills nor the capital needed to undertake successfully the kind of enterprise that would make the best use of their meagre resources. As a result of legal entanglements, moreover, about 25% of all remaining Indian land is now more or less permanently in non-Indian hands.

These difficulties have been intensified by the fact that the Indian population, which by the end of the nineteenth century had been reduced by disease and warfare to about a tenth of its probable pre-Columbian level and was confidently expected to disappear altogether, has in fact increased approximately fourfold over the last ninety years and is still rising at about 3% p.a., twice the national average. With every year, therefore, the Indian land-base becomes less able, in the words of the BIA, 'to provide a decent livelihood for the population it must support'.

Poverty is only the most tangible problem created by the government's determination that the tribes must be destroyed. Less easily measured, but probably even more catastrophic, have been the social and psychological effects on the Indians. For three generations the Bureau of Indian Affairs has sought to undermine the personal ties, the tribal identity and the cultural self-confidence of the native in order that he should be 'educated' for life in an alien world, and for most Indians during this period the only alternative to an impoverished and stultifying existence devoid of opportunity has been what seemed a complete abandonment of his family and his background. As a result, many native people are understandably depressed, lacking in initiative and self-assurance and unable to live successfully either in their own culture or the white man's, and their distress and sense of futility can be seen to some extent in the violence, drunkenness, apathy and despair on many reservations. Among Indians in school the drop out rate ranges from 45%–62%. Accidents, mostly alcohol-related and involving motor vehicles, are now the leading cause of Indian death, and cirrhosis of the liver, a disease almost exclusively associated with liquor, is the fourth most common cause. The Indian suicide rate is twice that for the population at large, and a comparison between reservations and country areas as a whole shows that while crimes against property are only half as frequent on reservations, crimes of violence are up to ten times more frequent. Significantly, these problems are generally markedly less severe in tribes which have managed to preserve their traditional culture relatively intact.

SOURCE: *The Original Americans: U.S. Indians*, MRG Report No. 31, 1976,

Discussion points

1. How have stereotypes of Native Americans changed over time?
2. How can holding a derogatory stereotype of a particular minority group help to justify oppressive treatment of that group?
3. How many Native American tribes or nations are there and what are some of the differences found between them?
4. What features of their life today make Native Americans the most oppressed minority group in the United States?
5. Do you think that this situation should be looked upon as a 'Native American problem' or a 'white problem'?

Key references

Brown, D., *Bury my Heart at Wounded Knee: An Indian History of the American West* (Picador, 1975). All the quotations in Extract 5.11 were taken from this source. It is an excellent antidote to traditional majority views of the American West and is a well-researched study of the minority experience.

Frideres, J. S., *Canada's Indians: Contemporary Conflicts*, (Toronto: Prentice-Hall of Canada, 1974).

Searle, C., *The World in a Classroom*, (Writers' and Readers' Publishing Co-operative, 1977). This book is a compilation of the writings of children in an East End London secondary school. It covers work they did on many world issues including Chile, South Africa, Chicano farm workers in California and the Sioux occupation of Wounded Knee in 1973. It is both a valuable and inspiring collection of materials.

Wilson, J., *The Original Americans: U.S. Indians*, (MRG Report No. 31, 1980).

Testimony-Chief Seattle, a resource pack (London: United Society for the Propagation of the Gospel).

6 A Multi-ethnic Curriculum

Multi-ethnic education and development education

Where does the study of majority/minority issues fit into the everyday school timetable? Should it fit in anywhere at all? The curriculum certainly does not require a new subject called Minority Studies nor is there particularly a need for such a label. The case studies in the last chapter began to answer the question *'How* do I teach about such issues?', a theme further explored in the next two chapters. As they show, many opportunities do exist for teaching about majority/minority issues and contact with some fifty schools in different parts of the country suggests that these issues *are* being studied in a wide variety of subjects. It was found, in a not necessarily representative sample, that this was most likely to occur in Social Studies, Religious Education, World History and sixth-form General Studies. In addition some work on majority/minority issues was also found in English, Geography, Environmental Studies, Humanities, World Studies, Community Studies, European Studies and Integrated Studies.

Some of the justifications for teaching about majority/minority issues have already been considered in chapter 1 and need not be dealt with again, but it might be useful briefly to consider the role of different subject areas here. Thus in Social Studies, Humanities or General Studies one might explore the conflicts in Ireland or Zimbabwe or the situations of groups like the Roma (the gypsies of Europe) or the Amerindians of South America. The study of world faiths in Religious Education can be linked to minority groups in Britain and the local community. A course in Modern History could look at the Palestinian conflict or Cyprus. In Geography the living conditions for Tamils on tea plantations may be more important than the climatic figures for tea growing and, as one of the case studies in the last chapter indicated, the Sahel drought is as much about models of development as it is about climatic

change. In World Studies one might look at the flashpoints of Namibia and South Africa and in European Studies at the call for greater autonomy from Basques, Corsicans and Bretons as well as the situation of migrant workers.

If we attempt to generalize from the above we can say that majority/minority issues are part of a broader concern for the study of cultural differences and similarities both within Britain and elsewhere in the world. This concern was well expressed in the DES Green Paper *Education in Schools* which had this to say:

> Our society is a multicultural, multiracial one, and the curriculum should reflect a sympathetic understanding of the different cultures and races that now make up our society. We also live in a complex, interdependent world, and many of our problems in Britain require international solutions. The curriculum should therefore reflect our need to know about and understand other countries.

Although the curriculum *ought* to reflect these concerns, it is not necessarily likely to, for there are various underlying forces which militate against this. If both the definitions of ethnocentrism and racism on page 12 refer to western culture generally then they must also have some bearing on what goes on in schools. Since schooling is a reflection of culture and, in part, exists to perpetuate it, it will partake of all the basic premises of that culture. As Katznelson (on page 8) and Husband (on page 13) suggest, British society tends to be both ethnocentric and racist in its outlook. In part this is a legacy of colonialism, it is reflected in the curriculum, and visible in a) the ignoring or misinterpreting of minority group needs within the UK, and b) the ignoring or distorting of other cultures in the world, particularly the so-called 'Third World'. We should not be surprised about this but learn to expect it and also how to detect it. To deny its existence however, whether in society generally or in education, is in itself an ethnocentric defence-mechanism.

There have been several responses to the ethnocentric curriculum. Thus multi-ethnic education is concerned with education for, and education about, the diverse cultural and ethnic groups within a given society. Multiracial education and multicultural education are terms also used in the same context. The term multiracial is less often used now because it could be taken to imply the existence of discrete racial groups, and, as the note at the end of this chapter points out, the word 'race' is associated with many myths and misconceptions. There is in some areas a preference for the use of 'multi-ethnic' as the term acknowledges the diversity of groups with particular needs.

Some definitions

There are, of course, still other differences of opinion amongst those involved in multi-ethnic education as these differing definitions show:

Multicultural education — the aim must be to inspire respect and appreciation for non-Western cultures.

Great priority is to develop a positive self-image in members of minority groups. This involves discovery of and pride in their own cultural heritage.

Aims to protect minority groups in British education system, e.g. by giving special help in language development.

Aims to promote better race relations by encouraging tolerance and understanding amongst the white majority.

The eradication of racism, in both individuals and institutions.

Knowledge, skills and attitudes to participate effectively and responsibly in a multicultural society and an interdependent world.

There is no difference between multicultural education and good education.[1]

Not all of these definitions of 'multicultural' education are mutually exclusive but consideration of their underlying premises reveals a wide spectrum of opinion as to the real nature of the issues. One can say, however, that whilst multi-ethnic education is often thought of as relating mainly to minority groups within the UK it clearly has an international or global dimension.

Other major responses to the ethnocentric curriculum take a variety of forms and use a variety of labels. The chief contenders are: education for international understanding, global education, education for global literacy, international education, peace education, world studies, and devel-

opment education. Clearly such differing terminology reveals a variety of origins, aims and objectives as well as ideological positions. Their overall concern, however, may be said to be the recognition of the need for a global dimension in the curriculum.

Within the UK many of the recent developments have come within the field of development education, a term originally used by the national and international voluntary agencies but increasingly being used in schools. Again when one looks at definitions of development education one finds a spectrum of opinion:

Development Education is promotion of knowledge and understanding about world development and about this country's interdependence with the Third World.

Dev Ed — the ultimate aim is to enable people to participate in society — world society but also national and local — with a view to making society more just, at all levels.

To instil attitudes of sympathy for poorer countries, and readiness to support aid agencies and the British aid programme.

Methods and process are as important as content — development education must be based on dialogue and action, not just chalk and talk, note-taking etc.

'Development education' is an ugly and incomprehensible phrase which needs replacing.

Dev Ed must begin at home. Relationships in the classroom and school. Political and social issues in the local environment.[2]

Thus whilst multi-ethnic education, initially with a national focus, also has a global dimension so development education, initially with a global focus, also has a national and even local dimension.

Not until fairly recently has any interest been shown in the possible interrelationships between multi-ethnic education and development education. This was largely because people were fully involved in either one field or the other and had little time to look at the overlap between the two. One of the spurs to this concern about the interrelationships was a government sponsored report arising out of a survey of public attitudes towards overseas development. Not only did the report speak of 'a common obsession with the domestic scene at the expense of a wider appreciation of world problems (which) may be described as a form of parochialism or "national introversion"', it also identified a relationship between negative attitudes to the 'Third World' and to immigration into Britain.[3]

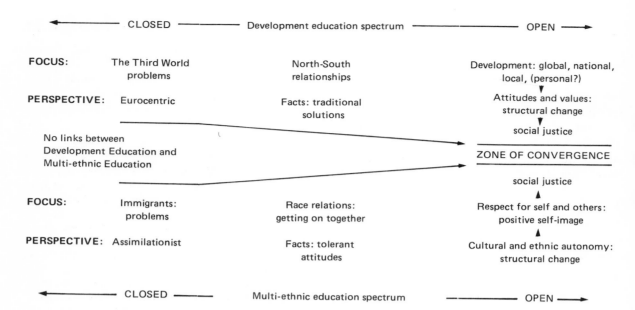

Fig. 6.1. Links between development education and multi-ethnic education
SOURCE: Hicks, David W., 'Two Sides of the Same Coin: An Exploration of the Links Between Multicultural Education and Development Education', *The New Era*, 60(2), March/April 1979.

Again such negative attitudes towards minority groups within Britain and other cultures in the world should not be surprising as they are part of our cultural heritage. How we teach about these matters is clearly crucial especially if multi-ethnic education and development education were seen to be at cross-purposes. One of the first articles on this theme did indeed point out that they often had a detrimental effect on each other.[4] Subsequently some of the differences of opinion in each field were noted as being part of a spectrum, (see Fig. 6.1). Thus if one is ideologically near the 'closed' end of either spectrum, development education and multi-ethnic education have little or nothing in common. It is only as one approaches the 'open' end of either spectrum that they can be seen as in fact 'two sides of the same coin'.[5] This is of course still very much at a theoretical level and what needs to be done now is to set out the practical classroom implications.

Although the focus of this book is not specifically on the multi-ethnic classroom as such it is important to map out some of the elements of what a multi-ethnic curriculum might include. It is essential because we live, always have lived, and always will live in a plural society. This applies equally to schools catering for students from ethnic minority groups and to those in all-white areas. Students therefore need (a) to be aware of the nature of this plural society; (b) to know how to gain from the benefits of such cultural diversity; and (c) to know how to cope with, and how to fight to reduce, the tensions inherent in such a society.

Effects of the ethnocentric curriculum

The opposite of a multi-ethnic curriculum is that which has traditionally been considered 'normal', objective and balanced. It is the curriculum which gave so much pain to Wilfred Pelletier (page 44), it is the curriculum which has frustrated so many Black British students (page 52). It is also the curriculum which necessitates minority groups' running supplementary schools for their children (page 22) and which often reinforces racial prejudices gained in childhood socialization (page 12). From a minority perspective — and increasingly from a rethought majority perspective — the normal curriculum can be seen as highly ethnocentric and based on a white, male, European view of the world. The dangers of this are manifest in its transmission of biased views and the belittling — often through omission — of other cultures as well as its perpetuation — often unwittingly — of prejudiced and racist attitudes. The effects of this on some minority group students are clearly shown in Extracts 6.1 and 6.2.

Extract 6.1

Black Self-Image

In a multi-racial society the white majority-group child shows evidence of being aware of simple racial differences from a very early age, sometimes as young as three years old. In the following years he begins to show feelings about these groups; these are simple evaluations, which invariably take the form of preferring and identifying with his own group, and showing some dislike or rejection of the other racial groups. These evaluations are picked up from adults, brothers and sisters, friends, teachers, and from children's literature and the mass media. Soon afterwards, around the age of 5, rudimentary versions of adult attitudes may be mouthed, and the first understanding of the social roles of whites and blacks appears. Versions of adult stereotypes are reproduced, and the process of absorption of the society's colour-values crystallizes into fully fledged racial attitudes.

For the black child brought up within the same society, things are rather different. He is surrounded by the same colour-values and attitudes, and they are made real to him; they pervade all the social life and the institutions of the society, and he cannot help but absorb them. They speak directly to him, for within those attitudes is a picture of his group, and by implication, of himself. The more derogatory is this portrayal, the more unacceptable is the 'identity' it imposes. Even without the more lurid stereotypes, which tend to accompany tense inter-racial situations, the inferior status of the minority underwritten by their colour, ensures them a devalued identity.

So as the white child develops a positive identification with his group and a preference for it over others, in line with the attitudes of the majority, the black child faced with the same climate of attitudes may develop a very much more ambivalent pattern of identification and preference. Obviously, it is difficult for the child to incorporate within his self-image a picture, apparently subscribed to by the majority of the community, which depicts him as somehow inferior. In inter-racial situations, as we have seen, 'race' is likely to be one of the most important aspects of the social reality, and so contribute centrally to the person's identity. For the black child, then, a crucial element of his identity – his race – is devalued, and in some cases it may be rejected.

This is the burden of the findings of any number of research studies. 'Black' minority-group children in a variety of different countries have shown an orientation away from their own group and towards the dominant white majority in experimental test situations. In some cases this has extended to a denial of their black identity and momentary escape into the fiction of a white one. Although this passes with age, there is no reason to believe that the conflicts which engender it do so. The socialization of racial attitudes in both black and white children undoubtedly form the foundations of adult racial attitudes ... This of course begs the question of how racism arises in a society in the first place.

For example, in the case of our own society, such an analysis would have to take account of our traditional cultural image of black people based on the history of our exploitative relationships with them, cultural colour values, traditions of nationalism and cultural ethnocentrism, and the history of competitive class and 'caste' attitudes towards 'others' deriving from class attitudes in a capitalist society. Then it would need to include an analysis of social and economic conditions at the time of the immigration – a decline in post-war expansion, contraction of demand for labour other than unskilled labour, selective strains in areas of the housing market, education system, social services, and the attitudes of those white people already affected by these strains (and this would be supplemented by an account of the political exploitation of these fears, and the imaginary fears of much wider sections of the white population, by politicians in pursuit of personal political capital). Finally, at the individual level, the analysis would include an account of personal dispositions towards prejudice among particular groups of the population due to personality organization, themselves the result of certain kinds of child-rearing practice and parental attitudes.

SOURCE: D. Milner, *Children and Race* (Penguin Education, 1975).

Extract 6.2

The young blacks who live in no man's land

by KEVIN O'LONE

Suppression,
Frustration,
So, him work up,
But him screwed up,
So, him rave up,
Again him screwed up,
Unemployment,
Social security,
The Ghetto.

THESE are the closing lines of a poem written by Pat Robinson, a 21-year-old black born in London. To him they sum up the frustration of a generation born in Britain to West Indian parents.

The plight of young blacks was highlighted in last week's report by the House of Commons Select Committee on Race Relations and Immigration. It said : 'The alienation of the young blacks cannot be ignored and action must be taken before relations deteriorate further and create irreconcilable division. The problems of the young blacks are those of the West Indian community at their point of greatest tension and strain.'

Pat Robinson agreed. 'I was born here, but I don't feel British. I don't feel I belong to the West Indies, although I spent eight years in Jamaica.

'You feel as if you're in a no-man's-land because you have an English accent and I love football, but you've got a black skin. You're not English. But the West Indies isn't home either ; it's some place thousands of miles away in the sun.'

Pat is relatively lucky. He has a job as a clerical officer with the Community Relations Commission and is active in youth work. 'But I still feel the frustrations of other young blacks. That's why I wrote the poem. I wanted to get across what we all feel ; getting the rotten jobs, being hounded by the police and just the whole business of not belonging.'

No 7, Grantham Road, Brixton, South London, is set in a row of run-down terraced houses. It is the centre for a job creation programme run by the Brixton Neighbourhood Community Association with money from the Manpower Services Commission. Twelve young people with a long history of unemployment are taking a course in social work.

The blacks at the converted house were wary of yet another white journalist. 'It's all been done before,' said Ige, 26, whose mother is white.

'The media pick on us every so often because we make good headlines — look at the sensationalised coverage of the Commons report in most papers. It was all about flashpoints and bloodbaths. Why didn't they say what should be done ?

'The media could do a lot to educate white people, but they play up things like the violence at last year's Notting Hill Carnival. Why hasn't THE OBSERVER sent a black journalist to see us ?'

Wariness gave way to anger. 'We got no chance,' said Angela, 18, who came to Britain from Jamaica at the age of six. 'We got no chance in school, we got no chance with decent jobs, we got no chance with the police.

'I've lost count of the times I've fixed up an interview for a job over the telephone and find it's gone when I get there. It still happens despite that Racial Equality Act. As soon as they see you're black, they get embarrassed and make up some excuse like " Oh, the job's filled." '

Elaine, 20, was born in England. She has been out of work for more than a year.

'All the heroes on telly are white and a lot of the villains are black. White people probably don't notice that, but we do. I was once stopped outside a supermarket and accused of stealing because I was black. When I showed the detective the slip, she walked away without even apologising.

'I worked as a tablemaid at an hotel and something was stolen. Five workers were black. We were all sacked, but none of the white ones were. Soon after we'd left they found out that the thief was one of those kept on.'

A recurring complaint was of harassment by the police. The young people said this was the reason for giving me only their first names.

Angela said : 'They're always stopping blacks or arresting them for no good reason. If you're on a bike, they'll stop you and ask if it's stolen. They've stopped me and looked in my bag many times.'

Ige said : 'This report like all the others will probably end up on some shelf and the media will go on to something else.

'Governments and local authorities could give us a fair deal and the media could educate the whites to what the problem's about and not just concentrate on sensationalised headlines.

'I mean from the start you get discrimination. The schools make no attempt to teach you anything about your history. I remember having a lesson about " The White Man's Burden ! " If they have a lesson about slavery, it'll be all about how some nice white men freed us. They'll ask you to stand up' in class and say " This is what a slave looked like." '

Pat Robinson agreed. For many blacks, school is prison where you have to for several hours a d Many West Indian pare think all the work should done at school and give help or encouragement w homework. 'Black kids s learn the best jobs are for them so they give up just mope around.'

This feeling was echoed three black schoolboys.

Peter Sullivan and friends were passing time at the entrance to Tube station, sheltering fr the rain. Peter, 16, was b in Guyana and came to tain at the age of three. said : 'School doesn't int est me much. The lessons boring. The teachers are interested in us.' Sometim I don't bother to go to sch and just go about with mates. I leave this year, t I don't know what I'll You daren't go out at nig by yourself because y might run into a gang white kids. So we go ab in gangs and the police always stopping us.'

Mr Paul Stephens Youth and Commun Officer with the Commun Relations Commission, sai 'Young blacks don't ha much going for them. I pumped into them t h they're second rate and go for only the menial jobs, a after a time they start lieving it.

'Adults born in the W Indies know where they ca from and have a sense identity. Young blacks bo here aren't so lucky. How you think they feel wh someone yells at them to back where they belong Adult West Indians tend to be somewhat meek and on with their job, but you blacks are far more milita and tired of getting seco best. Society has got to something for them becau all that pent-up frustrati will explode one day.'

SOURCE: *The Observer*, 3 April 1977.

What a multi-ethnic curriculum might involve

A multi-ethnic curriculum, whether for schools in all-white areas or whether in areas with minority group children, does not involve an extra 'subject' on the timetable but rather refers to the whole tone of the curriculum as well as the ethos of the school. It comprises a constant recognition of the multi-ethnic nature of society both nationally and globally. Every teacher, or, better, each school as a whole, could ask the following questions about its curriculum:

Does it reflect the real world locally, nationally and globally?

Does it highlight the range of contributions made by diverse cultures?

Does it utilize the skills of parents and other key people in the community?

Does it acknowledge that children are aware of, and need to discuss, racial differences and similarities at an early age?

Does it discuss the nature of race and the history of migrations?

Does it acknowledge the presence of racial intolerance in society whilst at the same time explaining the reasons for this and fighting to remove them?

These are only the more obvious questions and schools which cater for ethnic minority group students will also need to consider:

the dangers of the 'colour-blind' approach that sees all children as being, and needing to be treated, exactly the same;

the dangerously self-fulfilling nature of low pupil expectation;

the danger of ignoring the particular mother-tongue language needs of students;

the danger of overlooking the need for encouraging self-respect and cultural identity in a plural society.

The Education Committee of Ealing Community Relations Council has touched on some of the needs in a leaflet entitled 'Race relations and the secondary school curriculum: a statement of minimum requirements'. It is available from the Commission for Racial Equality, the address of which is given in chapter 11. They suggest that History syllabuses should continue the trend away from a UK-centred approach with a world history course that includes the history of the Indian sub-continent, African history, the institution of slavery and the post-emancipation history of Africans in the American continent (see the Tulse Hill syllabus description in chapter 7 for an account of how one school has tried to do this). Geography could give greater attention to the study of areas such as the Caribbean and Cyprus and also to the way in which world trade still reflects old colonial patterns. Biology should put the facts of race in perspective, as outlined on page 56. In English reading, discussion work and drama offer valuable contexts for exploration of prejudice, and also for looking at major cultural achievements from different parts of the world. The Literature and Society syllabus at William Gladstone High School described in chapter 7 shows one way in which this can be done. In Languages, the use of CSE Mode 3 and GCE options can make Punjabi, Hindi, Urdu, Hungarian, Arabic etc. available. In Art, Art History and Music and Dance, study can be made of African, Asian and Afro-American contributions. Religious Education increasingly pays attention to the major faiths of humanity. Maths and Science also need to draw their examples from a diverse field and give due acknowledgement to non-Western innovations.

Resources and support are available for introducing a multi-ethnic perspective into the curriculum and reference to these will be found in chapter 11. One of the most useful organizations for support here is the National Association for Multiracial Education (NAME) which has many branches throughout the country.[6] Amongst the groups involved in the production of learning materials it is worth mentioning the Afro-Caribbean Education Resource Project (ACER) which has set up a pilot scheme to collect, create and disseminate multi-ethnic learning materials 'intended to foster a greater awareness of the multi-ethnic composition of the school population and wider society'.[7]

As witness to the tensions and dilemmas of multi-ethnic education one might refer to the fate of the Schools Council Multiracial Education Project described in chapter 10. It includes one of the few sets of objectives for multi-ethnic education (see below) as well as some extremely useful criteria to be used for 'the selection of learning experiences'. One of the few recent books on the multi-ethnic curriculum was also written by one of the ex-project team members.[8]

Extract 6.3

Criteria for the selection of learning experiences

(a) An insular curriculum, preoccupied with Britain and British values, is unjustifiable in the final quarter of the twentieth century. The curriculum needs to be both international in its choice of content and global in its perspective.

(b) Contemporary British society contains a variety of social and ethnic groups; this variety should be made evident in the visuals, stories and information offered to the children.

(c) Pupils should have access to accurate information about racial and cultural differences and similarities.

(d) People from British minority groups and from other cultures overseas should be presented as individuals with every variety of human quality and attribute. Stereotypes of minority groups in Britain and of cultures overseas, whether expressed in terms of human characteristics, life-styles, social roles or occupational status, are unacceptable and likely to be damaging.

(e) Other cultures and nations have their own validity and should be described in their own terms. Wherever possible they should be allowed to speak for themselves and not be judged exclusively against British or European norms.

SOURCE: Jeffcoate, R., *Positive Image: Towards a Multiracial Curriculum* (Chameleon Books, Writers' and Readers' Publishing Co-operative, 1979).

Extract 6.4

A Classification of objectives in multiracial education

(A) **Respect for Others**

Cognitive (Knowledge)

All pupils should know
A1.1   the basic facts of race and racial difference;
A1.21   the customs, values and beliefs of the main cultures represented in Britain and, more particularly, of those forming the local community;

A1.22   why different groups have immigrated into Britain in the past and more particularly, how the local community has come to acquire its present ethnic composition.

Cognitive (Skills)

All pupils should be able to
A2.1   detect stereotyping and scapegoating in what they see, hear and read;
A2.2   evaluate their own cultures dispassionately.

Affective (Attitudes, Values and Emotional Sets)

All pupils should accept
A3.1   the uniqueness of each individual human being;
A3.2   the underlying humanity we all share;
A3.3   the principle of equal rights and justice;
A3.4   and value the achievements of other cultures and nations;
A3.5   strangeness without feeling threatened;
A3.61   that Britain is, always has been and always will be a multi-ethnic society;
A3.62   no culture is ever static and that constant mutual accommodation will be required of all cultures making up an evolving multicultural society like Britain;
A3.71   that prejudice and discrimination are widespread in Britain and the historical and socioeconomic causes which have given rise to them;
A3.72   the damaging effect of prejudice and discrimination on the rejected groups;
A3.8   the possibility of developing multiple loyalties.

(B) **Respect for Self**

Cognitive (Knowledge)

All pupils should know
B1.1   the history and achievements of their own culture and what is distinctive about it.

Cognitive (Skills)

All pupils should be able to
B2.1   communicate efficiently in English and, if it is not their mother tongue, in their own mother tongue;
B2.2   master the other basic skills necessary for success at school;

Affective (Attitudes, Values and Emotional Sets)

All pupils should have developed

B3.1   a positive self-image;

B3.2   confidence in their sense of their own identities.

SOURCE: Jeffcoate, R., 'Curriculum planning in multiracial education,' *Educational Research*, 18(3), 1976.

Some of the interrelationships between multi-ethnic education and development education have already been touched on and in drawing some of the threads together at this point it might be useful to consider how the following UN definition of development education could be applied to multi-ethnic education.

> The objective of development education is to enable people to participate in the development of their community, their nation and the world as a whole. Such participation implies a critical awareness of local, national and international situations based on an understanding of the social, economic and political processes.
>
> Development education is concerned with issues of human rights, dignity, self-reliance and social justice in both developed and developing countries. It is concerned with the causes of underdevelopment and the promotion of an understanding of what is involved in development . . .[9]

The 1974 Unesco Recommendation on International Education similarly refers to 'understanding and respect for all peoples, their cultures, values and ways of life, including domestic ethnic cultures and cultures of other nations', as well as 'action to ensure the exercise and observance of human rights, including those of refugees; racialism and its eradication; the fight against discrimination in its various forms'.[10]

In the light of the current North–South dialogue and the call from 'Third World' countries for a New International Economic Order (NIEO), the need for a global dimension in the multi-ethnic curriculum is paramount. The classroom resources are available for this and many of them are readily available from the Centre for World Development Education (CWDE) in London.[11]

Recent calls for the inclusion of political education in the curriculum can also be seen to have a bearing on multi-ethnic education since the study of politics is not merely about political parties and government but also about local and national issues, rights and civil liberties, and the study of power. The possibilities of political education have been explored over the past few years although it still remains for the multi-ethnic links to be clearly drawn.[12]

A curriculum which includes the study of majority/minority issues should enable students to explore questions of identity, power, rights and change. It should facilitate the asking of questions such as those below:

Identity

Opportunities to explore the tensions and perceptions involved in majority/minority relationships are also opportunities for learning more about oneself. Who am I? What makes me like I am? Why do I see other people, and other groups, in the way that I do? What is my culture and what are the distinctive things about it? How do other people see me? What does it feel like to be in somebody else's shoes?

Power

As one considers how different people and groups see each other it is also possible to begin to look at where power lies and how it is used. Where do I stand in relation to the use of power? Who decides what, why, and how? What power do I, or could I, have to change things? Am I acting in an oppressive way in any of my everyday relationships? What alternative ways of approaching relationships are there? What are their advantages?

Rights

Consideration of self-image and of the operation of power are closely linked to questions of rights and civil liberties. Many parallels can be drawn between majority/minority conflicts and the immediate relationships that students have with their peer groups and other groups in the school and local community. What rights should one have in these personal and social contexts? Similarly the student's own attitudes and prejudices will reflect the world in miniature, for questions of conflict and cooperation, dependency and autonomy, injustice and human rights are continually occurring in the classroom itself.

Change

Two useful components of learning are reflection and action. Reflection involves thinking back on what has happened, on what one has learnt, whether in written work, verbally or through drama. It gives students the opportunity to ask themselves 'How has this affected me? How might I use what I've learnt?' Action means actually doing something to affect the course of events, either in reality or in simulation, maybe in school, in the local community or with contacts farther afield. Only this real-ization can provide a meaningful 'earthing' for the learning experience.

As a final note, it would be wrong to think that a multi-ethnic curriculum on its own will effectively solve the tensions inherent in a plural society – it will not. Only fundamental changes in society will do that. Criticisms of the multi-ethnic curriculum have been justifiably made on these grounds and must be noted.[13] It is, however, an important beginning for those working within education and is one place at which the vicious circle of racism can be attacked.

A note on 'race'

There are many myths and misconceptions about race generally, as well as in the classroom, and it is worth noting a few points at this stage. It is a word which is used extremely loosely so that people may talk about white and black 'races' (distinguishing by skin colour), about the Jewish 'race' (distinguishing by culture), or even the English 'race' (distinguishing by nationality). All these uses of the word are incorrect.

Anthropologists recognize only three broad racial groups: Negroid, Caucasoid and Mongoloid. Bio-logically there are in fact very few differences between these groups and the word 'race' is in fact used as a *social* label. When one looks at groups that are socially defined as races it turns out that well over ninety-four per cent of all the differences are found *within* a so-called 'race' rather than *between* 'races'. Ashley Montagu writes:

> In the past the tendency has been strong to overstress the differences as if stressing the differences were an argument against the likenesses. Looking back now upon the history of the nineteenth century it seems fairly clear that this drive to find differences in the 'races' of mankind grew out of the general social climate of the day. A natural stratification of the races mirrored the social stratification of the classes, and in the light of the doctrine of 'the survival of the fittest' justified the exploitation and oppression of both.[14]

It is clear therefore that defining people as English or Irish, Hindu or Christian, black or white, is a *social* and not a biological description.

Similarly there has been no new scientific evidence to alter what a massive Unesco survey said in 1951 when it concluded that 'there is no proof that the groups of mankind differ in their innate mental characteristics, whether in respect of intelligence or temperament. The scientific evidence indicates that the range of mental capacities in all ethnic groups is much the same'.

Thus the recent NUT guide points out that although 'intelligence' tests may help predict children's school performance they say nothing about any supposedly fixed 'biological potential'. And also that the determinants of 'civilization' and the growth of different sorts of human societies should be sought in social, economic and historical factors, not in biology.[15]

It is in the light of the above points that teachers often prefer *not* to use the term multiracial, but multicultural or multi-ethnic instead. As has been said before 'race' prejudice is a pigment of the imagination . . .

7 Innovations in the Curriculum

What would a syllabus look like that specifically set out to include a multi-ethnic perspective? How might one set about designing materials that meet specific multi-ethnic needs? These two questions are answered in part by the four contributions to this chapter. The first three examples deal with World History, World Studies and Modern Languages, the last example with developing teaching resources to meet specific local needs. Naturally they have all arisen out of particular school requirements, and those schools are set in particular localities. Curriculum needs will thus vary but the patterns and models that are developed can be instructive when wishing to redesign a syllabus in more appropriate form. It is hoped that they will provoke discussion about curriculum development in their fields.

The *World History* syllabus at Tulse Hill School, Brixton and the way in which it came about is described first. The course for third-year pupils is described in detail as it is noteworthy not only for the global perspective it develops but also for the way this is related to the students' needs to develop their own perspectives.

World Studies at Groby Community College, Leicester also sets out in a different way to give both a global and multi-ethnic perspective. It is an excellent example of the sort of syllabus within which majority/minority issues can adequately be studied and also interesting for its explicit use of the Problems, Background, Values and Action approach to course design (see chapter 1).

Literature and Society is one of the courses from the Modern Languages Department at William Gladstone High School, London. It shows how the field of world literature can be used to highlight the achievements of various cultures, which in turn can help to promote a positive self-image in many students. The study of race in the media is also an important part of majority/minority issues.

Islam and Hinduism in Preston examines in some detail how the needs of a particular locality were identified and how they were met by teachers in that area. It reminds us of how needs vary from area to area but yet the principles are applicable over a variety of situations. It also begins to answer the question *'How* do I get hold of the materials I need?

World history

Extract 7.1

Unearthing a black tradition

Christopher Griffin-Beale

looks at the

world history course

developed by teachers at

Tulse Hill Comprehensive

in South London

Although " world history " is spreading in secondary schools — encouraged in London by ILEA's world history packs and TV programmes—the " home-produced " course at Tulse Hill Comprehensive, Brixton, remains remarkable both for the history staff's industry in developing it and the originality of their conception.

The course is organized around comparative studies of different kinds of contact between cultures, taking in the North American Indians' experience, the Maoris and Captain Cook, the cooperation between Indians and Moguls in Asia, as well as the black experience in England. The department's explicit aim is not only to develop historical skills—handling sources and weighing evidence—but to make a positive contribution to the multicultural educational policy advocated by the school and by the ILEA.

The course, though global in scope, stresses connexions with the school's locality, and was designed for the school's particular population : roughly half of the 1,250 boys are black, mostly born here, while many of the rest are Indian, Pakistani or Chinese. Yet the course's essentials could be duplicated elsewhere, even in a school with a more homogeneous intake.

The course's own history dates back to 1973, when the school mounted a week-end conference at Eastbourne about future policy, attended not just by staff and governors, but by inspectors and representatives of pupils, parents and the community.

The school had pioneered black studies for several years, but some dissatisfaction was developing with the notion of a segregated, labelled special course, especially since many of the humanities had already integrated something of black studies into their syllabi.

At the conference, the history department attracted strong criticism for their current syllabus—a fairly traditional diet of British and European political and social history. The world history course was the department's considered response. It took a good year to conceive, with several arduous working weekends for the whole department at The Croft, the school's residential study centre in Surrey.

It took a year to evolve the course's outline, and another to develop the resources, before the course was introduced in late 1975. There were few suitable written resources available, and not much money, although the project had the backing of the district inspector, who happened to be staff history inspector, and the help of ILEA's resource support group.

The department concentrated on the course for third-year pupils. Among the integrated humanities work in the first year, some historical foundations are laid : pupils look at Britain, and get a foretaste of the theme of contact between cultures in the arrival of the Romans, the Angles, Saxons and Normans. In the second year, they are introduced to historical skills through detective work on historical puzzles.

The third-year course opens with a look at all major regions and civilizations— Africa, India, Europe, the Incas and the Caribbean—as they were in the fifteenth century, before European colonization

and influence spread, and before the examples of contact that will be studied later. Each study, concentrating on the basics of social organization (in Europe, the decaying feudal system), is built around illustrated, duplicated work books.

The third-year mixed ability class I saw were having one of their first sessions on Africa. They had to make do with dog-eared booklets, whose improved replacements were delayed by the school's malfunctioning offset litho (such are the realities of curriculum development). This was their penultimate region of study—only the Caribbean remained. Their teacher, Chris Power, a senior housemaster, asked them to recap, and consider whether the regions manifested civilizations and what they had in common.

Given the usual variations in attention and response, the class nevertheless displayed an impressive recall of salient facts, together with a capacity to compare the regions and a recognition of the plurality of civilizations and their values. A lively argument developed about the human sacrifices of the Incas—were they cruel or not, and was this the kind of question a historian could ask ?

After they had identified the common characteristics of all the civilizations, Chris Power cited the common misconception about pre-colonial Africa's lack of civilization, and challenged them—an effective ploy—to disprove it from the material in their booklet, which they were able to do from information about the civilization of Timbuktu.

This work is a foundation for the study of contact between cultures which occupies the second half of the year, and is based on individualized materials, duplicated sheets which pupils select from a browsing box with a free—but guided— choice. The materials are classified by region, century and—most important— by themes : different kinds of contact: co-operation (including Captain Cook and the Maoris, and the Hindus and Moguls), exploitation (the Spanish and Incas), rejection, settlement, mission, forced movement (including transportation of white convicts as well as black slaves), voluntary movement, refuge (the Pilgrim Fathers and Huguenots), and resistance.

There are simulation games on trading and colonization, films from the ILEA film library, the World History TV programmes, and slides. For pupils with reading difficulties the written texts have been taped by sixth formers, leaving teachers free to give them special attention.

The most original material is the evidence of the long tradition of black people in England, gathered by Chris Power and Nigel File, the department's acting head.

There were black people in Britain centuries before the post-war waves of immigration—20,000 in London alone in 1764, according to a writer in the *Gentleman's Magazine*, who objected to these imported Negro servants because "they ceafe to confider themfelves as flaves in this free country, nor will they put up with an inequality of treatment".

Some solutions to "the problem" have a long history too· pupils encounter documents about the Committee for the Black Poor, which agitated in London in the 1780s to encourage black people to return to Africa, to settle Sierra Leone (repatriation, if not forced).

The staff have been able to build in a valuable local dimension to these themes Francis Barber, a freed slave who became Dr Johnson's trusted servant, lived in Streatham in the 1770s, and Granville Sharp, a tireless white campaigner for emancipation of *all* slaves, had connexions with Clapham and Battersea.

This material fascinates pupils, who are able to see that many hysterical assumptions about current "racial problems" are inaccurate and betray an ignorance of history. Many of the white pupils, Chris Power claims, have been among the keenest to take the material home to show their parents. At open evenings parents have expressed enthusiasm, and the department has had no complaints.

For black pupils, many of them struggling to receive their identity as black British, this evidence of a black tradition —not just in England, but specifically in South London—has a more powerful impact. One pupil wrote : "Black people have been here for 300 years, and they're here to stay."

The department are still amassing resources for the fourth and fifth-year course on the twentieth century, which offers an extensive study on Nazi Germany (a topic, they reckon, with "immediate moral lessons") and on the Second World War, with a special option on Commonwealth troops. Other topics include the Chinese Revolution, a history of British working people, or the history of the black experience.

In the sixth form pupils follow the AEB Mode 3 O level course of World Powers and then a London University A level syllabus (B) which seems to fit with the school's approach : last year six of seven candidates passed, half of them after only one year.

Despite several staff changes, the project's continuity seems assured by the head's support, and the commitment of two new staff : Donald Hinds, a Jamaican who has written a book about West Indian immigration, and Michael Tidy, with a decade of Kenyan teaching experience and several African history textbooks behind him.

Together the staff have plans to simplify existing resources, and expand the contact themes to include Cromwell and the Irish, and to have more on other well-established groups in England—the Jews, Huguenots, Irish, and Indians.

One might wish for more on the history of the indigenous working people —a topic neglected in most traditional syllabi—though this is an option in the fourth and fifth-year course. But generally the course's approach touches on many other traditionally recognized historical issues.

One visiting Catholic lecturer described the department's approach, not entirely approvingly, as "evangelistic". But they do not seem to be distorting any material through their approach, although they show a strong commitment to multicultural education.

Chris Power stresses that their approach is multi-*cultural* rather than multi-*ethnic* : the pupils may come from different cultures, but they are not of different nationalities since most of them were born here, many to parents who came as immigrants with British passports.

For the same reason, a course overwhelmingly devoted to, say, the Caribbean would not be an ideal solution for a multi-cultural school. Many "West Indian" pupils are more concerned about establishing their own black identity within Britain than harking back to a place they may have hardly visited. The Caribbean can usefully feature in the syllabus—one third-former this year has kept asking when they were going to study Jamaica. But for most pupils— black and white—the important questions, which Tulse Hill's course directly address, concern the relationship *between* cultures.

The course fosters a spirit of historical inquiry, and the necessary skills to accompany it, such as handling primary sources. But it is also history rooted in our society's multi-cultural future, to which so much official educational policy is committed.

SOURCE: *Times Educational Supplement*, 24 February 1978.

*Published in book form as *Black Settlers in Britain 1555–1958* by Chris Power and Nigel File (Heinemann Educational Books, 1981).

World studies

Extract 7.2

Living and Learning in the Global Village~aims and plans at a new school

by **David Selby and Hilary Cox,** Groby Community College, Leicestershire

This article is the main text of a paper recently submitted to, and approved by, the East Midlands Regional Examinations Board. It is reprinted here with grateful acknowledgement to the Board, and also to Groby College, whose copyright it remains.

Groby Community College is a new Leicestershire upper school for 14–18 year old students. In their first two years at Groby all students are to follow a core course in World Studies, starting in autumn 1978. The article which follows outlines the aims, rationale and content of this core course, and shows the scheme of assessment.

Aims

The aims of this World Studies Syllabus are as follows:

1) To encourage students to set their thinking about the modern world within a global framework.

2) To foster amongst students an allegiance to mankind in general as against an allegiance to national, local or sectional interests.

3) To help students become aware of the widening gap between the richer and poorer countries, and of the consequences likely to follow if global inequalities are not remedied.

4) To encourage respect for cultural diversity.

5) To help students identify and respect those values shared by mankind in general.

These aims are discussed in the Rationale that follows.

Rationale

'Our society is a multicultural, multiracial one, and the curriculum should reflect a sympathetic understanding of the different cultures and races that now make up our society. We also live in a complex, interdependent world, and many of our problems in Britain require international solutions. The curriculum should

therefore reflect our need to know about and understand other countries.'[a]

The basic premise of this syllabus is that there are certain definable problems of human organisation on this planet which can only be fully understood from a global point of view and which can only be treated on a global basis. Central to the syllabus is the concept of the 'global village', the word 'village' underlining the fact that the contemporary world is a single system with all its various parts interdependent. Developments of a social, political, economic, environmental or technological nature in any one quarter of the 'village' can have significant repercussions in many — possible all — other quarters.

'Viewed against a backdrop of the whole of man's history, the continuing transformation of the world from a collection of many lands and peoples to a system of many lands and peoples is a profound change in the human condition. The emergence of the contemporary world system carries with it far-reaching implications for the task of socialising and formally educating young people.'[b]

In the first place, it becomes vitally important that students be introduced to a new framework within which to develop their thinking and loyalties. Students should be shown that they have a double allegiance — an allegiance to their own nation and people and an allegiance to mankind in general — and that where a conflict exists between the two, the larger loyalty subsumes the smaller.

On the opposite side of the same coin, the prospects for the future, should global loyalty not transcend national loyalty, need serious consideration. In the socio-economic sphere, it is becoming imperative that students be made aware of the fact that the world's wealth is not equitably distributed and that, unless a global strategy is evolved to remedy the inequalities existing, the 'global village' may well lurch from crisis to crisis in their lifetime and beyond.

Finally, whilst making every effort to foster respect for cultural diversity, students should be encouraged to identify and respect those values shared by the whole species — the 'attitudinal glue', as it has been called, which can 'bind together the moral impulses necessary for human co-operation'.[c]

The 'global village' approach to studying the modern world (as against the 'places' and 'events' approaches common to Geography and Modern World History courses) presents problems in terms of syllabus construction in that it is, by definition, non-linear. To accept that the world is a single system with interdependent parts is to reject the notion that any particular problem, set as it is in time and place, can be understood by exclusive investigation of that one problem. Does 'Poverty in the Third World' go under the heading of 'Natural Resources', 'Over-population' or 'Global inequalities' as a study topic? Is the remedy for Third World poverty to be found in aid organisations and programmes, intermediate technology, population control, dismantling well-established trading systems or in a compound of these – and other – factors? Do we put Southern Africa in the conflict, human rights or race section of a syllabus?

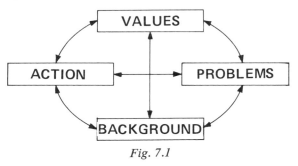

Fig. 7.1

Conceptual model

To extricate ourselves from the tangles and dilemmas raised by questions such as the above, we have adopted the useful conceptual model suggested by Robin Richardson for constructing World Studies syllabuses.[d]

The four concepts in the model are in themselves mutually dependent. A global problem is only perceived as such given certain values on the part of the beholder. Values, likewise, determine one's analysis of the underlying causes of a problem and one's decisions as to a particular course of action. Action (i.e. an attempt at tackling a problem) may well lead to a shift of values in the light of experience and to fresh insights into the problem and its underlying causes. From this central conceptual hub, Richardson has developed a 'World Study Topic Web', a diagram which maps out the field of World Studies as a school subject and which illustrates how closely interwoven are the topics likely to appear in a World Studies syllabus.[e]

In the syllabus that follows no attempt is made to draw attention to the many interconnections existing between the various topics listed. Nor is mention made of the ongoing interaction between background, problems, action and values which will be central to our classroom strategy. The listing of topics is convenient but the reader should not be deceived into thinking that the teaching team will religiously follow the order as set down on paper.

When we look at Poverty (Section II, 2), for instance, we will also give some consideration to the 'North-South Conflict' (Section II, 4), to the work of the United Nations in combatting poverty (Section III, 2), to the work of aid organisations (Section III, 3), to 'dismantling structural violence' (Section III, 7) and to population control (Section III, 8) although all of these topics will be given fuller consideration later in the course. Our teaching, in other words, will involve an elaborate system of cross-referencing.

Nor will the locality of the school be overlooked as a resource. It is, clearly, the case that failure on our part to identify events and situations illustrative of the syllabus within the locality would tend to invalidate the very concept of a single world system upon which the syllabus has been built.

Grassroots action

Whilst Section I of the syllabus deals with background and Section II identifies the key problems, Sections III and IV are concerned with what has been described as 'action'. Broadly speaking 'action' can be taken at two levels; it can be taken at 'the top' by those involved in national government or in international organisations or it can be taken at the grass roots by individuals or small groups. Section III deals with the former type of action and Section IV with the latter.

Under Section IV students will be given the opportunity to involve themselves in a project at grass roots level. The experience they gain may be reported and analysed as their research project. Alternatively, they can choose a research project title from within the twelve study areas listed in Section V of the syllabus.

Finally, a word on content. The syllabus is all-embracing and it may be thought to be too full. It should, however, be pointed out that a case-study approach will be adopted to many of the topics listed. An exhaustive approach to each topic would be both unrealistic and counter-productive. Furthermore, it is worth mentioning – although it is a point mentioned again later — that material for the final examination will only be selected from Sections I, II and III of the syllabus.

The syllabus

Section I: The Global Village

1. The term 'Global Village' introduced and explained.
2. Origins and Evolution (theories of the formation of the earth and of the structure of the earth's crust – plate tectonics and isostacy).
3. Sizes and Shapes (comparative study of differing size of land masses; the sea area and land

area compared; the annihilation of distance with modern technologies and transport developments).

4. Climatic Zones.

5. Natural Resources (including water) – their distribution and uses; the sea as a natural resource.

6. Human Resources (population figures, racial groupings).

7. Developed and developing countries; the Third World; the Fourth World – the terms introduced and explained (including basic facts).

Section II: The Global Village is a Village at Risk

1. Overpopulation.

2. Poverty and Affluence (including hunger and malnutrition; drought; the geography of world disease; the diseases of affluence and the diseases of poverty; incapacity in the face of natural disaster; illiteracy; the uneven distribution of wealth and income between the developed and underdeveloped worlds).

3. Conflict and Violence (including racial, religious and ideological conflict; war; the arms race; the threat of nuclear war; torture; refugees; conflict over the ownership of the sea bed).

4. Structural violence (oppression as perpetrated by organisations, governmental systems, trading systems and widely-held opinion which, in its effect, achieves the same end result as actual physical violence). Apartheid in South Africa; the role of women in certain societies; minority groups in Central and East Africa, Russia, India, Sri Lanka and Canada; migrant workers in Europe and, most importantly, the relationship between the 'rich world' and 'poor world' to be considered.

5. Reactive Violence (including anti-colonial movements; freedom fighting; terrorism; student and youth protest and, most important of all, the Third World response to structural violence as it has developed since the Oil Crisis of October 1973).

6. Destruction of the Environment (man's spoliation of the natural environment – pollution, resource depletion and misuse, the energy crisis, desertification and urbanisation).

Section III: Pointers Towards a Better World

1. Towards World Government and Co-operation (an outline history of world government theories and movements including the UN Charter for a World-elected Assembly; the emergence of political groupings transcending the nation state; international co-operation in weather prediction, communications and outer space).

2. The United Nations Organisation; its aims, history, work, structure and achievements; the aims,

work and achievements of its specialised agencies (including FAO, ILO, UNESCO, UNICEF, UNHCR, UNRRA, UNRWA, WHO) and specific case studies of same.

3. Some other international bodies and their work (including the Red Cross, Christian Aid, IVS, Oxfam, Save the Children Fund, VSO and the World Council of Churches).

4. International Policing, Law and Security (including United Nations policing in Korea, Suez and Cyprus, Interpol, Extradition Agreements and the International Court of Justice).

5. Human Rights (including the Declaration of Human Rights, the Declaration of the Rights of the Child, the European Court of Human Rights, Amnesty International, the Carter Initiative).

6. Peacebuilding. Peace movements, arms control and disarmament.

7. Dismantling structural violence on a global scale: UNCTAD; its work and conferences; aid programmes, Intermediate Technology.

8. Population Control – some national and global strategies.

9. Alternative lifestyles and technologies.

10. Conservation.

Section IV: Involvement

'In a global age where worldwide interdependence makes itself felt in the daily lives of most human beings, it is critical that individuals learn how they might exercise some measure of control and influence over the public affairs of global society, as well as over the public affairs of their local communities and nations.'[f]

'We must encourage and assist our students in identifying their own value and action priorities in light of their concern about particular global issues. We must help them discover their own strengths and learn how they can be most effective. We must help each person find his or her entry point for action.'[g]

This section will involve an examination by students of how they, as individuals, can contribute meaningfully to the welfare of the Global Village. Included amongst the forms of involvement to be discussed will be:

1. The UNESCO Associated Schools and Colleges Project and how it can help the individual foster international understanding.

2. Community Relations work.

3. Participation at local, national and international level in the work of an international environmental organisation (e.g. Friends of the Earth).

4. Participation in the work of IVS, United Nations,

Population Concern or a similar body at local or national level.

5. Money-raising to help fight world poverty, hunger and disease.

6. Projects connected with the school such as school recycling projects or monitoring the school's use of energy and other resources.

7. Running a 'globally-conscious' home (conservation etc.) and 'globally-conscious' shopping.

8. Local projects involving experimentation with or development of alternative technologies.

9. a) A voice in local politics. b) A voice in national politics. What channels are open to the individual so he/she can make known his/her views concerning global issues?

10. A global problems and solutions publicity compaign in the locality.

After brief consideration of the above in class, students working individually or in groups will be invited to involve themselves in a local project of their choosing and, later, to write up their experience and conclusions as their research project.

Section V: Cohesive Forces within the Global Village

These students choosing not to involve themselves in a project under Section IV will be asked to choose a research project title falling within one of the following areas:

1. Common factors in world beliefs and ideologies.

2. The universal appeal of sports, games and athletics.

3. Developments in the use of space.

4. The universal appeal of art, science, films, fashion, music, cookery or literature.

5. The study of an art form or craft of a particular country, culture or continent, with an examination of its wider influence and appeal.

6. Our concern to preserve the archaeological and architectural heritage of mankind.

7. Family, home life and children in particular parts of the world.

8. Travel, transport and tourism.

9. Communications systems and mass media.

10. World leaders (political, religious and cultural).

Objectives and Assessment

By the end of the two-year course the student should:

1. Be able to recognise and recall relevant information.

2. Have a knowledge of the key concepts in the syllabus.

3. Have given evidence that he/she can plan, organise and pursue independent enquiry.

4. Have shown that he/she can present the results of that enquiry, and other course work, clearly and accurately.

5. Have given evidence that he/she can explain in his/her own words the arguments surrounding current global issues and developments and can form his/her own judgement.

6. Be able to express his/her point of view clearly and accurately in speech.

These six objectives will be assessed through (1) course work; (2) a research project; (3) an oral examination; (4) two written examinations. The course work will constitute 20% of the overall assessment, the research project 30%, the oral examination 10%, and the written examinations 40%.

Assessment of Objective 1 (recognition and recall of relevant information) will constitute 22% of the overall assessment; of Objective 2 (knowledge of key concepts) also 22%; of Objective 3 (ability to plan and organise independent enquiry) 15%; of Objective 4 (presentation of results) 10%; of Objective 5 (ability to explain and form judgements) 25%; and of Objective 6 (ability to express views in speech) 16%.

Course work

Assessment of course work will be based on the standard of the student's ten best pieces of work, two arising out of Section I of the Syllabus, four out of Section II and four out of Section III. One 'piece of work' we define as being a relevant written response or written and graphic response to any part of the course or syllabus.

It might be an essay on a particular topic, a critical review of a film seen, a piece reflecting on ideas put forward by a visiting speaker, a story intended to highlight some aspect of a global issue, or it may take some other form.

The course work will be assessed with regard to Objectives 2 (7 marks), 4 (5 marks) and 5 (8 marks).

Research project

A research project will be undertaken by each student. The project may be an account and analysis of practical work undertaken by the student following consideration of Section IV of the Syllabus. Alternatively, a title can be chosen from within one of the areas listed in Section V of the Syllabus.

Prior to commencing their project, students will be asked to prepare and present a 'plan of campaign' containing a project title, a description of how the project will be tackled, and an initial list of resources to be consulted. This plan of campaign will be incorporated into the project together with subsequent amendments made by the student in the light of ongoing research. Written work together with any illustrations, photographs, diagrams etc, will be presented bound in a folder.

The research project will be assessed with regard to Objectives 2 (3 marks), 3 (15 marks), 4 (5 marks) and 5 (7 marks).

Examinations

There will be an oral examination of not less than ten minutes on any three topics pre-selected by the student. This exam will assess Objectives 1 (2 marks), 2 (2 marks), and 6 (6 marks).

A written examination on Sections I, II and III of the Syllabus will be taken by students at the end of the course, and will consist of two papers.

Paper I, lasting 1½ hours, will contain 50 questions requiring one or two-sentence answers and testing the candidate's ability to recall information (Objective 1). There will be 2 marks for each question, thus a possible total of 100 marks, to be scaled down to 20.

Paper II, lasting 1¾ hours plus 15 minutes reading time will contain three sections. The first section will require short paragraph answers and will test knowledge of key concepts (Objective 2); the second will consist of 10 questions requiring short answers based on stimulus documentary and/or visual material (Objective 5); the third will be a major essay question testing knowledge of key concepts (Objective 2), and the ability to explain the arguments surrounding current global issues and developments and the ability to form an independent judgement (Objective 5).

References

[a] *Education in Schools,* consultative document by the Department of Education and Science, July 1977.

[b] Anderson, L. and Becker, J., 'An Examination of the Structure and Objectives of International Education', *Social Education,* 1968.

[c] Henderson, J., 'A Note on World Studies – the Key Concepts', background paper for a meeting of the Education Advisory Committee of the One World Trust held at the House of Commons, Westminster, 29 April 1975.

[d] Richardson, R., 'Studying World Society: some approaches to the design of courses', *The New Era,* Vol. 58, No. 6, December 1977, p. 182.

[e] Richardson's World Topic Web appears in Richardson, R., *Learning for Change in World Society,* 1976, p. 6. The topic web and conceptual model emerged out of discussions held at conferences of the World Studies Project, which is funded by the Department of Education and Science.

[f] Anderson, L. and Becker, J., 'Education for Involvement', *The New Era,* Vol. 58, No. 2, March 1977, p. 43.

[g] Shiman, D. and Conrad, D., 'Awareness, understanding and Action: a global conscience in the classroom', *The New Era,* Vol. 58, No. 6, December 1977, p. 166.

SOURCE: *The New Era,* 59 (4), July/Aug. 1978.

Literature and society

Extract 7.3

Literature and Society: a Mode III CSE with Middlesex Regional Examining Board

Introduction

The Modern Languages Department at William Gladstone High School has, over the past two years, attempted to insert a significant multi-ethnic area of knowledge into the school curriculum. Although in the Social Studies Department various cultures are studied historically and geographically, their creative works are not included. We believe that a multi-ethnic literature course is needed to bridge this gap in the present curriculum as it can clearly lead to an even greater intercultural understanding.

During the academic year 1976–7 the department started such a literature course for the third year. The response from the students was very postitive in terms of the quality of work produced and the motivation. Approximately 47 students of mixed ability and from a range of cultural backgrounds have consequently opted to take the Literature and Society, Mode III CSE course for four periods a week in their fourth and fifth years. We feel we have achieved our aim in avoiding creating a specific course for a specific group of students, (for example, a Caribbean literature course attracting mainly West Indian students) as we have succeeded in involving a broad range of students. The Bullock Report, when recommending that the culture of the students of overseas origins should be an important part of the curriculum, stated: 'We see implications here for the education of all children, not just those of families of overseas origins.'

By teaching the students to value many different cultures the course is aiming, primarily, at a greater intercultural understanding, whilst at the same time it is broadening and intensifying the students' response to various kinds of literature. In so doing, their understanding of their own multicultural community should be positively developed.

The literature has been carefully selected to give a balance of different cultures so that an interest and an appreciation of the differences between cultures will be promoted and viewed with greater knowledge and understanding. At the same time the similarities will be stressed and particularly where problems in society are explored in the literature, links will be made to similar problems in other groups to show that they are not unique to one set of people. The study of literature, which is a strong instrument for empathy, encourages students to consider the thoughts, experiences and feelings of people who exist beyond their immediate daily awareness and so may have an effect on any existing ethnocentric attitudes. It may also encourage students to distance themselves from some of their immediate problems. To quote once again from the Bullock Report, literature 'equally confronts the reader with problems similar to his own and does it at the safety of one remove. He draws reassurance from realizing that personal difficulties and feelings of deficiency are not unique to himself'.

Literature has also been chosen to accentuate the positive aspects of culture and this should equally help to promote a positive 'self-concept' in many students who have not been aware of the creative works of their own cultural background and will now be able to experience a pride in them and also be able to share this experience with students from other cultural backgrounds.

Besides the literature and background studies, the section on biographies and autobiographies has been included to encourage the student to place herself/ himself and others in a social and historical context, and thus to value one's own history and other people's.

As educationalists we are not only responsible for extending the students' view of the world but also we must challenge some of the perceptions they already hold, which may have been passed on to them in this society. For this reason an investigation of the media has been included as an integral part of the course, as it is a significant factor in the construction of one's attitudes and beliefs. This part of the course will mainly concentrate on the study of images of race as presented in the media. The method of investigation is based on the work of the semioticians Guy Gauthier and Roland Barthes.

With these aims in view the following CSE Mode III syllabus has been drawn up.

A. Core of syllabus

The students will study at least four of the following books in depth plus their social, cultural and historical context. The teacher will choose at least one book from four different sections to ensure as wide a range of cultures as possible and these will be studied together in class. One book from the European section will be compulsory. Students will be encouraged to read complete novels (as recommended by the Bullock Report) and not just a collection of extracts. The sections are as follows in alphabetical order.

(a) *African Literature*

Things Fall Apart: Chinua Achebe
No Sweetness Here: Aidoo Ata Ama
Second-Class Citizen: Buchi Emecheta
Roots of Time: Jefferson and Skinner
Nine African Stories: Doris Lessing
The Study of Literature: edited by H. L. B. Moody
Weep Not Child: James Ngugi
Young and Black in Africa: A. Okion Ojigbo
The Fisherman: Tom Okoyo
Tribal Scars: Sembene Ousmane

(b) *Afro-American Literature*

Young and Black in America: Alexander and Lester
To Be A Slave: Julius Lester
Long Journey Home: Julius Lester
The Journey: Murray and Thomas
The Scene: Murray and Thomas
The Search: Murray and Thomas
Major Black Writers: Murray and Thomas
Black Perspectives: Murray and Thomas
Three Against Slavery: Philip Spencer
Black-Eyed Susans: edited by Mary Helen Washington
Black Boy: Richard Wright

(c) *Asian Literature*

Untouchable: Mulk Raj Anand
I Take This Woman: Rajinder Singh Bedi
East End At Your Feet: Farrukh Dhondy
The Whispering Earth: K. S. Karanth
From Citizen to Refugee: Mahmood Mamdani
My Village, My Life: Mohanti Prafulla
The World of Premchand: Premchand
A Mentor Book of Modern Asian Literature: Dorothy
   Blair Shimer
A Bride For The Sahib: Khushwant Singh
Contemporary Indian Short Stories: Ka Naa
Subramanyam

(d) *Caribbean Literature*

Bluefoot Traveller: edited by James Berry
Backfire: edited by N. and U. Guiseppi
Out Of The Stars: edited by N. and U. Guiseppi
Moon On a Rainbow Shawl: Errol John
Miguel Street: V. S. Naipaul

Joey Tyson: Andrew Salkey
A Brighter Sun: Samuel Selvon
Ways of Sunlight: Samuel Selvon
The Lonely Londoners: Samuel Selvon
The Sun's Eye: edited by Ann Walmsey

(e) *European Literature*

The Jewish Wife and other Plays: Bertolt Brecht
The Diary of Anne Frank: Anne Frank
Andorra: Max Frisch
A Scot's Quair: Lewis Grassic Gibbon
Childhood: Maxim Gorky
An Irish Navvy: Donall MacAmhlaigh
Hal: Jean MacGibbon
Portrait of the Artist as a Young Dog: Dylan Thomas

B. Social Background

(a) *Book, film and TV programme reviews*

Written or taped reviews are to be submitted over the
five terms. These should be concerned with aspects of
culture and race. A variety of books will be provided by
the school to encourage voluntary, independent
reading. Where necessary the teacher should guide
the student's reading to cover a variety of areas as
recommended in the core syllabus.

(b) *The Presentation of Race in the Media*

This section will mainly be based on the study of the
British Film Institute's course on Racial Images which
includes slides, film extracts and full length films.

(c) *Autobiographies/Biographies OR Projects on
various aspects of culture and race*

(i) Autobiographies/Biographies
The students will be encouraged to compile small
booklets about themselves or someone else,
preferably a person who has come from another
culture, and so produce some original research into a
person's history and culture.

Extracts will be used from some of the following
biographies, autobiographies and books about culture
in British society.
Lifetimes: Group Autobiographies (Manchester
Polytechnic)
1. A Mancunian Couple
2. A Russian and a Mancunian
3. A Couple from Runcorn and the Isle of Man
4. A Barbadian
5. An Irish Couple
6. A Couple from Durham
7. A Mancunian
Small Accidents: Sandali Sabir
Memories: George Paul
A Licence to Live: Ron Barnes

Millfield Memories: Doris Knight
Daddy Burtt's For Dinner: Rose Lowe
A Hoxton Childhood: A. S. Jasper
Poverty: The Forgotten Englishmen: Ken Coates and
   Richard Silburn
Into Unknown England: edited by Peter Keating
or

(ii) Projects
The students will be required to demonstrate a detailed
knowledge in a chosen area which will be closely
supervised by the teacher. This project may include
written work/tapes and illustrations and may, where
possible, involve contact with the local community.

Links are being made with schools in Zaire and
Tanzania which may prove to be useful sources for
research.

Assessment

A. *Regional Assessment 50%*

1. Written Examination 1½ hours (35 marks)
The candidate will be required to answer three
questions in an essay form chosen from three different
areas of study specified under section A of the
syllabus. The teacher will determine which book will
be studied for the examination.

2. Oral Examination 10 minutes taped (25 marks)
The candidate will be required to discuss clearly, and
intelligently, showing an understanding of at least one
of the books studied in detail. Assessment will be
based on:
(a) clarity of expression
(b) a good literary appreciation of the book displaying
      a knowledge of the following areas:
   (i)   characters
   (ii) motivations
   (iii) culture
   (iv) location
   (v)   literary styles and techniques
   (vi) ideas expressed by the author in the book
(c) an ability to relate ideas to other areas of study or
      personal experience.

3. Project or Autobiography/Biography (40 marks)
The candidate will be required to do either a project or
an autobiography/biography. The minimum number of
words will be 150.

B. *School Assessment 50%*

1. Essays – Continuous Assessment
The candidate will be required to submit five essays of
between 100 to 700 words from the areas specified in
section A.

2. Book/Film/Television Programme Reviews – Continuous Assessment

The candidate will be required to produce five reviews during the five-term course as proof of individual study. These may be related to any sphere of multicultural studies and should cover as many varied fields as possible. Each review should not be less than 100 words written or three minutes taped.

3. Media Studies – Continuous Assessment

The candidate will be required to submit one essay from this topic. The minimum number of words will be 100.

Specimen Written Examination Paper Summer 1979; Time: 1½ hours

Write *THREE* essays making sure that each one comes from a different section.

Section One – African Literature

Nine African Stories: Doris Lessing

1. 'Tommy took the little animal gently in his hands, and his tenderness for this frightened and lonely creature rushed up to his eyes and he turned away so that Dirk couldn't see – he would have been bitterly ashamed to show softness in front of Dirk, who was so tough and fearless.'

What incident is this referring to? Discuss Tommy's and Dirk's relationship and how they are drawn together.

2. Write about what you learnt of the atmosphere and cultures of Rhodesia as Doris Lessing describes it in these stories.

Section Two – Afro-American Literature

Long Journey Home: Julius Lester

1. 'All he knew was how to be a slave.' Discuss how Julius Lester shows slavery as having a marked effect on the minds and behaviour of the slaves. Refer to at least two stories.

2. What are your most vivid impressions of life as a slave? Refer in detail to the stories you have read to support your answer.

Section Three – Asian Literature

East End At Your Feet: Farrukh Dhondy

1. From your reading of this book, which problems experienced by the Asian community are special to them and which do you think are common to many families? Refer closely to the book to support your answer.

2. Discuss the role illusions and dreams play in the lives of some of the characters in this book and how they differ from reality.

Section Four – Caribbean Literature

Miguel Street: V. S. Naipaul

1. Describe the incidents in these short stories which show how the community in Miguel Street believes in pulling together and supporting each other.

2. Describe some of the humorous episodes in the book making clear what makes the reader laugh.

Section Five – European Literature

The Diary of Anne Frank: Anne Frank

1. Give examples to illustrate Anne's statement that she is well-known for 'my exuberant cheerfulness, making fun of everything, my high-spiritedness and above all, the way I take everything lightly'.

2. Compare and contrast Anne's relationship with various members of her family. What outside pressures also influence the family's attitudes to each other?

SOURCE: Middlesex Regional Examining Board and Scilla Alvarado, William Gladstone High School, Brent

Resources on Islam and Hinduism

Extract 7.4

Islam in Preston and Hinduism in Preston

The development of teaching materials based on the religious and social practices of Asian communities living in a northern town
by Stephen Harrison, Head, Revoe Junior School, Blackpool

Needs identified

In the late 1960s and early 1970s teachers working in industrial areas of the UK were faced with the challenge of considerable changes in the composition of their classes. The Asian men who had emigrated to this country in the previous decade were by now being joined by wives and fiancées; subsequently the number of children of Asian origin in schools grew rapidly in many areas.

This new phenomenon presented teachers with two challenges. The first was that of teaching English to children of all ages whose only speech was in one of a number of Asian languages. The second, more elusive challenge was that of learning about the cultures of these newcomers and of adapting the curriculum so that it might reflect the presence of these new groups in society.

The majority of teachers had received a substantial part of their training in Sociology. The value systems, morality, aspirations and lifestyles of the various social classes in British society were studied at length and the deprivation experienced by children from working class homes (whether economic or linguistic deprivation) was a subject colleges expected all their students to comprehend. Names like Bernstein, Labov, Lawton, Rosenthal and Jacobson tripped from the tongues of all ambitious students at every tutorial and seminar.

It was obvious to many teachers that if a knowledge of working class culture was a pre-requisite of teaching in urban society then it followed that a knowledge of Asian cultures ought to be similarly important for teaching in a multi-racial society. The colleges were painfully slow in responding to this need. In 1972 Townsend and Brittan[a] reported that, of 596 probationers questioned, only 66 claimed to have had tuition on the education of immigrants and, of these, 6 had received only one lecture.

Other bodies, apart from the colleges, determined to fill this gap in teacher expertise. It was the partial failure of such bodies to provide adequate information that resulted in the need for locally based materials.[b,c]

The LEAs and bodies such as the CRC attempted to fill the knowledge gap, and a number of textbooks appeared which sought to reflect the new nature of British society.

In-service courses for teachers proved to be uneven in value. Many local authorities turned, understandably, to the universities for speakers on Asian culture. The response was often the provision of lecturers on Islam who were expert on the events of the Prophet's lifetime, the military expansion of Islam, the closing of the gates of Ijtihad, but with little or no contact with Muslims from Pakistan or India. The interpretations many such speakers chose to place on the Quran were quite unrelated to interpretations

Muslims from rural backgrounds in the Indian sub-continent would place on the same book.

In retrospect it seems odd that we in the British Isles, with its enormous variety of religious practices all encompassed within the Christian community, should assume that people from as far apart as Rawalpindi, Dacca, Broach, Cairo and Istanbul behave in a uniform way simply because they all call themselves Muslims.

The alternative to academics was often an Asian, but the same colour of skin is no guarantee of shared experiences. An Asian doctor of middle class origin might be said to have more in common with his fellow white professionals than with the illiterate rural peasant from Bangladesh.

A number of publications produced at the beginning of this decade were designed to reflect the changing nature of our society, by now termed a 'plural society'. It soon became obvious to teachers involved with the Asian communities that many such publications failed to reflect the plural society accurately.

East Comes West[d] was comprehensive in its treatment of the major Asian religions but, in my view, missed an opportunity of identifying those aspects of background which transferred from the Indian sub-continent to the UK.

We learn that Hindus rise between 4 and 5 a.m., go to a local river and immerse themselves prior to morning prayer. The obvious question was to what extent a large Hindu family in the inner city, subject to bus and train timetables, and in many cases without access to a bathroom, can continue to carry out the early morning bath. Similarly the suggestion that Hindus pray three times a day and Muslims five, is one that demands examination in the light of the demands of an industrial society.

One of the more popular textbooks[e] on Islam contained a photograph of Muslims at prayer in the Shah Jehan Mosque in Woking. The photograph depicts men and women sitting alongside each other in worship. The picture is totally unrepresentative of what goes on in the majority of British mosques. In most, women attend only rarely and where they do they are accommodated in separate galleries or rooms. One assumes that the photograph was taken when the Woking mosque was controlled by Ahmadiahs, a group who regard themselves as Muslims but who are not so regarded by most UK Muslims and are classified as a non-Muslim minority in Pakistan.

One other major problem for teachers and pupils is that Asian groups in this country are dynamic. Their numbers, attitudes and emphases are in a state of flux.

These changes are most obvious where East African immigration has supplemented Indian immigration. It is therefore extremely difficult for writers to reflect actual practices of Asians across the country.

As recently as 1973 Michael Lyon[f] wrote: 'Gujaratis share a common language and regional culture which to a large extent overrides the religious differences between Hindu and Muslims, and even between sub-castes.' Such an assessment was (and still is) quite mistaken in the context of Preston where over 10,000 Asians of Gujarati origin live, but it does apply even today in Skelmersdale where the Asian community is small and expresses a sense of community through linguistic and geographical bonds rather than through religious ties.

Dilip Hiro in 1970 stated that 'almost all Gujaratis are Hindus,[g] a statement that ignores the regional variations in the UK such as those in Lancashire where Gujarati Muslims far outnumber Gujarati Hindus in Preston and Blackburn.

Finally, in attempting to meet the needs of teachers, some publications persisted in using the terminology and assumptions of much earlier books on Asian religions. A well documented example is the use of the word 'Mohammedanism' instead of 'Islam'. Teachers using such a word to describe the religion of children they may be teaching, not only do them an injustice but may also deeply offend those pupils with a considerable understanding of their own faith. It is sad to report that this error is still being made today.[h]

It was in view of the fact that the usual channels failed to provide teachers and pupils with adequate information and materials that the need to look elsewhere became apparent. In describing the shortcomings of established agencies I have tried to refer to mainline publications to which many teachers were exposed, but a similar pattern emerges if one examines the more specialist literature of the period.

Responses

A direct result of the extent of misinformation was the establishment of a working party of teachers. The group's aim was the identification of the specific needs of Asian children. The working party floundered almost immediately, proving to be too divided in its attitude to priorities and too unwieldy to promise much in the way of useful teaching material.

The Curriculum Development Officer subsequently encouraged two of the teachers involved with the working party to work together on a specific theme which would not be so wide-ranging as to prove elusive, and yet might offer a significant contribution to the information available to teachers.

An inquiry was begun into the beliefs, rituals, organization, social customs and recent history of the Muslim community in Preston. The decision to concentrate on the Muslims was based on two considerations. The Muslim community was the most homogeneous of the Asian communities in the town and in addition had a national reputation as an active flourishing group. The first purpose-built mosque this century had been erected there in 1970 and the town was attracting other Muslims, who came principally to provide their children with a 'good' Islamic education at the various mosques in the town.

The inquiry consisted of many long conversations with members of the Muslim sects within the town. First contacts were divided between personal acquaintances, based on contact via Muslim pupils, and members of the local hierarchy who were concerned with the day to day running of the communities' affairs.

Contacts mushroomed to include people such as the CRO, the architects and quantity surveyors of the mosques, benefactors to the communities and, when occasion allowed it, women members of the various groupings in the town.

The materials produced were based on questioning and on observation. Where the answers to questions did not square with observed practice it was often necessary to pursue lines of secondary inquiry in order to gain a clear picture of theory and practice.

The first stage in the development of materials was a book, *Islam in Preston,* which was completed in a little under two years. At this time the book was aimed at the in-service training of local teachers. In order to facilitate such an aim it was felt that, rather than simply referring to objects in the mosque, home or culture, which would be alien to the teachers, it would be advisable to have examples of artefacts used by Muslims. Thus, rather than simply expect teachers to imagine what a prayer-mat looks and feels like, it seemed preferable to provide one for the teachers to see and feel. Where objects could not be provided for the teacher, slides were provided. The style of Asian toilets, the design of Minbars and Mihrabs could only be adequately understood if a picture could be made available.

Similarly, rather than describe the prayer positions, it seemed obvious that they ought to be recorded on slides. This proved difficult at first as the Muslims did not wish to be photographed, and even today two of Preston's mosques do not allow photographers inside. Eventually, when our motives and sheer doggedness were acknowledged, we were able to gain slides of Muslims at prayer, although the subsequent cine film had to be taken in a building other than a mosque.

The County Adviser for Immigrant Education was invited to comment on the scope of the materials. He suggested a far wider application than that initially intended and encouraged those involved to aim at producing materials for use in schools as well as materials to assist teacher knowledge. Crucially at this point the Adviser provided the resources necessary, both in terms of finance and professional support. Other Advisers, DEOs and members of the Inspectorate were invited to offer their suggestions as to the full potential of the materials and areas for subsequent development. The County Library Service was involved at this juncture and provided support for the project. The library purchased a large number of books on Islam which were arranged into appropriate sets and made available to any school which decided it could make use of the project materials.

Prior to the presentation of the materials to teachers, certain other developments took place. In accord with current curriculum development theory the draft texts of the books were sent to local Muslims and to the Department of Arabic and Islamic Studies at Lancaster University. As most curriculum development projects filter down to teachers from universities or colleges via HMI, CEO, advisers and headteachers, it was felt that the pedigree of this project ought not to be questioned as being inconsistent with the best contemporary knowledge.[i]

The support of headteachers was also recognized as vital if the materials were to be given adequate trials in schools. The authority therefore convened a meeting for all local headteachers and departmental heads.[j] A number of headteachers committed their schools to using the materials in a trial situation which was monitored by the Curriculum Development Officer,[k] advisers and a student working in the field of curriculum development.[l]

Training sessions were provided for the teachers who were to be actively involved in working with the materials. Separate sessions for the secondary and primary sectors were regarded as essential for discussion of teaching styles and recommended length of study. The materials were designed to facilitate discovery-based methods but teachers were allowed considerable freedom in how they taught and what areas they chose to emphasize. At the request of a member of the Inspectorate, the project team defined their view of the teacher's role in the secondary level, as being that of neutral chairman.

Contents of the Books

Book 1: Islam

Islam In Preston provides the history of Muslim

settlement and organization in Preston. The patterns of immigration: single males, married couples, whole family units, housing patterns. The priorities of the Islamic organizations within the town altered in accordance with the changing composition of the community.

The better known areas of Islamic history only feature in the book when they have a direct bearing on contemporary events. Two examples from the book will illustrate the point.

Zakat

One of the 'five Pillars' of Islam, Zakat is usually referred to in standard popular textbooks, but a reference is usually all there is. This alms-tax has undergone considerable change since its inception, changes wrought by the different types of organization dominant in the Islamic world and also by the changing nature of society. The major theological schools define Zakat in a number of different ways.

In *Islam In Preston* we determined to describe the rules applied by Muslims in this country, the organization for the collection of Zakat and the areas and methods of distribution to the poor.

Similarly, sectarian groupings are delineated and the divisions related to the theological schools of the wider Islamic world. The vast majority of Muslims in the UK are Hanafites but such a blanket description is not sufficient in understanding the theology of this majority for even within the Hanafite rite there are a number of identifiable sub-groups.

Salat

The book describes the Salat (prayer) in detail, each movement is also shown on slide and cine. The place of women in society and their position and actions at the mosque are given considerable attention. It is interesting to note that women perform the Salat differently to men, yet textbook illustrations always depict men at prayer. As half the Muslims in the world are women we felt it important to provide slides of a woman praying.

The attitudes of Muslim parents towards their children is a subject which is given some prominence, as is the curriculum used in the education of Muslim children at the mosques.

List of resources at present available to schools

Book: *Islam In Preston*.
Slides: 96 (68 of which are linked to the text).
Cine-film: full Salat; also details from Salat; with
   sound.
Cassette tape: Salat; optional prayers; Azzan (call to prayer); with English translations.
Copy of Quran: in English.

Arabic alphabet and Arabic primer used in mosque
classes.
Namaz cards: monthly prayer cards; in English.
Id cards exchanged by Muslims at festivals: some
similarities with Christmas cards.
Prayer Mat.
Prayer Hat.
Bottles of Perfume used by the men at Friday prayer.
Incense sticks.
Prayer beads.
Wedding Invitations.
Urdu primer and Urdu books on history of Islam used
in mosque classes.

The trials in schools produced encouraging results.
Most of the schools taking part welcomed the
materials as strengthening their RE/Social Studies
curriculum. The secondary schools followed up their
trial use by purchasing complete packs and
establishing the project as a permanent aspect of the
curriculum.

In the Primary sector a further aspect of the trials
proved to be of significance. Schools with a high
percentage of Muslim pupils reported wide
repercussions from the use of the materials. The work
of the Muslim children in the schools showed a
marked improvement. This improvement was not
confined to the immediate project but spread across
the whole of the curriculum. Two causes were
identified by those involved. In the first place the
inclusion of aspects of their own culture into a subject
regarded as worthy of study at school improved the
self-image of Muslim children. Secondly, they were
able to identify more readily with the school than had
previously been possible.

The schools made it clear that they would welcome
the opportunity to expand this kind of work if more
materials could be made available. In response to this
request the second of the kits was produced, the
project was called 'Hinduism in Preston' and was
made available to schools in Autumn 1978.

The format of 'Hinduism' differed from that of
'Islam' in a number of ways. Most of the changes were
in response to suggestions made by teachers as to
how such materials might be better designed to fit the
needs of teachers in specific situations.

Book 2: Hinduism

One major difference lies in having included an
historical chapter on the development of Hinduism
from earliest times. This departure was based on two
considerations. In 'Islam' teachers were expected to
use standard textbooks to give themselves a greater
background knowledge. This expectation was only
partially fulfilled. Those teachers who failed to follow

up suggestions for further reading were at a
disadvantage in guiding their pupils into areas of
personal research. Nor were these teachers as ready
to respond to detailed questioning and while many
attempted to 'look-up' answers to questions the
'crucial' point was passed for many pupils. The second
consideration related to the different natures of Islam
and Hinduism. Hinduism is so vast a subject, and the
literature on it so diverse and variable in quality that it
seemed unreasonable to expect teachers to approach
the topic completely cold.

In accommodating the greater degree of diversity
within Hindu ritual and practice than within Islam it
was also necessary to increase the range of slides.
Over 140 are at present available to schools. The
place of marriage as a major sacrament, in fact the
only great sacrament which has transferred wholesale
to the UK, was sufficient to include a special chapter
with appropriate slides on a Hindu wedding.

List of resources available to schools
Book: *Hinduism In Preston*.
Slides: 140 (108 linked to the text).
Copy of Vedas in English.
Bells used in Puja (worship).
Ghee: clarified butter used in Puja.
Ghee dishes.
Steel trays used for food offered to Gods at Arti.
Incense.
Incense holders depicting various deities.
Statues of Krishna; Ambajii: Hanuman; Ganesh; Siva.
Diwali Cards.
Wedding Invitations.
Sandalwood paste.
Posters depicting various deities and scenes from
Hindu mythology.

Wider usage

The materials have filled a gap which commercial
publications have shown little sign of filling. The
emphasis throughout has been on actual practice and
belief combined with objects from the culture and
religion and comprehensive illustrations with slides.
The greatest gratification derived by those connected
with the kits has been the extent of the wider usage of
the materials. The packages have had different
attractions for different bodies and groups, many of
which have adapted the kits to fit their own needs.

LEAs from as far apart as Cleveland, Birmingham
and Redbridge have requested materials for schools'
use. Colleges of education throughout the UK have
done likewise, some of these colleges encouraging
their students to use the books and kits as models for
their own projects. Community Relations Councils
have utilized the kits in providing information for local

organizations directly involved with minority groups. Copies of the books have gone out to EEC countries and Scandinavia, and, like coals to Newcastle, some have been requested in the Middle East.

In the Lancashire area generally there has been a strong demand from voluntary bodies for speakers, equipped with kits, to address local groups. This demand from the community at large prompted a further adaptation of the materials. A radio series was produced by BBC Radio Blackburn, the aim of which was to provide the general public with a basic knowledge and some understanding of the religions and cultures of the Muslims, Hindus and Sikhs in the North-West.

The series ran for twenty weeks in 1978 and the major part was recorded in Asian homes and places of worship. Asians themselves provided descriptions of their beliefs and practices, although the historical content was presented in question and answer form between the producer and myself. Subjects such as arranged marriages, female emancipation and the calls for separate schooling were dealt with at length. The series has been made available to other local radio stations in the UK.[m] The programmes have also been placed in the County Cassette Library and are now available as a further aspect of the kits. This was particularly useful as the cassettes provided in the Islam Kit were not well received by teachers and subsequently removed from the planned resources in the Hindu Kit.

Future developments

It is worth noting that the customs and practices described in Preston are representative of Asian communities in many parts of the UK. In visits to Asian communities throughout Britain it is only in Bristol that I have been struck by considerable variations in practice.

One aim of the developers was that *Islam* and *Hinduism* might act as models for local studies throughout the country. Some areas have found so few dissimilarities that the text has been reproduced wholesale for local teachers. In other areas, particularly the North of England, the chapters on the history of immigration, local organization, ethnic origins and mosque/temple curriculum are being re-written from a local slant, the rest of the book being left intact.

In Preston the third and fourth kits on Sikhism and Christianity became available in 1979. Meanwhile *Islam In Preston* is already failing to reflect the ever-changing nature of Islam in the town and is to be revised, enlarged and reprinted.

Chapter 7

References for Extract 7.4:

[a] Townsend, H. E. R. and Brittan, E. M., *Organisation in Multi-Racial Schools* (Slough: NFER, 1972).

[b] Harrison, Stephen W. and Shepherd, David, *Islam In Preston* (Preston Curriculum Development Centre, 1975).

[c] Harrison, Stephen W., *Hinduism In Preston* (Preston Curriculum Development Centre, CDC, 1978).

[d] Holroyde, P. and others, *East Comes West* (Community Relations Commission, 1970).

[e] Droubie, R-El, *Islam* (Ward Lock Educational, 1970).

[f] Lyon, Michael H., 'Ethnicity in Britain: The Gujarati Tradition', *New Community*, vol. 2, no. 1, 1973.

[g] Hiro, D. *The Indian Family In Britain* (CRC, 1970).

[h] Lobo, E. de H., *Children of Immigrants to Britain* (Hodder and Stoughton, 1978), p. 5.

[i] For the relevance of this, see Cronbach, L. J., 'Course improvement through evaluation', *Curriculum Design* (Croom Helm, 1975).

[j] For the importance of Heads, see Madonald, B. 'Humanities Curriculum Project' in *Evaluation in Curriculum Development: Twelve Case Studies —* Papers from the Schools Council Project Evaluators on Aspects of their Work (Macmillan, 1973).

[k] An official report edited by the CDO, R. J. Wells, was subsequently issued by the LEA. Further details are available from Miss Wells, 5 Camden Place, Preston.

[l] Unpublished B.Ed. Thesis: 'An Innovatory Piece of Local Curriculum Development: Islam In Preston — A Case Study.' P. Harrison, University of Lancaster.

[m] Further details of the radio series, 'Window On The East', available from Ian Cook, Education Producer, BBC Radio Blackburn, King Street, Blackburn.

8 Experiential Learning

The themes subsumed under the headings majority/ minority issues and the multi-ethnic curriculum are all potentially difficult areas to explore, yet they can be explored successfully if the factors of controversy and identity in a group are looked upon as resources, rather than 'problems' in the classroom. The fact that issues are controversial can be part of the subject matter to be studied. Also all students in the social situation of the classroom will be concerned about their own identity, about how others see them and how they affect other people. If it is also remembered that several of the objectives referred to in chapter 6 were affective ones, it seems important to explore the use of activities which are experiential. Experiential learning puts students in situations, through role-play or simulation, where they *experience* the problems of communication or perception for themselves. From these experiences can come a new awareness of individual and group needs and increased understanding for fuller discussion and debate of particular issues.

The seven activities that follow have been drawn from several sources but all in their way are aimed at exploring feelings, perception, attitudes and values in a wide range of conflict/co-operation situations. It is important to remember that they can be used in a variety of contexts and the original suggestions for their use, when given, accompany them. Obviously in the context of majority/minority issues it is feelings about empathy, trust, co-operation, aspiration and prejudice that might be stressed. In no case can an activity be used in isolation. It can only be really useful if it is part of the continuing work, whether used to introduce a new topic, to conclude a study, or to illustrate a particular point.

Getting It Together provides an opportunity for students to experience non-verbally some problems to do with co-operation, empathy, participation, sense of identity when a member of a group, sharing, and seeing a problem as a whole.

Closed and Open provides an opportunity for students to experience non-verbally a situation in which they have to guess the perceptions and intentions of another person; and to experience some problems connected with trusting, and being trusted by, the other person.

Blind Trust enables students to experience and talk about feelings of trust and mistrust, dependence and independence as well as sensitivity, fear and sensory deprivation. Examples of follow-up projects (not necessarily all directly related to majority/ minority issues) are also given.

Levels of Aspiration enables students to see how aspirations may be related to self-image and to experience feelings of achievement or failure in a playful context. It also relates to how others see one and can lead to discussion of the forces that can shape one's aspirations.

Ideal Group allows students to explore the supportive aspects of membership of a group, feelings of conflict, separation, independence and loneliness. This can lead to discussions of the various meanings of groups, group identity as well as isolation and rejection.

Building a Just Society gives students the chance to think about ideas of justice and freedom as they set about organizing their own community. What patterns of organization evolve? What debates and arguments arise? One could also specifically build into this a minority group (different beliefs or dress) and see what relationships develop between them and the majority.

Experiencing Underdevelopment is a cross-cultural simulation game which allows students to experience a culture's perception and understanding, or lack of understanding of another culture.

With all these activities it is extremely important that extended and careful 'debriefing' takes place to ensure the maximum benefit. Initially students will 'stay with' the exercise and need to discuss exactly what happened in it. Subsequently, and equally important, this needs to lead to a consideration of how this illuminates the context in which it has been used. There is nothing infallible about the exercises and they need to be planned carefully and tailored to particular situations and student/teacher needs. Their sources, where other useful material may be found, are given at the end of each exercise below.

Extract 8.1

Getting it Together

Preparation

This is an exercise for five people. In the classroom it can be done by just five students, with everyone else watching. Or alternatively, the teacher can prepare enough material for the whole class – say, for six groups of five.

The preparation for one group of five is as follows. It has six stages. First, rule five squares, each of identical size, on a piece of card or stiff paper. A convenient size is 12 centimetres square. Second, rule each square into a pattern, as shown in the diagram. Measurements must be made very carefully, and the recurring ratio must be 2 : 1. (Hence if the squares are 12 × 12 cms nearly all the smaller shapes will have at least one edge of 6 cms). Third, mark the smaller shapes each with a letter, as shown below. Fourth, cut the squares into shapes. Fifth, group the shapes into five sets, according to their letters. Sixth, put these five sets into five envelopes, and mark the envelopes with the appropriate letters.

Procedure

A group of five students is formed, and each student is given one of the five envelopes. The instructions should be presented verbally by the teacher and students should have a chance to clarify them. It may also be very useful if the instructions can be written on the blackboard, so that they remain a constant reminder. They are as follows:

1) When the exercise starts, but not before, open your envelopes and take out the contents.

2) The exercise will then continue until each of you

has a square: the five squares must all be exactly the same size.

3) You may pass a piece of card to another member of the group, but you may not reach out and take one.

4) There is to be no talking during the exercise, nor any other kind of communication – no winks, gestures, kicks under the tables, scowls, shakes or nods of the head etc.

5) You may at any time decline to take any further part. And the teacher too has the right to stop the exercise if he or she wishes.

What usually happens

At least one square is formed which, although indeed a square of the right size, is not one of those illustrated at the foot of this page. This will hold up the group as a whole, until the person concerned dismantles it.

Discussion

A good start for subsequent discussion is to ask 'what happened?', and systematically to recall the various exchanges, hold-ups, breakthroughs. But then, if possible, students should be encouraged to verbalise some of their feelings. Frustration and irritation will be readily mentioned. But there is also the anxiety of someone who can't make a square; and their envy of others who can. There is the self-satisfied complacency of the person who makes a square easily. There is the initial difficulty, because of anxiety, of empathising with the other members of the group, or of seeing the task as a whole. There is the horror of the person who has to dismantle ('sacrifice') their own square for the good of the group as a whole. And there is the eventual delight when the task is finally achieved.

With regard to issues in the wider world, the exercise dramatises something about sharing, about aid (the difference between real, insightful generosity on the one hand and merely discarding something on the other), and about democratic participation.

It also very strikingly dramatises the tension which often seems to exist between self-confidence and co-operation. First, a person tries to get their own square. And similarly in life generally, a person or

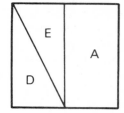 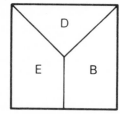 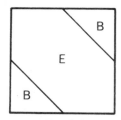 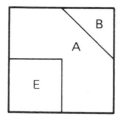 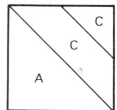

Fig. 8.1

group may aim first for security, a firm base to work from. This seems sensible at the time, but may nevertheless make subsequent co-operation more difficult.

Acknowledgement

In its basic format, this exercise was first published in the NEA Journal, USA, October 1969.

SOURCE: Richardson, Robin, *Learning for Change in World Society: Reflections, Activities and Resources* (London: World Studies Project, 1976).

Extract 8.2

Closed and Open

Preparation

No preparation is required.

Procedure

Two students sit facing each other across a table. They both have their hands under the table. The teacher acts as umpire, and says '1, 2, 3, Now!' On the word 'Now!' the teacher slaps the table, and at the same split-second the students have to bring their right hands above the table, either as a closed fist, or as an open palm. If they both have closed fists, they get one point each. If they both have open palms, they get two points each. If there is a mixture, then the one with a fist gets four points; and the one with a palm gets none.

This happens five times altogether. A note of the points scored is kept on the blackboard, or a large sheet of paper.

IF	STUDENT A	STUDENT B
✊ ✊	1	1
🖐 🖐	2	2
✊ 🖐	FIST 4 AND PALM 0	

Fig. 8.2

After the exercise has been clearly demonstrated in this way by the teacher and two students, the class can be split into groups of three (1 + 1 and an umpire), so that everyone can have a go.

Variations

Instead of conducting the exercise with two individuals it can be useful and interesting if the competitors are small groups, and if they have a chance to discuss secretly amongst themselves what they're going to do — fist or palm.

Discussion

It is useful if the teacher can manage to avoid words such as 'game', 'contest', 'against', 'win', 'lose' during the instructions. For a major question is how students perceive this exercise. Is it as a contest, to be won against an opponent? Or as a problem, requiring co-operation with another person for its solution?

The point is that 'two palms' involves the best possible outcome for the two people considered together. But it involves trust — each has to trust the other to see the situation in the same way as himself, or herself. If each distrusts the other, and both show fists, then this is the worst possible outcome for both considered together. Students should preferably be left to work all this out for themselves, rather than have the points expounded by the teacher. Some students will see in a flash — entirely intuitively — what the exercise is about. Others will be slower.

The next stage in the discussion involves applying the exercise to issues in the world at large. It is in fact based on the so-called Prisoners' Dilemma story, and is intended, in the first instance, to be about disarmament. If both players show palms, then this is like two countries disarming. It is to the benefit of both. But if they can't trust each other not to take advantage then they will both arm, and this costs them both a lot of money and resources.

If the exercise is conducted between two groups, rather than between two individuals, students will experience some of the problems associated with trying to persuade other people within one's own group to trust, or not to trust, the people in another group. There can also be discussion of the images and assumptions which groups develop about each other. Do students automatically expect the worst of each other, or the best of each other? Why?

Certain conflict situations in the modern world can be partially illustrated by this exercise, and in particular the role played by national stereotypes, prejudices, images of the enemy. There are parallels also in the everyday lives of the students, and of the school. That is, occasions when it would be to the

Fig. 8.3

general advantage of both parties if they could be 'open-handed'. They yet cannot trust each other, and therefore see their relationship as a contest or conflict.

This distinction between 'a conflict to be won (or at least not be lost)' on the hand and 'a problem to solve between us' on the other is a very useful one. Students will probably be able to give many examples of this distinction, from their own observation and experience.

SOURCE: Richardson, Robin, *Learning for Change in World Society: Reflections, Activities and Resources* (London: World Series Project, 1976).

Extract 8.3

Blind Trust

Procedure

The members of the class are divided into pairs; one is 'blind', with eyes closed or well covered, the other is his/her leader. The pairs are instructed to walk around for about 10 minutes; depending on circumstances, this can be inside and/or outside. Doing both is better because of the greater variety of experiences possible.

The instructions must include, (1) no one is to talk during the whole exercise and (2) the leader should not turn the walk into an obstacle course for the 'blind' pupil. Sometimes there is a tendency to 'tease'. This should be discouraged; most of the walking should be fairly easy and the leader should try to be creative in finding a variety of experiences for the blind pupil such as trying to identify objects by touch, being left alone for a few minutes, running (on smooth ground) and being exposed to a variety of sounds. The teacher can mention these possibilities specifically, but it is better just to ask the pupils to use their own imagination in creating a variety of experiences.

After about 10 minutes, the paired pupils switch roles and continue their walk for another 10 minutes. The teacher can ask for this switch to take place in the classroom or leave the timing and location up to the pairs.

Variation

The 'blind' pupils in the pairs do not know who their partner is. Half the members of the class cover or shut their eyes. The other half are the leaders. They select their partners from the 'blind' group without any talking. After the 10-minute tour, all pairs return to the classroom and the selection process is then repeated with the leaders becoming the 'blind' group. In all other respects the procedure and instructions are the same as above.

Discussion

Concepts

We are all born with total trust . . . and then, what happens?
Relationships between trust and mistrust, dependency and independence.
Dependency – what are our reactions to being dependent?
Communication of emotions through bodily posture, movement and tension.
Role of past experiences in trust and mistrust.
Unfamiliarity and mistrust: increasing mistrust of those more unlike oneself, e.g., opposite sex, different social class, different race or culture.
Earn trust, earn power.
Sensitivity to the environment – how did one's awareness of the environment change with loss of sight?

The trust walk is generally a strong experience for pupils. They come back wanting to talk; it is useful for the teacher to stay completely out of the discussion at first. The pupils begin talking about *events* that took place. But the experience has *emotional* effects, i.e., feelings of fear, helplessness, trust or mistrust in one's leader, responsibility for another's safety and guilt if there was an accident and, for those few who relax completely while blind, a feeling of freedom and release from decisions. If the pupils spontaneously discuss these emotional aspects, the teacher can help them explore the meaning and significance of their feelings. However if their discussion is confined to the *events,* their own avoidance of the emotional components can be pointed out to them as a starting point.

Some of the concepts listed can be brought into the discussion as it goes beyond the experience itself. These are easily related to the pupils' experiences with their friends and in their families, in school and in the community. The discussion should also move to the workings of the social system and the actual ways in which different social institutions handle trust and responsibility; for example, factory workers punch time cards; people cannot purchase certain drugs without a doctor's prescription; the doctor puts his medical certificate on his office wall; do we have standardized national school examinations because teachers cannot be trusted to evaluate pupils? How are rules related to mistrust . . . family and school rules, safety regulations for food, medicines, traffic, etc.? How are immigration laws related to mistrust? Can we imagine what a society would be like if there was complete trust amongst all persons? Is there such a society or group? Are there racial, cultural, social class and national differences in the level of trust amongst the people? Why?

If the pupils have been both indoors and out, they may be interested in a discussion of feelings about environments. Was there a change in awareness of air temperature, sounds and smells when going outside? In what ways does one suddenly become more aware of the environment, and how do our different senses contribute to this? Do you remember places that looked beautiful but where the temperature, sounds or smells were terrible, or where the activities of other people spoiled the atmosphere? Why do certain environments, both indoors and out, affect us emotionally?

Follow-up projects

1.   *Family* – Pupils do a study of changing (or unchanging) family patterns, related to trust and mistrust. They compare their own family 'rules' with those their parents and grandparents had as children.

Additional data sources include autobiographies, novels and books for parents on raising children. This study could be followed up with a parent-pupil evening meeting beginning with a trust walk and ending with a discussion of experiences and feelings about family and school rules as they relate to responsibility and trust. A meeting of this kind is useful in introducing parents to the ideas of the curriculum approach.

2.   *School* – Similar to (1) except that the subject is the school.

3.   *Senses* – Repeat the blind trust walk but for the purpose of exploring the human senses. Before beginning, the pupils are instructed to concentrate on their other senses and they may try to see if they can tell when they are approaching a wall. Most will experience sounds as extremely loud; this is an example of how our brain's system for selective attention involves inhibition of sensory input. Some pupils may want to try to walk without vision or hearing. The only practical way to eliminate hearing is to have the pupil carry a small transistor radio with an earphone in place and the volume turned up high.

4.   *Lending money* – Design and carry out an experiment on interpersonal trust. For example, see if strangers will lend money on the basis of a promise to mail it back the next day? What difference is there if the pupil needing the money is a boy or girl, is neatly or untidily dressed? Are old or young, males or females more likely to lend money? Make hypotheses about the results before gathering the data, and then make a theory. There are many other kinds of interpersonal trust situations which can be studied experimentally.

5.   *Secrets* – Can you trust fellow pupils (or teachers) to keep a secret? Design an experiment to examine some of the relevant factors. For example, are girls more likely to keep secrets about other girls, but to divulge them if they are about boys? Is the same thing true between racial, religious, ethnic and social class groups? Why?

6.   *International mistrust* – The mass media are filled with spy stories, both factual and fictional. A project could examine some of the political, psychological and moral aspects of spying, which may be carried on *within* countries as well as *between* countries.

7.   *The United Nations system and other international institutions* – (e.g., the International Court of Justice) can be examined as ways of handling trust and mistrust amongst nations.

8. *Managing conflict* — Where there is little or no trust: e.g., racial or religious conflicts. Do a 'case study' comparing conflict management situations with and without a loss of trust. Refer back to the pupils' own emotional reactions during the trust walk for an understanding of the emotional component.

Applications to school subjects

History — projects like 1, 2, 6, 7, and 8 are relevant to history courses. A historian has labelled the twentieth century 'The Age of Anxiety'. Does mistrust cause anxiety?

Geography and environmental studies — do a comparison of aspects of trust, mistrust and responsibility with different kinds of man/environment conditions; e.g. Eskimos, isolated mountain villages, areas of repeated natural disaster, urbanized regions, small islands, etc. How do our feelings change in different man-made and natural environments, e.g., in tiny or huge rooms, with candle or fluorescent light, on top of a mountain or deep in a valley? Are the different kinds of dwellings people live in an indication of their trust in others?

Biology — is trust necessary for co-operation? Look at co-operation/competition, the hunter and the hunted, in different animal species. Are fear and mistrust instincts or are they learned, or both? What is the physiology of the emotions the pupils felt on their blind trust walk? Project 3, emphasizing sensory reactions and the selective attention and inhibition process, is especially relevant to biology. How do the sensory worlds of different animals compare? We know little scientifically about sensation but it is an interesting and important topic for biology and moral education.

SOURCE: Wolsk, David, *An Experience-Centred Curriculum,* Educational Studies and Documents, No. 17 (UNESCO, 1975).

Extract 8.4

Level of Aspiration

This unit uses a simple game as a basis for looking at the origins of individual and cultural differences in what pupils want to achieve or accomplish — their level of aspiration.

Equipment

One small plastic cup and ten paper clips for each two pupils. Any set of small bottles, jars, cans, etc., with open tops about 3–4 cm in diameter will do; and metal or rubber washers, tacks or small nails can be used instead of paper clips. It is best to test out various combinations of the cups and objects to be certain that the task is not too easy or too hard (see *Procedure* below). Paper, pencils.

Procedure

Pupils work in pairs (it is good for the teacher to participate). Each pair is given a cup and ten paper clips. The task is to place the cup on the floor, stand directly above it, hold the paper clip next to one's face and try to drop the clip into the cup. Before starting, each pupil is to guess how many of the ten paper clips he/she can drop into the cup and then to write this number on her/his own piece of paper. Then, each pupil does the task and writes her/his score next to the guess. The whole exercise is then repeated with new guesses and the new scores from each pupil. If a paper clip hits the bottom of the cup and bounces out, it is still counted as a 'hit'. (An average of about 50 per cent hits is ideal.) All the guesses and scores are then written on the blackboard in the following form:

Pupils	1st guess	1st score	2nd guess	2nd score
1.				
2.				
3.				
Total Average				

Discussion

Concepts

Self-evaluation — winner or loser?
Nature of abilities, talents, skills — what are we born with and what can we learn?
Need for achievement and fear of failure — which do we think about first and which is more important to us?
The forces that shape our level of aspiration — family, friends, culture, religion, nationality?
What does *experience* teach us — the persistent fighters and discouraged 'quitters'?
Group, national and international levels of aspiration.

Variations

Instead of paper clips 1p or $\frac{1}{2}$p coins can be used. It is in fact very difficult to keep them in the cups (use yoghourt pots) as they tend to bounce out. Students tend to revise their guesses drastically in the light of experience. How do one's aspirations vary if everyone else expects one to do well, or badly? How does this relate to self-image, and also to teacher expectation of students?

SOURCE: Wolsk, David, *An Experience-Centred Curriculum,* Educational Studies and Documents, No. 17 (UNESCO, 1975).

Extract 8.5

Ideal Group

In a large room cleared of furniture, the class divides into groups of five or six. Each group forms a linked-arms circle, all close their eyes and for the rest of the time they are not to speak or open their eyes. The teacher provides a commentary for a series of five phases which involve the pupils in imagining, and feeling different aspects of being part of an ideal group. During the first linked-arms-in-circle phase, the commentator describes some of the positive supportive aspects of group membership. Next, the group members touch each other to find identifying features (eyes, glasses, wristwatch, sweater) which will assure their being able to recognize each other later with eyes still closed. The third phase, with each group reformed in their circles, consists of a long drawn-out separation, a slow pulling apart, during which the commentator talks about conflicts between the desire to keep the group together and the need, now, to separate. After separation, each person goes off by himself while the narrator talks about independence and loneliness. After several minutes of silence, the last phase consists of each one trying to find the other members of his group as they come together for a big 'reunion party'.

The discussion which follows focuses on the various meanings of groups, the individual experiences in the exercise and its relationships with other group experiences. Is man biologically a social animal? Can you imagine yourself living totally alone? Or with one other person? The pupils may themselves know stories of children supposedly brought up by animals in the forests.

What is the feeling of loneliness? Is it not hard to describe? Why? Is complete trust necessary for an ideal group? Does the group start out with this or does it develop later? How? Did you feel much trust with your ideal group? How many people are needed for an ideal group?

When you are grown up and if you have a family of your own do you think it may be an ideal group? How? The ideal family can be compared to the characteristics of today's family life. One interesting way to do this is to discuss how the family is *perceived* by *hearing* (noise, quarrelling, discussing, television, violin practising), *seeing* (the home as it looks, clothing, neatness, space), *touching* (caressing, beating, working together), *tasting* (food and drink, meals and snacks) and *smelling* (odours in and around the house).

Given below is a framework of ideas. The commentator is to use his/her own creativity and feelings and experience in improving a commentary. As it is only meant to provide some structure to the participants' own fantasy processes, it is important that there be long pauses between statements . . . time for fantasy. However, the slowness and pauses should not produce a sleepy, monotonous type of speaking. The commentator should put some feeling and emotion and animation into the scenario. It is best to do this without anyone watching; pupils not participating should be asked to leave the room.

Phase I

(Each group has formed a circle with arms over shoulders interlocked) *Try to forget that you know the people in your group and that they know you . . . this is an entirely new experience, outside of the here and now, so put all of that out of your mind and start afresh. Keep your eyes closed and make no sounds.*

'You are with your ideal group . . . friends you love to be with . . . whom you know all love to have you as part of the group. You cannot imagine a better group of friends. You can always be yourself . . . everyone is open. You always have good times together . . . fun, laughter, good talk, sharing, helping, working together.'

Phase II

(Touching each other to find identifying characteristics.) *'You cannot always be with your group. But before you separate you want to be sure you can easily find each other again. So, keeping your eyes closed and making no sounds, break the circle up and go around to all the other members of your group. With each one you should find some identifying thing, like spectacles, clothes, shoes, etc., which will be enough for you to find the person later. When you are finished the members of the group should lock arms again.'*

Phase III

(Pulling apart, separation. The commentator should try to prolong this phase as long as possible.) *'Now you are together again, but you know that has to end soon. But you do not want it to end. You know it is time to separate but you want to hold the others back . . . not to let them go just yet . . . one more minute of so . . . but you have to go . . . no, not just yet. We really must! When you are free, walk slowly backward until you reach the wall of the room. Then, just stand or sit there.'*

Phase IV

(Loneliness and independence) *'Now you are by yourself . . . all alone. You miss your group . . . but it is good to feel independent. No one is watching you or expecting things from you. You are free to do what you want. But there is no one to share it with. Loneliness.'* (*Stop the narration for about 3–5 minutes. Quietly change your own position in the room so it is not quite as easy for the groups to find each other.*)

Phase V

(Reunion, Celebration) *'Now's the time when you've arranged to be together again . . . it is time for a celebration with your group. So, keep your eyes closed, search for your friends, and when you find someone from your group, stay together and look for the others. And, when you are all together, have your celebration!'*

SOURCE: Wolsk, David, *An Experience-Centred Curriculum,* Educational Studies and Documents, No. 17 (UNESCO, 1975).

Extract 8.6

Building a Just Society

One way to begin thinking about justice and freedom is to imagine starting a new society from scratch. Imagine for example, a plane crashing on an island somewhere. About 150 people including the crew, plus quite a lot of children. And for some reason, no chance of escape in the near future. Here on these pages there's a reminder of some of the things the people would have to decide, and some of the things they might be thinking and feeling. Where would your own voice be if you were with them?

We've survived for ten days. How do we organise ourselves?

'Some people are natural leaders.' We need a small governing group or committee, with a chairman. It's fairly obvious to me, and I'm sure it's equally obvious to pretty well every intelligent person on this island, who the obvious people for this committee should be. By all means let's have an election. I'm confident that the right people would be elected, as I said. For of course they would make life generally awkward and embarrassing if they weren't. The point is that some people are natural leaders, and other people are by nature rather passive. This is a fact of life.

It's already obvious who the natural leaders on this island are. They have emerged. Let's have a ruling committee of seven, to take all important decisions. They must of course be in close contact with the masses, who after all elected them, and they must always do their best to explain their decisions properly and intelligibly, and persuade — not force — people to go along with them. We certainly don't want a police state. But also we don't want anarchy. Decisions have got to be taken, this is a fact of life. And we must all of us — all of us — stand by them, when they have once been taken.

'Talk, talk, we must sit down and talk.' All important decisions must be taken by the whole community meeting together. This includes the decision that all important decisions should be made in this way, so I don't know how we start! But everyone has got to be consulted and involved — even if they don't want to be consulted and involved! The silent majority mustn't be allowed to be silent. Now that we've established the basic possibility of surviving we must sit down and talk, talk, talk.

The strong boys who were so clever at building the shelters, and at getting all that lovely food, mustn't be allowed to dominate. Nobody must be allowed to dominate. Let us meet each other, and talk to each other — in small groups, and in large groups, and two people face to face. Let us have a meeting at least once a week, when every single man, woman and child is present, and let it last for hours if necessary; this is the only way to create a society. Also let's have a meeting whenever there's a crisis. Talk, talk, we must sit down and talk.

Violence. What do we do?

One day a man on the island called H. gets involved in a sudden quarrel with another man, about which of them is to fetch some drinking water. He loses his temper, picks up a stick and, attacking the other man from behind, hits him several times and kills him. This happens in full view of some other people, who are however too slow to prevent it. The victim was a married man, with three children.

'I'll do the deed myself.' He is dangerous and lunatic and must be got rid of. I've no doubt at all that he'll attack someone else if we don't get rid of him. He loses his temper very easily, loses all control of himself, and lashes out. Who'll be the next if we don't take strong action now? I look at that poor woman, I hear her helpless weeping, I see the staring uncomprehending eyes of those three kids condemned now to grow up fatherless. I'll do the deed myself, cheerfully, cleanly, without any mess, it needn't really involve anyone else.

'What sort of society is developing here?' I don't know what we do with H, but I do know we mustn't do anything in too great a hurry. What sort of society is developing here? Maybe H was driven to violence because of the society that this already is? He seemed a harmless enough fellow to me until this happened. Have we been in too great a hurry to build our shelters, and organize our fruit gathering and fishing expeditions, and have we failed to notice the frustrations which were building up inside the weaker members of our community? Poor pathetic little H, he's not a danger, he can't be. What sort of society are we already? What sort of society do we want this to be? These are the questions. We must look at them *now,* before there's another tragedy.

Marriage and children. What do we do?

When buildings on the island were first put up, separate houses were made for the married couples who had been on the plane. But otherwise the sexes lived separately. But now a number of pairings are beginning to take place, and there are at least three couples who have declared (in one way or another) that they would like to set up house together.

'We've got to have some hard and fast distinctions.' Of course we must have proper marriages, a proper ritual, with feasting for the whole community, and a special event to celebrate the building of a new house. We must have dancing, and singing and music. And we must have something like the old marriage service. Or we could have the actual old service.

'Do you take this woman . . . for better or worse . . . do you promise . . . I do.'

I'm sure we must have some hard and fast distinctions. I mean, *either* two people are officially together, and they live together, and they may have children together, *or* they are single. Don't let's blur things. But in any case, we surely need, in addition to the ceremony, some sort of official permission so to speak? If the community at large doesn't think two people are suited to each other then surely we ought to try to discourage them from getting married?

'Don't make a fuss.' What I say is that if two people want to live together, then let them, and don't let's make a fuss about it. They'll need to build themselves a hut in the village. Let's get it quite clear that it's nobody's business apart from the two people concerned. When the house is finished they just move in. If any children come along, then my suggestion is that they should be brought up in a communal nursery. We can't expect people to bring up their own children, it would take up too much of their time.

Rebellion. How do we handle it?

One day three young people – two men and a girl – have a big argument with some older people. There's a bit of a fight, and one of the older people gets hurt. The younger ones run off, taking with them some valuable equipment. They set up camp not far away from the main settlement, and fortify it, and shout aggressively at anyone who comes close.

'We need young life.' This is a tragedy, a terrible tragedy, but we have got to learn from it. It's quite clear that the task now is to rehabilitate these unhappy young people. I know I sound sentimental, but someone's got to make a stand on this. I suggest our whole society has got to make a stand on this. War is wrong. Violence is wrong. We must not use force. We must welcome these young people back into the fold, show them that we understand them, forgive them. And we must adapt our society, I'm sure it's true that we are getting too rigid. We need young life, new ideas.

'We've already got the proper channels.' Quite simply we've got to stamp this out once and for all. Every able-bodied man in the community to lay siege to their encampment. Starve them out, or else go in and get them. There's no need to be gentle. When they've been captured they've got to show penitence. Publicly. Shave their heads. Make them grovel. If they refuse to co-operate then they must be banished. Let them have one of the boats, and let them sail

away, and good riddance. Let them know that if they ever come back they'll either be killed or else must have their heads shaved and must be entirely compliant. When once we have dealt with them we must have a long cool look at our so-called educational system. This mustn't ever happen again. People have got to learn to respect the laws and the social order. They should drink it in with their mother's milk and throughout their childhood and youth. Don't get me wrong. I'm not a diehard reactionary. I know there are things wrong. But we've got the proper channels for making protests. We've got to have order. We can't survive if we don't have order.

SOURCE: Richardson, Robin, *Fighting for Freedom* (Nelson, 1978), one of four books in a World Studies series.

Experiencing Underdevelopment

Purpose

This is a simple, but effective, simulation game for use in conjunction with the first case study in chapter five: the Aboriginal struggle. It can be used to illustrate one or all of the following issues:

(i) The experience of one particular minority group.
(ii) Human rights with particular reference to a minority group.
(iii) Questions relating to development and under-development.

(*Note*: Issues of development and underdevelopment are increasingly popular themes for teaching. They generally take place, of course, in the context of 'Third World problems'. It is often useful therefore, as here, to take examples of inequality and injustice from a rich part of the world. We also create our own 'Third World' nearer to home.)

Requirements

1. Six or seven sets of cards shown in Fig. 8.4.
2. Envelopes for storing each set of cards.

3. Nothing present in the room to indicate that this exercise is about Australia!
4. Tables and chairs or desks arranged so that pupils can sit in groups of five.

Optional but extremely useful:

5. Extracts from *Natural People's News* on Aboriginal affairs in the news.
6. The film *Strangers in Their Own Land* available from Concorde Films.

How to play

1. Children are seated in groups of five.
2. Each group is given an envelope containing the fifteen fact cards; these are taken out and laid face down on the table.
3. The following instructions are then given by the teacher: 'For the purpose of this activity you are not going to be yourselves. You are going to become another group of people, and you will find information about yourselves on the cards that are face down on the table.

Each member of the group takes it in turn to pick up a card at random, and then reads aloud slowly and clearly the information written on it. Go round the group doing this until each person has read out three cards.'
4. Continue as follows: 'Remember that each item of information you read out is not about someone else, it is about *you* and your group! After all the cards have been read out, without comment, they can be laid face up on the table – you have built up, as it were, a picture or simple jigsaw about your situation.'
5. It is important to stress that as the cards are read out people are reading about *themselves*. As a group they are then asked to discuss four questions:

(i) How does it *feel*, being in the situation you have just described?
(ii) What are you going to do about it, i.e. what options, if any, do you actually feel you have for action to improve your situation?
(iii) *Who* do you think you are, i.e. which minority group are the cards based on?
(iv) *Which* of the fifteen facts about yourself do you feel are the most difficult to live with?

6. Groups should be encouraged to write down their thoughts during this discussion phase. It is best to

No residence rights
You have no legal right to live where you do although you are on your traditional territory.

Control of movement
The authorities can, and do, forbid you to go and visit relatives and to have visitors.

Communications
Telegrams are the only means of communication with the outside world, and all are vetted by the authorities.

Low wages
Special provisions are made for you to receive wages that are less than (maybe only 25 per cent of) the legal minimum.

Health care
The authorities halted an anti-trachoma (eye disease) programme because, they said, two of the team were enrolling people to vote in the coming election.

Mining
The authorities can, and do, give mining companies permission to enter your territory and opencast mine on it.

Business
You are not allowed to enter into any trade or business in the community without permission of the authorities.

Possessions
You are not allowed to own electrical goods (except kettle, radio, iron and razor) without permission.

Malnutrition
In one large city 25 per cent of your group's children suffer from serious malnutrition; 80 per cent of these are under 3 years of age and are therefore likely to suffer brain damage.

Blindness
Your people are twenty times as likely to suffer blindness (from trachoma) as the rest of the population in the country.

Culture
Both your language and culture are considered inferior, unimportant and of little worth.

Self-esteem
You are constantly reminded by others outside your group that you are of no worth as a person and useless to society.

Resentment
The many injustices that you face every day result in a general feeling of resentment towards the authorities.

Resignation
Continual enforced subservience often leads to despair and resignation over your condition.

Racism
In the society in which you live racial discrimination is generally taken as normal.

Fig. 8.4. Experiencing underdevelopment: fact cards

supply questions (i) and (ii) only at first. Give a reminder after five or ten minutes that groups need to go on to the second question. Only ask for consideration of the third question when the first two have been thought about fully, as the third one often tends to preoccupy people!

7. After sufficient time has been allowed for discussion ask each group to report back. Note down comments on the blackboard or OHP under the two headings: How does it feel? What shall we do?

Outcomes/debriefing

1. Responses to the question 'How does it feel?' will generally be one-word answers, such as, depressed, angry, resentful, rebellious, etc. It is important to elicit as wide a range of responses as possible. What often happens is that a spectrum of feelings emerges, ranging from apathy and despair to anger and resentment.

2. Responses to the question 'What will you do?' will often correlate with the feelings expressed previously. Again a wide range of responses should be elicited, and they will often range across a spectrum that runs from suicide/drink/do-nothing via standing up for one's own culture/rights and seeking legal redress to the belief that non-violent, or even violent, direct action are the only ways of achieving redress.

This range of responses is important for in fact it illustrates just those responses to discrimination and oppression found in the real world. Subsequently, one might want to discuss how some minority groups have actually reacted in all the various ways mentioned with particular reference to why Aborigines have responded to their situation in the way that they have.

3. Responses to the question 'Who are you?' will vary depending on previous knowledge – both genuine and stereotyped – of other groups, countries and cultures. Often the situation described in the cards is thought to be located in a poor country rather than a rich one.

Important note: It is necessary to be precise in explaining which group situation the class has been experiencing. Most of the facts on the cards relate to the situation of Aborigines living on reservations in Queensland. They were certainly true in the early 1980s. Although seven of the cards apply to the

Aborigine situation more generally, the eight specific ones only apply to life on some Queensland reservations. The city referred to under 'malnutrition' is Sydney.

5. When eliciting responses on which aspects of life might be the most difficult to cope with it is useful to list them in two columns: those which are subjective (culture, self-esteem, resentment, resignation, racism), and those which can be objectively measured (the remainder). It is then possible to enquire about the differences between the two lists, leading to identification of the distinction between subjective and objective discrimination (see pages 6–8).

Follow-up work

Clearly this simulation game could be followed up in a variety of ways. One would be to ask the question 'How did Aborigines come to be in the position that they are in today?', which would involve working back from the present to the past. Materials for doing this can be found in chapter five and further supplemented by reference to Jan Roberts's *From Massacres to Mining*. Another option would be to examine the struggle over land rights today and to set this in the context of discussion on, say, the *UN Declaration on Human Rights*.

A third possibility arises out of the title given to this activity and the reference already made to the popularity of teaching about development and underdevelopment. Such teaching, of course, generally relates to 'Third World' development or, more appropriately, global issues of North–South development. It is very instructive, however, to apply questions which are commonly asked about world development (i.e. about differences *between* countries) to minority groups *within* countries.

The following exercise can also be done usefully in pairs or small discussion groups. It needs to be incorporated into a larger unit of work on development. Its purpose is to provoke discussion about the various possible meanings of 'development'. Pairs or groups are asked to select from the nine statements below the three with which they most agree.

Meanings of development

1. *Economic growth*
Development means economic growth for without this no country can survive. This must be initiated

from the top. Gross National Product is the best indicator we have of development.

2. *Interdependence*
Development requires an appreciation of the nature of interdependence, both within countries and between them. In particular it means recognising the mutual interdependence of North and South.

3. *Human being*
Development means primarily the development of human beings rather than of things. This means that people are the focus, not projects, and that *they* are consulted first about their real needs.

4. *Basic needs*
Development means starting at the bottom where most people are, not at the top. It involves responding to the basic needs of the poorest sector of society, e.g. health, employment, food.

5. *Models*
Understanding development requires an appreciation of the various models of development that are in favour at different times and places, their differing ideologies and in particular non-European perceptions on development.

6. *Participation*
Development requires that people are able to participate in their own affairs. This involves having control over one's own life and destiny and not being subject to those who wield power unjustly.

7. *Local*
Development must begin at home with relationships in the classroom and local community. Any interest in the North–South debate must arise first out of understanding social and political issues locally.

8. *Morality*
Development is basically a moral issue, which requires a massive transfer of resources and aid from the overdeveloped, rich countries of the North to the underdeveloped countries of the South.

9. *Underdevelopment*
Development is impossible until it is realised that underdevelopment is a process, not a state, begun during the colonial period and still continuing. Development therefore begins when underdevelopment stops.

If these 'definitions' and the questions they raise are applied to a particular minority group several interesting avenues for discussion emerge. For example, what does it really mean if, with reference to a group such as Aborigines, development is about human beings, basic needs and participation? What does an Aborigine, as against a white, strategy for development look like? If underdevelopment is a process rather than a state, in how many ways is it perpetuated, and by whom? If issues of development can only be understood by reference to situations in one's own country and local community, who and what should we be looking at close to home?

Part Three
Classroom Resources and Support

9 Evaluating Resources

All children have to attend school for eleven years, and if they see no other kind of book, they will see and read a school textbook. These will have been chosen by teachers from a publisher's list or exhibition . . . Yet teachers have not been trained to handle biased materials. They are often insensitive to racist content. Many school books written in the 1970s appear to be more colourful versions of books written in the 1940s, with no change of approach in the handling of subjects, or the ideas within them. Colonial poses are struck; the white man is still in charge.[1]

Member States should promote appropriate measures to ensure that educational aids, especially textbooks, are free from elements liable to give rise to mis-understanding, mistrust, racialist reactions, contempt or hatred with regard to other groups or peoples.[2]

How do you react to suggestions that the teaching materials you use might be biased? Do you shrug it off, or ask what *sort* of bias, or say that publishers wouldn't allow biased school books? The point is, of course, that all authors (and there is nothing particularly special about writing a school book) have their own attitudes, values and implicit assumptions about the world and the subject matter of their book. Whether they are writing about the world or about Britain, their perceptions are influenced by history, upbringing, culture and class. Parts of chapter 3 touched on the problems of socialization and the cultural bases of racism, and, just as these factors influence the 'normal' curriculum, so they appear in the teaching materials we have at our disposal.

In discussing the evaluation of resources two things are clear. The first is that the multi-ethnic curriculum, by definition, must set out to minimize, if not eliminate, all types of ethnocentric bias. This will generally mean avoiding a white, male, European perspective on the world all the time. The second point is that, due to the cultural and institutionalized nature of racism, one should initially *expect* most resources to contain such bias. One's awareness of the presence of racism in society at large and in teaching resources in particular will depend on a variety of factors. If you teach in inner London with children from several ethnic minority groups in your school and the National Front stirring up racial hatred, you will quickly become aware of the subtleties of racism. In the middle of Cumbria or East Anglia the plural nature of society is not apparent, racism a word that is rarely used and bias in teaching materials seldom considered.

Whilst quite a lot has been written about racism in books, it is only available in scattered form and much of the best work is based on the American experience. As a result of the understandable racial unrest in the 1960s (see chapter 4) attention was drawn to the unsuitability of most teaching materials when considering Blacks, Native Americans, Chicanos, Asian Americans and so on. Pressure was then brought to bear on the publishing houses and very gradually changes began to occur in books. Stereotypes of minority groups are being removed, Black children are included in reading schemes, and attempts are being made to avoid sex-role stereotyping. In the UK much of the initiative for this has come from librarians and teachers in multi-ethnic areas. The main emphasis has probably been on children's books, reading schemes and fiction. Much remains to be done on subject textbooks. An excellent exhibition on bias in books can be hired from the London branch of the National Association for Multiracial Education (NAME) and details for obtaining this, as well as references to books on this topic, are given in the resources section of chapter 11. The Minority Rights Group, too, is engaged in a two-year project (1978–80) on this theme and details are given in Appendix 2 on page 109.

Questions to ask

Several questions can be asked about any book. Does this book foster awareness, sensitivity and empathy over majority/minority issues? Are minority group culture and history dealt with in a positive way? Is it made clear that the minority itself is not the problem but rather majority attitudes and social structure? Does the book illustrate the breadth of minority response to discrimination? Will it have a positive effect on minority self-image and esteem?

Checklists and guidelines

One useful way of trying to evaluate resources is by using a checklist which sets out the main points to look for. Three examples follow in Extracts 9.1, 9.2 and 9.3.

Extract 9.1

Ten Quick Ways to Analyse Children's Books for Racism and Sexism

Both in school and out, young children are exposed to racist and sexist attitudes. These attitudes—expressed over and over in books and in other media—gradually distort their perceptions until stereotypes and myths about minorities and women are accepted as reality. It is difficult for a librarian or teacher to convince children to question society's attitudes. But if a child can be shown how to detect racism and sexism in a book, the child can proceed to transfer the perception to wider areas. The following ten guidelines are offered as a starting point in evaluating children's books from this perspective.

1. Check the illustrations

● *Look for stereotypes.* A stereotype is an over-simplified generalization about a particular group, race or sex, which usually carries derogatory implications. Some infamous (overt) stereotypes of Blacks are the happy-go-lucky water-melon-eating Sambo and the fat, eye-rolling 'mammy'; of Chicanos, the sombrero-wearing peon or fiesta-loving, macho bandito; of Asian Americans, the inscrutable, slant-eyed 'Oriental'; of Native Americans, the naked savage or 'primitive' craftsman and his squaw; of Puerto Ricans, the switchblade-toting teenage gang member; of women, the completely domesticated mother, the demure, doll-loving little girl or the wicked stepmother. While you may not always find stereotypes in the blatant forms described, look for variations which in any way demean or ridicule characters because of their race or sex.

● *Look for tokenism.* If there are non-white characters in the illustrations, do they look just like whites except for being tinted or colored in? Do all minority faces look stereotypically alike; or are they depicted as genuine individuals with distinctive features?

● *Who's doing what?* Do the illustrations depict minorities in subservient and passive roles or in leadership and action roles? Are males the active 'doers' and females the inactive observers?

2. Check the story line

The Civil Rights Movement has led publishers to weed out many insulting passages, particularly from stories with Black themes, but the attitudes still find expression in less obvious ways. The following checklist suggests some of the subtle (covert) forms of bias to watch for.

● *Standard for success.* Does it take 'white' behavior standards for a minority person to 'get ahead'? Is 'making it' in the dominant white society projected as the only ideal? To gain acceptance and approval, do non-white persons have to exhibit extraordinary qualities—excel in sports, get As, etc.? In friendships between white and non-white children, is it the non-white who does most of the understanding and forgiving?

● *Resolution of problems.* How are problems presented, conceived and resolved in the story? Are minority people considered to be 'the problem'? Are the oppressions faced by minorities and women represented as causally related to an unjust society? Are the reasons for poverty and oppression explained, or are they accepted as inevitable? Does the story line encourage passive acceptance or active resistance? Is a particular problem that is faced by a minority person resolved through the benevolent intervention of a white person?

● *Role of women.* Are the achievements of girls and women based on their own initiative and intelligence, or are they due to their good looks or to their relationship with boys? Are sex roles incidental or critical to characterization and plot? Could the same story be told if the sex roles were reversed?

3. Look at the lifestyles

Are minority persons and their setting depicted in such a way that they contrast unfavorably with the unstated norm of white middle-class suburbia? If the minority group in question is depicted as 'different', are negative value judgments implied? Are minorities depicted exclusively in ghettoes, barrios or migrant camps? If the illustrations and text attempt to depict another culture, do they go beyond over-simplifications and offer genuine insights into another lifestyle? Look for inaccuracy and inappropriateness in the depiction of other cultures. Watch for instances of the 'quaint-natives-in-costume' syndrome (most noticeable in areas like costume and custom, but extending to behavior and personality traits as well).

4. Weigh the relationships between people

● Do the whites in the story possess the power, take the leadership, and make the important decisions? Do non-whites and females function in essentially supporting roles?

● How are family relationships depicted? In Black families, is the mother always dominant? In Hispanic families, are there always lots and lots of children? If the family is separated, are societal conditions—unemployment, poverty—cited among the reasons for the separation?

5. Note the heroes and heroines

For many years, books showed only 'safe' minority heroes and heroines—those who avoided serious conflict with the white establishment of their time. Minority groups today are insisting on the right to define their own heroes and heroines based on their own concepts and struggles for justice.

When minority heroes and heroines do appear, are they admired for the same qualities that have made white heroes and heroines famous or because what they have done has benefited white people? Ask this question: Whose interest is a particular figure really serving?

6. Consider the effects on a child's self-image

● *Are norms established which limit the child's aspirations and self-concepts?* What effect can it have on Black children to be continuously bombarded with images of the color white as the ultimate in beauty, cleanliness, virtue, etc., and the color black as evil, dirty, menacing, etc.? Does the book counteract or reinforce this positive association with the color white and negative association with black?

● What happens to a girl's self-image when she reads that boys perform all of the brave and important deeds? What about a girl's self-esteem if she is not 'fair' of skin and slim of body?

● In a particular story, is there one or more persons with whom a minority child can readily identify to a positive and constructive end?

7. Consider the author's or illustrator's background

Analyse the biographical material on the jacket flap or the back of the book. If a story deals with a minority theme, what qualifies the author or illustrator to deal with the subject? If the author and illustrator are not members of the minority being written about, is there anything in their background that would specifically recommend them as the creators of this book?

● Similarly, a book that deals with the feelings and insights of women should be more carefully examined if it is written by a man—unless the book's avowed purpose is to present a strictly male perspective.

8. Check out the author's perspective

No author can be wholly objective. All authors write out of a cultural as well as a personal context. Children's books in the past have traditionally come from authors who are white and who are members of the middle class, with one result being that a single ethnocentric perspective has dominated American children's literature. With the book in question, look carefully to determine whether the direction of the author's perspective substantially weakens or strengthens the value of his/her written work. Are omissions and distortions central to the overall character or 'message' of the book?

9. Watch for loaded words

A word is loaded when it has insulting overtones. Examples of loaded adjectives (usually racist) are *savage, primitive, conniving, lazy, superstitious, treacherous, wily, crafty, inscrutable, docile,* and *backward.*

● *Look for sexist language and adjectives that exclude or ridicule women.* Look for use of the male pronoun to refer to both males and females. While the generic use of the word 'man' was accepted in the past, its use today is outmoded. The following examples show how sexist language can be avoided: *ancestors* instead of *forefathers; chairperson* instead of *chairman; community* instead of *brotherhood; firefighters* instead of *firemen; manufactured* instead of *manmade; the human family* instead of *the family of man.*

10. Look at the copyright date

Books on minority themes — usually hastily conceived—suddenly began appearing in the mid-1960s. There followed a growing number of 'minority experience' books to meet the new market demand, but most of these were still written by white authors, edited by white editors and published by white publishers. They therefore reflected a white point of view. Only very recently, in the late 1960s and early 1970s, has the children's book world begun even remotely to reflect the realities of a multiracial society. And it has just begun to reflect feminists' concerns.

The copyright date, therefore, can be a clue as to how likely the book is to be overtly racist or sexist, although a recent copyright date, of course, is no guarantee of a book's relevance or sensitivity. The copyright date only means the year the book was published. It usually takes a minimum of one year— and often much more than that—from the time a manuscript is submitted to the publisher to the time it is actually printed and put on the market. This time lag meant very little in the past, but in a time of rapid change and changing consciousness, when children's book publishing is attempting to be 'relevant', it is becoming increasingly significant.

SOURCE: The Council on Interracial Books for Children, New York.

Extract 9.2

Practical guidelines to assessing children's books for a multi-ethnic society

Children in our schools are being educated in a multi-ethnic society. The books children read affect the attitudes and ideas they form of this society. We have a responsibility, therefore, to examine every book in the light of its contribution to:

(a) *the preparation of each child for his or her role in a multi-ethnic society.* We should not underestimate how greatly books help a child to recognize and value the contributions of those from other cultures. Such an understanding may very well help a child — of whatever background — to challenge the racial prejudice encountered in life.

(b) *the way each child sees him or herself.* A positive self-image, particularly in the case of children from ethnic minorities, can be enhanced by appropriate books.

There are two ways in which children usually encounter books. Often, a teacher presents a book to read from or as a textbook, and by doing this, endorses the book with his or her own authority and implicit approval. But frequently, too, a child withdraws from the outside world into a one-to-one communication with an author, by curling up privately with a chosen book. In this situation, a child is immensely receptive, and, where the book is negative or harmful, there is no one to intervene — nor is there in the case of images children receive when they flick through books or simply look at pictures.

The following criteria have been drawn up in response to requests from teachers and librarians concerned with these issues. They provide an added dimension to take into account, alongside the traditional standards by which we select good books for children.

1. *Ethnic-minority characters* should feature in the books we seek. We need books showing them in everyday pursuits, such as going to school, work, shopping, and so on, so that these activities, or indeed any experiences, should not be seen as the exclusive preserve of white people. If a book is set in a multiracial city such as London, both text and illustrations should reflect the whole population, as in Methuen's *Terraced House* books. More good books

of this kind are being published, and sources of information about them are also increasing.

2. *How people from ethnic minorities are portrayed is all-important.* In books such as *Hal* (Penguin) or *The Young Warriors* (Longman), they are shown as decision-making and self-respecting characters with whom children can identify. We can carry this further, by also seeking books that illustrate the contribution that adults from ethnic minorities have made, and are making, to society: as in *Toussaint L'Ouverture* (Collins). Avoid fiction such as Willard Price's *Cannibal Adventure* or the *Biggles* series, where 'goodies' and 'baddies' are divided according to their race.

3. As publishers begin to include characters from ethnic minorities in their new books, we need to *guard against:*

(a) *tokenism* – the arbitrary, solitary and standardized black face or character.

(b) *stereotyping* – defined by David Milner in *Children and Race* (Penguin) as 'the attribution of supposed characteristics of the whole group to all its individual members (which) has the effect of exaggerating the uniformity within a group, and its distinction from others'. Stereotyping is an invidious reinforcer of prejudice and is, sadly, evident in many illustrations and, more subtly, in texts. Still too prevalent are books such as those in the *Mumfie* and the *Dr Doolittle* series, where black men are invariably portrayed as stereotyped buffoons – the obvious butt for racist jokes. Allen Ahlberg's *Here are the Brick Street Boys* is an example of both tokenism – the one black face on nearly every page – and stereotyping – the damaging cannibal 'joke' with which it ends.

4. *Illustrations deliver their message quickly.* Good illustrations depict particular people in particular settings, thus avoiding the pitfall of caricature. But all too common are the kinds of illustrations, of which comics are the most extreme example, where one face with a variety of hairstyles and clothes serves for several characters, and the face of a character from an ethnic minority is inevitably a stereotype.

Publishers are finding it difficult to find illustrators who can successfully portray individuals from ethnic minorities. Some, such as Hamish Hamilton, have chosen to use photographs instead, and their series of four books written by Joan Solomon provide a model. The photographer has used a group of children from diverse backgrounds and cultures, who are friends and therefore interact naturally before the camera.

5. *Issues of hostility and prejudice* should be dealt with honestly where they arise, not ducked, disguised or distorted. Books such as Paul George's *Memories* (Commonplace Workshop) do just this, and have

enormous appeal for teenagers. Books which use racially derisive and derogatory terms gratuitously are unacceptable. Where they occur in older publications, they can be faced and discussed with young readers, and should not be glossed over.

6. *The language in books can communicate prejudice.* Value-laden terms, such as 'savage' and 'childlike' used about particular groups, are potentially destructive and still occur frequently in history and geography books. Language can distort even more subtly. Cassell's Anchor book *Crow and the Brown Boy,* published in 1976, describes the reaction of 'the brown boy' when he is discovered by white boy Jim hiding in the bushes – his eyes roll. Needless to say, Jim's remain steady.

Dialect is also a language issue. Where it is used to demean or to caricature, it is inappropriate. It can, however, make a positive contribution to children's respect for one another and the way they speak, as in James Baldwin's *Little Man, Little Man* (Michael Joseph), Charles Keeping's *Cockney Ding Dong* (Kestrel), or C. Everard Palmer's *Baba and Mr Big* (Deutsch).

7. *Look carefully at facts* and the implications that may be drawn from them, whether in textbooks, historical fiction or in topical novels. Recurring forms of distortion which take the place of accuracy are exemplified by:

(a) *Families in Other Places* (*Penguin Primary Project*) which depicts all non-white people as naked and living in primitive rural conditions. A more balanced perspective can be found in Marc Bernheim's *In Africa* (Lutterworth) which shows a range of lifestyles in rural and urban Africa.

(b) The Oxford Junior book *Africa* with its paternalism, white philanthropism and the premise that only with the coming of the white man can the history of a nation begin. Contrast this with Basil Davidson's *Discovering Africa's Past* (Longman), where European colonialism is set into a long and richly-varied historical past.

Much more could be written on the issue of facts, whether in geography, biography or science. The subject is wisely dealt with in a pamphlet by Chris Proctor *Racism in Textbooks.*

8. *The original date of publication* (which is usually given on the back of the title page) can be significant. This is not to diminish the considerable value of many old books, but, as Chris Proctor says: 'History does not change, but attitudes do.'

There is an increasing number of books that both contribute by their quality to children's literature and also meet our criteria for use in our multi-ethnic society. This is the time to ensure that such books take their place, alongside the old favourites, on classroom and library shelves.

SOURCE: Gillian Klein and Crispin Jones, ILEA Centre for Urban Educational Studies.

Extract 9.3

Images in Textbooks

Purpose

To provide an opportunity for students to look critically at the textbooks which are currently in use at their school; in this way, for them to become familiar with certain influential images and assumptions which are present not only in school textbooks but also in the press and television, and in political propaganda.

Preparation

It is useful to have some extracts from textbooks which clearly present a view different from the one prevalent in one's own country. There are several possibilities.

Activities

There is of course a variety of possible activities, depending on the age and knowledge of the students. They include the following:

Students look at extracts and then re-write the captions for the photographs in their social studies and history textbooks. For example, blatantly anti-Communist or anti-Western captions can be written.

Students look at the pictures and accompanying text in their own textbooks and try to imagine how their counterparts in other countries would react to these if they were to see them.

Students study closely some extracts and compile a checklist of questions which could be asked about school textbooks; and they then study some of the textbooks in use at their own school, bearing their questions in mind.

Students are given a checklist by the teacher, and they use it to examine extracts; or books in use at their school; or booklets, posters, films etc.; or television programmes and newspapers. There is a specimen checklist on this page, which can be adapted.

A Checklist of Questions

1. Top Nation

Does the book suggest or state that 'our' country or power-bloc is more civilized, inventive, peace-loving, sensible, tolerant etc. than others?

2. Foreign Devils

Does the book suggest or state that a certain other country or power-bloc is completely evil, is scheming destruction, trying to dominate the world etc.?

3. Acts of God

Does the book refer to so-called natural disasters (floods, earthquakes, drought, etc.) without mentioning that it is normally the poor who suffer from them, not the rich?

4. Sexism

Does the book imply that men are superior to women, or that traditional sex roles (breadwinner, homemaker) are unchangeable? And is the word 'Man' used to mean all human beings rather than just males?

5. Self-interest

Does the book look at world affairs – for example, the system of world trade – from the point of view of just one country or type of country?

6. Ignoring the background

Does the book refer to 'problems' such as poverty and pollution without referring to the social and economic background?

7. Ignoring human nature

Does the book criticize certain social systems (e.g. capitalism or communism) without referring to the attitudes and behaviour of individuals?

8. Catching up

Does the book imply that all countries should try to get richer and richer – for example try to 'catch up' with the United States? And does it imply that this is not only desirable but also actually possible?

9. Happy Savage

Does the book imply that 'primitive' or 'backward' people have happy carefree lives free from the problems of 'civilization'?

10. Between the lines

Does the book suggest, though perhaps not state, certain assumptions which would definitely not be shared by people in other countries? For example, in the examples in the maths and science books?

11. Ignorance

Does the book state things which few if any knowledgable people would agree with, regardless of their political views? For example, that poverty and hunger are caused mainly by the population explosion?

12. Problems, Problems, Problems

Does the book describe problems (poverty, war, pollution, etc.) without referring to what can be done, and has been done, to tackle the problems, and the background to them?

13. Leaders

Does the book imply that world events are caused by 'leaders' — 'great' men and women, who wage war, make treaties, pass laws, etc., apparently regardless of the millions of 'ordinary' people?

14. All or Some?

Does the book speak of, for example, 'the French' when it really means, 'the French government', or 'many French people' or 'some French people', etc.? Does it similarly make a blanket use of terms such as 'rich countries', 'developing countries', 'Third World' countries?

15. Misprints

Does the book contain misprints which perhaps reveal the assumptions and bias of the printer and proofreader?

16. Own Bias

Does the book admit that it is itself biased? Does it say what its bias is? Does it at least admit that its subject matter is controversial?

17. Challenge

Does the book challenge you to re-examine your own assumptions — for example, those which are present in questions such as these?

18. Excellence everywhere

Does the book draw examples of excellence from all parts of world society? Given the present maldistribution of power and wealth in world society, does the book in particular draw attention to excellence in non-Western cultures and societies?

SOURCE: *Learning for Change in World Society: Reflections, Activities and Resources* (World Studies Project, 1979).

The portrayal of minorities in textbooks

Minorities are all too often popular as the subject for schoolbooks because of their 'exotic' interest. Their treatment thus not only often reinforces popular stereotypes but also dwells on the past rather than the present conditions under which a minority group lives. Six books and one filmstrip are considered here. Between them they look at five minority groups and are a relatively random selection from UK educational publishers.

Some brief evaluations

A Closer Look at Eskimos by Jill Hughes (Hamish Hamilton, 1977)

This is a well produced and attractively illustrated book for the upper junior/lower secondary age range. Its date would suggest an up-to-the-minute attempt to look at this minority group. The book is not paternalistic in its approach, indeed Inuit culture is portrayed in a positive fashion and the first spread is entitled 'Inuit: the people', giving the group their own preferred name. On the face of it the book appears a useful study, until, however, one considers the over-all picture that is given. It is, like so many books dealing with minorities, a picture of the past. Indeed near the beginning it says 'many of the features of traditional Eskimo life described in these pages have vanished . . .' Yet twenty-six out of the twenty-seven pages are about these traditions. We learn that the Inuit lives in stone and turf houses in winter and skin tents in the summer and igloos when they are travelling. There are even diagrams on how to build a snow house. It would appear that all travel is by dog sledge, no reference to skidoos here, and rifles are not used for hunting.

The major omission is of course the actual life the Inuit are leading today. This is dealt with in three paragraphs on the last page, together with an up-to-date illustration which seems quite out of place after the rest of the book. True, it refers to the disadvantages of trying to adapt to an alien culture, to 'the first evils of White exploitation' and to surviving the 'benefits' of modern industrialized society, but the way in which this is done is mere tokenism, tokenism to the present.

Beguiling in its attractiveness and non-racist in its language, this book nevertheless does a grave disservice to the Inuit in ignoring them as a people with their own problems of life today.

Pia in Alaska by Sven Gillsater (Wheaton, 1969)
Well illustrated with colour photographs, this book describes a child's visit to Alaska and to the island of St. Lawrence in the Bering Sea. Inuit culture is generally described sympathetically and because the book deals with an *actual* community in the late 1960s the problems of stereotyping are minimized. One difficulty arises with the use of the child's viewpoint throughout, in that she occasionally makes unfavourable comparisons with her own European culture, for example, talking of language: '. . . Pia sometimes wondered if it did not hurt her throat, the way she half-swallowed the strange sounds of her language.' Presumably comments such as this are put in to emphasize what a child's perspective might be although the few examples are not necessary for the story and spoil an otherwise very sympathetic description. Igloos are put in perspective in the first pages and the illustrations leave no doubt about the 'modern' nature of dwellings on the island. Comparisons that are made between Inuit and white culture do not discriminate on behalf of the latter.

The themes covered seem a little eclectic: friends, fishing, school, wildlife, but again presumably relate to the fact that a child's viewpoint is being described. It gives a much better picture of Inuit life today than the book by Hughes in that it does attempt to describe things as they are *today*. If it had been written from an adult viewpoint, yet with children in mind as the target group, more could have been conveyed of life on the island.

From discussion with teachers and looking at teaching materials, it is probable that these two books are fairly typical of treatment of the Inuit at school level. What is missing is an appreciation of the destructiveness of the clash between Inuit and white society, of the continuing exploitation by whites and quest for identity by the Inuit. No better source is available on this than Hugh Brody's *The People's Land: Eskimos and Whites in the Eastern Arctic* (Pelican, 1975). What is needed now is a school text that looks at some of these issues — issues alive now! A case in point would be the *Observer* Colour Supplement of 25 June 1978 which examined the clash between conservationists, wishing to protect the world's whales, and the inhabitants of Point Hope whose way of life and very identity rest on whaling.

North American Indians Starters Long Ago (Macdonald Educational, 1974).
Since the title of this series for young children refers to the past one cannot really fault the book for not referring to the present. One can still ask the questions from the checklists, however, in relation to the past experiences of the group. The text is limited to fairly brief factual statements about habitation, hunting, crafts and traditions with which one would find little fault. What is particularly revealing, though, is the treatment of Indian–white relationships, the way they are described and the omissions from the story. For example, on the arrival of Europeans: 'At first the Indians were friendly. They sold goods to the settlers.' If they were friendly *at first* obviously something is soon to change; by referring to the Indians rather than the whites the onus is already on the former. Indeed, the next page reads: 'Later the Indians became angry with the settlers. Sometimes they attacked their camps.' This would be fair enough, as long as we find out why they were feeling angry, i.e. white encroachment on their territory. But no explanation is given. Instead we find that 'Many Indians were forced to leave their homes.' No reference to whites forcing this move on the Indians.

Soon comes a description of fighting between Indians and cavalry who 'protected white settlers'. The cavalryman in the picture appears to have been shot in the back, undoubtedly treacherously attacked from behind. There might still be a chance to retrieve the text after reference to attempted peace settlements, but suddenly the last page is reached. It announces: 'Now there are only a few Indians in America. Most of them live in special camps called reservations.'

The very fact that this is a book for top infants and lower juniors makes the bias by omission all the more serious. Stereotypes are formed at an early age and materials such as this only reinforce them. The fact that the language needs to be very simple does not necessarily make small alterations difficult.

Indians of the North American Plains by Virginia Luling (Macdonald Educational, 1978).
The title of this series is 'Surviving People' and the book goes a long way towards explaining the problems of survival for this minority group. There is no stereotyping or unfavourable comparisons with

white 'norms', in fact care is obviously taken to give a Native American viewpoint. The reader is told early on that 'the real discoverers of America arrived 12,000 years before (Columbus)' and that the way of life of the Plains Indian was destroyed by the whites. The inevitability of clashes between settlers moving west and Native Americans whose lands were being encroached on is described sympathetically and reference is made to the fact that it was Native American, rather than white, atrocities that always hit the headlines.

A particularly good point about the book is that it does pay attention to the situation of Native Americans today. It is at least more than the token one page (six out of forty-six in fact), although it would still be interesting to see current issues explored even more fully. Are not the events at Wounded Knee in 1973 as important as those in 1890? However, the effect of white efforts to 'civilize' Native Americans, of not being allowed to speak their own language, and of unsuitable curricula in schools today are all touched on.

In that it does partly deal with the present, the book is an improvement on many others. The impression one is left with, however, is still one of the past, an impression that the beautiful headdress on the front cover reinforces.

Peru: the Quechua Royal Anthropological Institute (ILEA and Basil Blackwell, 1978).
The strengths of this project lie in its response to requests from teachers and its joint development by the Royal Anthropological Society and ILEA social science teachers. Its style and layout – in the form of a core book, study guide, teacher's guide, colour slides and four case studies – are excellent. The project covers most details of life relating to the Quechua Indians in the Peruvian Andes, concentrating on the key idea of power, as found in the structure of authority and patterns of trade. It is an extremely well balanced example of what a project related to a particular minority, or any other group, should be like. None of the criticisms suggested by any of the checklists could be levelled against it, and this is of course the way all teaching materials should ideally be.

The fact that each of the case studies (on buying and selling, compadres, fiestas, and laws and leaders) looks at an aspect of the relationship of inequality

between town and village makes the key idea of power continually clear.

Gypsies by J. R. Love and C. Edwards (Harrap, 1977).
This topic book is part of a series called 'Issues' and is set out in case study format around an imaginary incident between gypsies and a local council. There are maps and photographs, case notes, articles and letters from newspapers, as well as numerous discussion questions. The intention of the book is undoubtedly to make a social issue interesting for older secondary students. Whether it does this or not, it is still done in an insensitive way.

Although extracts from books about gypsies are quoted and in places gypsies allowed to speak for themselves, nowhere is empathy really possible. Nowhere is gypsy culture described positively, nowhere can one find what it feels like to be a gypsy and *proud* of it. The tone of the book is no particularly paternalistic but one is in fact given very little information about gypsy culture. There is plenty of information in the book about the problems gypsies cause but it implicitly appeals to the reader's sense of fairplay for any empathy with the gypsies. Using this topic book, unless it was deliberately balanced by more sensitive resources, would undoubtedly reinforce all the unfavourable stereotypes including that of blaming the victims for their own oppression.

Everyday Life Among the Australian Aborigines EP filmstrip No. 6355.
This filmstrip epitomizes all that is bad about teaching materials on minority groups. It consists of thirty-one frames with a brief paragraph about each in the accompanying notes. The fault lies not so much in what is said but rather in what is *not* said. The pictures are almost exclusively about traditional life: crafts, hunting, fishing, cooking and religious ceremonies. The last one shows Aboriginal stockmen on a cattle station. In brief the twentieth century does not exist at all. This is, of course, the major fault with most materials about minority groups. One has only to compare the approach of this filmstrip with the Mapoon books (see chapter 5) to see just what is missing. The filmstrip and notes do a grave disservice to these peoples in ignoring the

white/Black culture clash in Australia and the continuing Aboriginal struggle for rights.

Even in these seven brief reviews the portrayal of minorities has ranged from the sympathetic to the insensitive. The impact of such materials on student perceptions will clearly vary, but to offer that which is in any way racist – even if it is so by default – is to do an injustice to both students and the peoples described. Minority groups live in the present not in the past, and if future materials acknowledge this then the portrayal of minority groups in books will have taken a step forward.

10 Some Current Developments

Curriculum development projects that relate to the study of majority/minority issues are, as one might expect, not very common. At the same time those that do impinge on this area are likely to be controversial for reasons that should by now be clear. Three such projects are described in this chapter.

The Schools Council Multiracial Education Project

As mentioned in chapter 6 this Schools Council project has yet to surface, if indeed it ever does. In Extract 10.1 Lucy Hodges describes the background to this project and the history of the controversy surrounding it. Much of the debate has centred around the first section of the project which aimed to illustrate the context within which multi-ethnic education has to operate e.g. institutionalized racism. Although now dated, the report would provide a useful contribution to the multi-ethnic debate.

The problems and effects of teaching about race relations

Extract 10.2 deals with this project carried out at the University of East Anglia under Lawrence Stenhouse, originally arising out of work done by the Humanities Curriculum Project. It also describes the aims of the National Association for Race Relations Teaching and Action Research (NARTAR) which is closely related to the work of the project. Project materials are about to be published and show how a controversial issue such as that of race relations can be tackled in the classroom.

The Schools Cultural Studies Project – Northern Ireland

This school-based/university linked curriculum project (Extract 10.3) is one of the few to have focused specifically on controversial issues including minority groups. The project's concern with conflict, culture and politics suggests an appropriate context for majority/minority issues and also relates them to Ulster's own problems.

The Netherlands Institute for Peace and Security

Space does not allow for the work of the Peace Education group at this institute to be described in detail. Teachers have developed materials on teaching about conflict in the classroom and also for teaching specifically about minorities. They are designed for students in the 12–13 age range and some of the earlier work of the team has been described by Robert Aspeslagh in his article 'Peace in the Classroom: Notes from a project in progress', *The New Era*, 59 (2), March/April 1978. Further details of the project can be obtained from Robert Aspeslagh at: Nederlands Instituut voor Vredesvraagstukken, Alexanderstraat 7, PO Box 1781, 's Gravenhage, Netherlands.

Extract 10.1

Off to a prejudiced start?

There is a lot more to the Schools Council multiracial education controversy than meets the eye—not least the story of its chequered three-year life.

The council project was born out of a proposal put to it by the NUT and the National Association for Multiracial Education. (The latter body does not go along with the union's objections.) Aristides recorded at the time—*TES* September, 1972—that one of the sketchiest research proposals ever put to the council got through the programme committee.

It was a three-page outline proposal drawn up by Mr Bert Townsend of the NFER. The aim was to produce teaching materials for a multi-racial society at a cost of £126,500 and the team began with a mini-project worth £10,000 to find out what multi-racial schools were doing about teaching race relations.

Things went wrong almost immediately. As soon as the project got under way in the autumn of 1973 Mr Townsend resigned to take up a job elsewhere. The four seconded teachers—Mr Rob Jeffcoate, Ms Shirley Hadi, Ms Rosalind Street-Porter and Miss Mary Worrall—were left on their own for the next six months.

They worked "democratically" collecting materials and trying to work out where they were going. But it was difficult for them to make major decisions in the absence of a director.

During this time, however, they decided to change the specifications of the project. Their original commission was to produce teaching materials. Instead they decided that what was needed was to develop a rationale or philosophy for curriculum development in multi-racial education. The age range of pupils they were looking at was reduced from five to 18-years-old to five to 13-year-olds.

A second director, June Derek, an expert in teaching English as a second language, was appointed. The project continued but still not without problems. There were political differences between her and members of the project team and eventually she left in 1975 to get married and live abroad.

A third director, Mr David Milner, was appointed, but fell ill almost immediately and was eventually replaced for the last year of the project by Dr Clare Burstall. She was also deputy director of NFER, the organization which was carrying out the research for the council.

After Mr Milner's departure the council decided the time had come to draw the project to a close. Vague suggestions of funding for a fourth year for disseminating the work were no confirmed and the project ran out of what became a £170,000 grant in 1976 when the teachers contracts came to an end.

However, much of the writing remained unfinished. The teachers had to do it in their spare time and Mr Jeffcoate was given the task of editing it.

When the draft document finally surfaced at last month's meeting of the council's programme committee it had not been seen by the project's consultative committee. (This had not met since the project came to an end.) The consultative committee—which included a NUT executive member, Mr Jack Bowdler—supported the project all along. Mr Jarvis denies that the union did so. He was also a member of the consultative committee but only attended one meeting as he explains in his letter on page 20.

(The project team members have not seen the edited draft either. They have asked the council for copies—so far without luck.)

As has been widely reported, the teachers' representatives on the programme committee, including Mr Jarvis and Mr Max Morris, ex-president of the NUT and head of a large multi-racial comprehensive in North London, objected strongly to the document's introduction.

They have variously called it "propaganda", "anecdotal", and "a slander against teachers". As can be seen from the extracts reproduced below, the introduction —which was written by Ms Street-Porter—illustrates how prevalent racist attitudes are in schools and in the rest of society. It gives the reasons why radical changes are needed in the curriculum.

The project team is now fighting a rearguard action to save the document, which was to have been published as a handbook of curriculum ideas for teachers.

Confusion reigns about what is going to happen to section one: whether the introduction is going to be "suitably edited" or scrapped. The team said in its statement: "The need for editing is not in question. What is in question is the preservation of the total argument the book presents.

"Briefly, the argument is that effective curriculum development (section two) depends on schools making a sensitive appraisal of the changing racial reality in which children are growing up and of the ways they are responding to it (section one). Any attempt to interfere with the logic of our argument or the force of the evidence quoted to substantiate it would make a nonsense of the book."

The teachers are unhappy with the way the document has been described in the press because reports have concentrated on the controversial section one, and particularly on the racist quotes. The team claims in the statement that the document is essentially a detailed discussion of curriculum issues derived from three years' cooperative work with teachers.

Hundreds of schools were visited in 25 local authorities and the project team spent most of their time working in conjunction with teachers, assessing what the children needed and developing ideas for a multi-racial curriculum. They were then tried out on pupils.

Miss Worrall explained that she concentrated on one or two schools in two or three authorities. What she got out of it was case studies of the sort of work that was going on in schools.

The other project team members operated in the same way, concentrating to some extent on areas or ideas that particularly interested them.

The team has never pretended that the study was a piece of research or a survey of attitudes. It was trying to assess the negative influences on children and put forward ideas about how to combat them. It was in the business of helping teachers, not criticizing them, it argues.

The row, however, may not die down yet. A summary of a report evaluating the project and telling the story of its difficulties, which was prepared by Elaine Brittan, now a research officer with Harrow, is also to be published by the council. Although her report supports the team's work it is believed to be critical of it in parts and of a lot of work that goes into multi-racial education generally.

It is widely accepted that the team over-extended itself by trying to do too much in too many local authorities.

Meanwhile, back at NUT headquarters discussions are going on with a view to putting up a new proposal for curriculum development materials to the council. This is not a direct result of the recent row but something the union was committed to at its last annual conference. It will have to show it has done something by the time of the next conference at Easter.

Racial reality: what all the fuss is about

The controversial first section of the Schools Council report looks at what it calls the "multi-racial reality" which faces all children in Britain.

Claiming that this is the only way to develop an adequate multi-racial curriculum, the introduction says: "The most significant feature of that reality is racism." This means it is better to be white in contemporary Britain than black or brown because if you are white you are likely to live in a better house, receive a better education and get a better job, it adds.

"A bald summary perhaps, but it expresses the kernel of the truth, and it is worth adding that one of the manifestations of racism is the education system — the under-performance of minority race children—was a motivating force behind the establishment of the project."

Schools definitely have a part to play in changing this state of affairs. "We have found many schools and teachers around the country reluctant to concede that this is so, either because they fear that intervention will be interpreted by outsiders as 'political' rather than 'educational', or because they feel they can achieve nothing against the batter of hostile forces in the wider society."

It is impossible to be completely apolitical, says the report. "Schools, by doing nothing, reinforce the negative ideas communicated to children by other agencies. The omission of anything positively multi-racial in schools says as much about the value it places on racial minorities (and confirmation) of negative stereotypes the children have encountered elsewhere.

"Schools have to demonstrate overtly their involvement in, and allegiance to, the concept of a truly multi-racial society—not least because failure to do so militates against the likelihood of educational success for racial minorities."

A selection of quotes are given to illustrate attitudes found by the project team. A teacher in a multi-racial primary school, for example, is quoted as saying: "Race simply is not an issue in primary schools. Before secondary age children don't notice colour. They don't see themselves like that. You would be putting it into their heads if you brought it up."

Another example was an exchange between a teacher and a visitor to a school.

Teacher: I don't think children are conscious about black and white when they are in the classroom at all. They may have words on the side and call each other black bastards or something like that as they sometimes do. . . . I think they hear their parents using these words and I don't think they really mean them.

Visitor: Do you think it has an effect on the black children—if a white child calls a black child some name?

Teacher: No. I think that In school black and white work together at all, it doesn't mean anything at all.

The project team adds that teachers' opinions about children's attitudes are so varied that it is impossible to illustrate them all. "Those we have chosen are not meant to be completely representative, but they are typical of opinions expressed by teachers in many parts of the country."

Children's comments contradict what the teachers have to say. The report cites the example of a class of seven-year-olds from a multi-racial inner city school who were taken to the seaside. Within the hearing of some of them, a local child said to another: "I don't like those Sambos on the beach. They dirty it up."

Another example was of a Pakistani boy and white girl, both aged eight, who were having a fight in the playground. A teacher intervened and was asked by the girl: "Ganhar says honky houses stink.

But it's not true, Miss, is it? Paki houses stink."

The authors point out that these examples show an early awareness of race " which in some cases takes the form of open hostility based on a confused version of the facts."

Britain has changed radically over the past 20 years from a predominantly white to an increasingly diverse multi-racial and multi-cultural society in which there is a lot of hostility, says the report.

'I never thought black people would be in books'

It is unwise to assume no positive intervention is needed to help children with this.

Because race is seen as a problem, teachers may feel there is something harmful in children talking about it at all, say the authors. "From this perspective it is not surprising that the idea of encouraging positive racial awareness and attitudes by the introduction of multi-racial materials into the classroom on any extensive scale appears to be divisive, to run the risk of ' stirring it up ', and to have less to recommend it than a simple policy of ignoring the problem in the hope that it will go away."

Children do not show their real selves in school because they try to conform and will, for example, refrain from speaking Creole for fear of being corrected or laughed at.

The important thing is for teachers to question, says the report. An example is given of what happened when a teacher talked first to a black girl and then to a white boy, aged eight, about the idea of introducing books containing blacks.

Teacher: What did you think when I held up the book first of all ?

Sharon: A bit shocked.

Teacher: Why were you shocked?

Sharon: Because I never thought black people would be in a book.

Teacher: Were you pleased?

Sharon: Yes.

Teacher: Why did you think black people couldn't be in the book?

Sharon: Because all the books we used to read when we were in the infants were about Peter and Jane and Paul and Janet and all that.

Teacher: Do you think it's a good idea to look at books with black children in them, so that you can learn about them ?

White boy, David: No.

Teacher: Why not ?

David: Because we can't eat the same food as them. It might poison

us. They got a different country.

Teacher: What about some of the friends in your class, who were born in this country, some of your black friends ? Do you think they should read the same books as you ? What sort of books should they read ?

David: The white, these books (Ladybird reading scheme), the white books.

'They're sensitive and tend to be aggressive'

The report discusses the way in which children form their attitudes about other races from a very early age as well as Britain's racist history, the media's attitudes and the effects of discriminatory immigration acts. Some teachers think parents bring their children up to be over-sensitive to race, say the authors. A teacher is quoted as saying:

"I think coloured children have got chips on their shoulders which stem from their parents. They're very sensitive and tend to be aggressive. . . ."

A black parent said that, far from having a chip on his shoulder " we reject the use of the term. . . . We prefer to say that we are sensitive to the attitudes of the people here ". The report goes on to argue how important it is for parents to support children when they have been subjected to racial abuse such as: " John, is it true that you lived in a tin hut at home ? "

The influence of newspapers and television is also important in creating attitudes, says the report. A nine-year-old black girl, fostered by a white family, was reported to have been called names when *Love Thy Neighbour* programme was released. She was called " nig-nog " and asked if she practised voodoo by her mates.

Children also pick up attitudes from teachers. The report quotes the following incidents related by a teacher:

" I was teaching a small group of West Indian children in a West Midlands' boys secondary school. They were withdrawn for extra language tuition. The room had a glass door, which meant that anyone passing had a clear view of the group inside. On this occasion, a fairly senior member of staff passed the door, paused and looked in. He opened the door, grinned at me, and said in a voice loud enough for all to hear : ' Excuse me, is this Dudley Zoo ? ' ".

Examples are given of children picking up racist attitudes:

" I think that Pakistanis have as

much right as we do but this does not happen. We think of Pakistanis as black, germy people. This is not true. They have funny spots, but not germy, but if they were in their own country many would die of an illness and some would die in the war. . . . I think they came to be safe and have money and a proper home and family. . . . I don't think they should be sent back to their own country. At some time it must be stopped or England will be crowded. Already there are fifty-five million immigrants in England and Great Britain."

The report says that many teachers maintain that calling another child "wog", "black sambo", "filthy paki", "banana arms", "black bastard", "go back to the jungle where you belong", "monkey brains", is no different from calling a child "fatty", "four eyes" or "spotty". "Certainly all are unpleasant and upsetting for the individual concerned, but racial name-calling is of a qualitatively different order", it says.

The authors argue that schools should provide positive confirmation of the identity of every child, as an individual and as a member of a racial group. The should also encourage respect in all children for the identities of individuals and the groups they belong to. Examples are given of how this does and does not happen at the moment.

One difficulty is the resistance to the use of the word "black". Some teachers also object to blacks wearing woolly hats. Schools should not just confine themselves to "isolated or occasional multiracial inputs" into the curriculum, says the report. "What is required is a constant and pervasive intervention across the gamut of everyday learning experiences which can be sustained from the beginning to the end of statutory schooling."

The report suggests ways in which the school should improve relationships with parents and others. The school should know which ethnic groups live in the area and how long they have been there together with the ethnic group and cultural background of every child in the school.

Each adult in the school should know about the parents and make contact with them by such methods as home visiting. Schools should also establish close links with one another.

The authors question the way teachers split up ethnic minority groups so that they do not sit together in the classroom because it can make things much worse. Children who cannot speak English fluently need to sit with those they can communicate more easily with, says the report. Teachers need to be very sensitive to stereotyping the races, especially when it comes to meting out discipline. "Black children are frequently described by teachers as being 'apathetic', 'withdrawn', 'boisterous', 'aggressive', 'volatile', 'difficult'", say the authors. "It has to be recognised that children who feel themselves to be categorized in this way, almost 'expected' to act in a given manner, will tend to conform to the expectation."

Schools should recognise in some way the English dialects spoken by different ethnic minorities. "Schools need to recognise that these children are, in fact, operating skilfully in a variety of language forms and registers, and are capable of making switches appropriate to the situation.

"Once that is recognized, schools can decide when it is appropriate to use the mother tongue—for instance, in creative writing, classroom conversation and drama—and when a child should be taught to use standard English as the form of communication.

"The policy on which the school decides should be explained to the children, so that they understand why there is a necessity to switch dialects under certain circumstances, and also understand that no dialect is 'superior' to any other."

Children's traditional dress and diet should be respected, and the school's physical environment made to reflect a multi-racial society.

A haphazard history . . .

A feeling of *deja vu* overshadows the row. Not only has the council's programme committee been trying for the second time to throw out a controversial report on the subject but the NUT's general secretary, Mr Fred Jarvis, has again been discovered absent from Schools Council meetings where he could have put his oar in earlier.

The stormy history of the NUT and Schools Council race research goes back some years—specifically to a set of teaching materials on race, known as the Stenhouse race pack. Mr Lawrence Stenhouse was director of the council's humanities curriculum project, which set out to provide discussion materials on controversial topics with young school leavers.

His packs on war, the family, sex, law and order and education were published without question but the race pack never saw the light of day because of a block vote on the council programme committee by the NUT.

That was in January, 1972. Controversy raged for some months after and letters flooded into the *TES*, including one from Mr Jarvis, who was then deputy general secretary of the union. His objection to the Stenhouse approach was that its concept of the teacher as neutral chairman was not appropriate for the treatment of the subject of race

This time the union is objecting to the introduction to the current council project on the grounds that it is too biased and does not treat race neutrally enough.

Stenhouse's idea was to increase the understanding of 14 to 15-year-olds rather than to change attitudes. The material was carefully put together but included some disturbing stuff about Black Power.

The council treated it cautiously at first. It was sent to an outside consultant after which the project team was asked to produce a smaller, more balanced pack. Mr Jarvis failed to turn up to the sub-committee which worked out the reediting and a month later the programme committee, which includes representatives of local authorities, the DES and the National Foundation for Educational Research, decided not to publish.

At the time Mr Jarvis was quoted in the *TES* as saying: "It is important to stress that far from running away from the subject of race—as one press report has suggested—the programme committee is anxious that the Schools Council should do more in the field."

SOURCE: Lucy Hodges, *Times Educational Supplement,* 24 February 1978.

Teaching about Race Relations

Extract 10.2

NARTAR: an introduction

People who are teaching 14-16-year-olds in the areas of humanities and the social sciences, or drama, are already quite likely to deal with the theme of race relations, either because it is an established part of an examination syllabus, or simply because they feel that the topic is important in view of the increasing ethnic diversity of British society. Nevertheless, there seem to be many teachers who would argue that this is undesirable in that it might lead to a worsening of attitudes between different ethnic groups or that, in the case of all-white schools, the topic is irrelevant. In fact whether a school teaches about race relations or not seems to bear little relation to its ethnic composition. What this variety of response does seem to reflect is the doubt and uncertainty that surrounds the issue of improving race relations.

In the absence of reliable evidence of the positive effects of such teaching on attitudes, the risk of increasing racial prejudice and intolerance might reasonably be seen as sufficient grounds for avoiding the topic in the classroom.

Indeed, limited research in the 1960s[a] did indicate that teaching in order to undermine prejudice might in fact have the opposite effect. The Schools Council Humanities Curriculum Project, although it conducted a research which indicated small but consistent gains in interracial tolerance from its work, nevertheless ran into considerable problems when it came to exploring race relations in the classroom, to the extent that the publication of its materials was vetoed by the Schools Council.

It is not simply the uncertainty which is common to any teaching which may involve changes in attitude that has inhibited the development of programmes of teaching about race relations. In most situations teachers do know, if only from talking to other teachers, what sort of responses they need to be prepared for, and how other teachers have coped with the different situations that can develop in the classroom. But the school which is concerned to give some coverage to race relations will not generally have access to this kind of information. Few teachers are in a position to pass on relevant personal experience, let alone the more generalised view that could be gained from an investigation of the experience of other teachers.

The National Association for Race Relations Teaching and Action Research (NARTAR) exists to do just that. Their aim is to make available to other teachers both the experience of teachers who have taught about race relations – and have studied their own teaching – and the findings of the research project in conjunction with which their teaching took place.

NARTAR is primarily an association of teachers who have already shared their own experience of handling the theme of race relations, in the context of a wide ranging investigation of 'the Problems and Effects of Teaching about Race Relations'. To their own insights and analysis of their work has been added those of professional researchers from the Centre for Applied Research in Education at the University of East Anglia. All NARTAR members have studied these findings and have a commitment towards passing their understanding on to other teachers. As disseminators they are therefore able to draw on a broad spectrum of experience which reflects the diversity of approaches and situations in the forty different schools that worked in the research project. It is hoped that NARTAR will therefore be able to offer some relevant experience to all teachers who are interested in teaching about Race Relations, whether they work in all-white or multi-racial schools, in urban or in rural areas.

This does not mean that ready-made solutions to any given situation are proposed. It cannot, for example, be said that a certain style of teaching will work best in a particular school situation. Approaches can only be suggested that may be effective. NARTAR disseminators can contribute to a dialogue which may enable teachers to make decisions about their own teaching in the light of the experience of others.

The limitations of the research project that NARTAR was set up to disseminate should, however, be noted. First, this project, which was funded by the Social Science Research Council and the Gulbenkian Foundation, was concerned with the effects of a concentrated teaching span of between six weeks and one term, on fourth year secondary school students. There was an assumption that this was about the maximum time that a school would give to this topic in a humanities or social studies curriculum. Secondly, for the purpose of the research, teachers adopted one of three teaching strategies. Some teachers will consider the division between these strategies to be artificial, and would tend to use a variety of teaching techniques. The strength of this approach to the research project is that teachers who adopt a research approach to their own teaching will more readily be able to distinguish the problems and strengths which are peculiar to a particular teaching strategy.

[a] Miller, H. J. (1967) A study of the effectiveness of a variety of teaching techniques for reducing colour prejudice in a male student sample (aged 15-21). Unpublished MA thesis, University of London.
Miller, H. J. (1969) The effectiveness of teaching techniques for reducing colour prejudice, *Liberal Education*, 16 pp. 25-31.

Design of the Project

The research team at the University of East Anglia wanted to work with teachers across a range of styles and standpoints. Rather than take a particular line and assess a specific approach to teaching about Race Relations (as had been attempted in the Humanities Curriculum Project) they hoped to sample the variety of teaching methods which could be employed. Working with teachers, they devised three possible approaches which became known as Strategy A, Strategy B, and Strategy C.

Strategy A was the Humanities Curriculum Project (HCP) technique where the teacher adopted the role of a neutral (some would prefer 'impartial') chairman of a discussion group. Evidence, usually in the form of printed material, would be fed into the discussion at appropriate points by the chairman and subjected by the group to critical study. This approach to teaching about Race Relations had already been tried in six schools working with the Humanities Curriculum Project and so some research into the effects of this strategy had already been done. On that occasion, however, it was decided to go no further, and so no teaching materials on Race had been published. In the new project fourteen schools took part and these were all schools where HCP was already in use, so that Race Relations simply slotted in as a topic. Strategy C was improvised drama, and this also took place in schools where drama teaching was already well established: ten schools worked with the project using this style. Strategy B, which ultimately included sixteen schools, was the exception in that it was not based on an existing and well defined approach.

The research team hoped that the Strategy B approach would meet the Schools Council recommendation that teachers should take 'a positive line' on race relations issues in their teaching. It was left to the teachers concerned to work out exactly what the strategy would be when they met together in conference. They broadly agreed that their aim should be 'to educate for the elimination of racial tensions and ill-feeling within our society, which is and will be multiracial, by undermining prejudice, by developing respect for various traditions, and by encouraging mutual understanding, reasonableness, and justice'.

The aim expressed by teachers at the Strategy A

(HCP) conference was 'to develop an understanding in the area of race relations of social situations and human acts and to the value issues which they raise' and was therefore consistent with the general aims of the Humanities Curriculum Project. Compared with this the aim of the Strategy B teachers was more positive in intention though the approach itself was non-authoritarian. The role of the Strategy B teachers was defined as follows: 'The teacher should be an example of a person critical of prejudiced attitudes and opinions held by himself and by society at large, and who is trying to achieve some degree of mutual understanding and respect between identifiably different human groups'. The third strategy to be employed (Strategy C) was Educational Drama. The reason for the inclusion of this strategy was the fact that teachers using drama are often working in areas of conflict, emotion and attitude. Since drama depends upon learning through social interaction it was considered to be a useful way of examining any facet of human relations. The other majority component of drama, the solving of problems and decision making through 'as if' situations meant that the teacher could seek parallel approaches to race relations without dealing 'head on' with inflammatory situations. The aim of the teachers was to examine and illuminate those factors which relate directly to relationships in multi-ethnic groups.

Teachers in all the Strategies were provided with a pack of teaching materials, consisting mainly of extracts from books and newspapers, together with photographs. All teachers were asked to be partners in the research by recording and studying their own teaching, by gathering information on their schools and by reporting on their experiences and problems. It should therefore be emphasised that the findings of the project relate to teachers who had adopted an actively critical and analytical approach to their own teaching.

The result of this was almost 1,000 hours of classroom recordings, and recorded discussions of pupils assessing the work without a teacher present. Most of the teachers provided written comments in addition to tapes and they were also interviewed by members of the central research team. It was thus possible for the team not only to hear what went on in each classroom but also to know what the teachers and pupils thought about it.

The teaching took place in the Spring term of 1974. At the end of the previous term and also at the end of the teaching period a large scale programme of psychological testing was run across all the schools and on control groups in most of the schools. A further battery of tests was completed by many of the students concerned a year later. The tests were selected in such a way as to make it possible to relate prejudice towards other ethnic groups to different aspects of personality and educational development.

In April 1974 teachers from all the experimental schools met together in a conference where they were able to exchange experiences. It was at the end of this conference that an urgent need for further action was expressed, and it was this that led ultimately, in January 1976, to the setting up of NARTAR at the end of a conference on the research findings.

Some Hypotheses Emerging from the Research

The project contains a majority of white pupils. In the main results are about white teachers teaching 'about race relations' to white or multiracial groups in humanities, social studies, or drama.

Variations from school to school and class to class are rather large; so all generalizations have to be regarded as hypotheses for the teacher to test or to judge rather than as conclusions for the teacher to accept.

Direct teaching about race relations in a wide range of contexts in the humanities, social sciences and drama will tend by and large to increase interracial tolerance rather than to increase racial prejudice. But even in groups where the majority improves, a substantial minority becomes more prejudiced. The balance is better than when it is not taught at all.

There is evidence of a widespread trend in this age group towards increased hostility towards Asians, and teaching about race relations moderates or eliminates this trend rather than actually improving attitudes towards Asians.

Strategy A and Strategy B are both about equally effective in combatting prejudice, and the data give no basis for suggesting one strategy rather than the other. Schools will be wise to adopt whichever strategy fits in with their own teaching tradition and the skills of the teachers involved.

Strategy C (drama) appears to produce little advantage on its own when measured by our rather cognitively biased tests. However, teaching about race relations through drama does not, even on these tests, lead to overall deterioration of attitude. Tests fairer to drama might well be expected to show improvements. However, it does appear that it would be unwise for schools to rely on drama alone as a means of teaching about race relations.

Black and Asian pupils have more positive attitudes to other races than have white pupils.

There is ample evidence that this is a particularly

difficult topic to teach: teachers need mutual support in teams and probably support from outside agencies such as the advisory services and teachers' centres. There is inevitable stress involved for the conscientious teacher.

Materials are, of course, of use, but it is likely that a very wide range of materials can be advantageous or disadvantageous according to the sensitivity with which they are used and the context in which they are used. Materials cannot be 'tested' and recommended on that basis as almost certain to work well in all situations.

Most important of all is access to the experience of other teachers, to the reactions of a wide range of pupils and to accounts of real classroom situations.

SOURCE: NARTAR, c/o Centre for Applied Research in Education, University of East Anglia, University Village, Norwich NR4 7TJ.

Extract 10.3

The Schools Cultural Studies Project

Educational research and curriculum development in Northern Ireland has been extremely limited in its scope and scale. In the past, relatively little attention appears to have been given, in the formal curriculum of many second-level schools in Northern Ireland to the treatment of controversial issues and current trends in contemporary Ulster culture. Trends and issues in contemporary culture have constituted a large part of a number of recent British curriculum projects e.g. the Humanities Project (University of East Anglia), Integrated Studies (Keele University), Moral Education (Oxford University), and Social Studies 8-13 (University of London and Liverpool) to name only a few. Naturally, there is no specific mention of Northern Ireland problems in these projects. On the whole, these projects concern themselves with issues of a controversial nature in politics, morals, religious beliefs, and aspects of interpersonal behaviour. These projects generally aim at encouraging pupils to be more tolerant, understanding and reflective about contemporary issues.

The Schools Cultural Studies Project (SCSP) was conceived in 1973 and will terminate in June 1980. The project is jointly sponsored by the Joseph Rowntree Charitable Trust and the Northern Ireland Department of Education. The Project is a school-based/university linked curriculum development project embracing twenty-six second-level schools, both Catholic and State schools, including comprehensive, secondary intermediate, and technical schools in Northern Ireland.

The Schools Cultural Studies Project is based on two very fundamental assumptions: first, that schools have a significant part to play in resolving the difficulties that have beset Northern Ireland society in recent years, and second, that teacher involvement in curriculum design and development will be crucial in any contribution made in and through schools. The project seeks to encourage and support teachers and others who have an educational responsibility for the following:

(i) the development of creative experimental approaches in schooling and curriculum;
(ii) to assist pupils to clarify personal values by adopting and using the skills of the valuing process;
(iii) to cultivate and increase modes of sensitivity and tolerance, and
(iv) to encourage personal awareness and mutual understanding in social relationships among school pupils in Northern Ireland.

The pursuit of these general objectives has led the project to concentrate its resources upon the development of a five-year social studies course for second-level schools that aims to explore new approaches to teaching about Northern Irish culture and society in schools. By 'Social Studies' is meant aspects of the social science disciplines of anthropology, economics, political science, sociology, as well as the more traditional subjects of history and geography. Social Studies also includes those areas of cultural enquiry which relate to the role of the individual in society; the understanding and solution of controversial social, religious and political issues, and the clarification of personal values.

SCSP as School-Based Curriculum Development

The project does not wish to conform to the standard model of curriculum development project, viz.

(1) identification of a subject in need of research and development;
(2) assembly of a project team;
(3) preparation of new materials;
(4) trial and revision of materials;
(5) write final report;
(6) disbandonment of project team.

Despite its success in changing curriculum thinking, this model suffers from a host of weaknesses. First of

all, it is assumed that what is needed are new materials that are prepared by 'experts'. Secondly, project teams have found it difficult to relate their work to programmes of teachers' education; and teachers are usually treated as 'Clients' rather than as participants in the curriculum development experience.

Given the weakness outlined above. SCSP materials and teaching strategies are designed, written and tested by groups of second-level teachers, from both sides of the community, working in conjunction with the central project team (five full-time members, including two seconded teachers) in a 'workshop' setting held within the New University of Ulster. Workshops are held one day every fortnight. Teachers from a variety of schools bring along their experience and work with colleagues on writing new materials, and have an opportunity to consider alternative teaching strategies and content. In this 'school-based' model trial materials are discussed and modified in the light of experience. The model casts the teacher in the role of cultural change agent; a role in which the teacher takes an active part in curriculum decision-taking.

One of the major benefits accruing from the school-based curriculum development model is increased teacher development in terms of writing materials, testing novel teaching strategies and becoming more informed about curriculum theory. Materials must only be viewed as one aspect of the project. Far more important is the creation of a network of informed teachers who possess the skills and theoretical background for making curricular changes in the future.

The Social Studies Course

The project's main contribution has been the development of a five year social studies course composed of twelve units of work. The units have been designed to take account of three components: (1) social science knowledge; (2) reflective thinking and inquiry methods, and (3) values clarification skills.

The course has been structured through the use of a number of 'key' concepts e.g. 'self', 'role', 'function', 'interdependence,' 'conflicts', 'culture' etc., that have been selected to provide a framework for understanding. Concepts are viewed as tools for understanding social phenomena.

The treatment of Northern Ireland controversial issues is attempted through a gradient approach. Rather than confronting the pupil with such issues in the early stages of the course, the pupil is gradually introduced to complex problems of conflict, culture crisis and political discord. The course leads to a direct study in the fifth year of controversial issues of a social, religious and political nature facing Northern Ireland society.

The programme is set out as follows:

Year 1 ALL KINDS OF PEOPLE-MYSELF

Unit 1A Myself Who Am I

Unit 1B Myself-Life: Mine and others.

These units emphasise such concepts as 'self', (including physical appearance, food, interests etc) as well as 'beliefs', 'attitudes' and 'values'. The aim is to foster an awareness of self and others, including their lifestyles and cycles in past and present.

Year 2 ALL KINDS OF PEOPLE-MYSELF

Unit 2A Myself and My Family

Unit 2A examines the 'structure' of the family in a sociological framework; especially the family in Northern Ireland. The pupil is also introduced to alternative styles of family life in other cultures.

Unit 2B The Functions of the Family.

This unit focusses upon the concept of 'function'. The concept is used to refer to the many tasks that the family must perform to exist as a social unit.

The unit provides an opportunity of examining the functions of four different family settings:

(1) A rural family in Ulster in 1914.

(2) An urban family in Belfast in 1935;

(3) A family in urban Belfast in 1976.

(4) The family in another culture in 1976.

The unit employs a fictional family 'the Quigley's' and their relatives throughout the four sections. It is hoped that through such detailed study, pupils will more fully understand their own family, and the families of their friends.

Year 3 ALL KINDS OF COMMUNITIES

Unit 3A Community

This unit focusses upon the concept of the residential community. The aim is to create an awareness of the

(1) *Community in the Past:* Aspects of the traditional community are analysed. Attention is given to the recording and collecting of 'evidence' on the local community in the past. Study is made of the traditional community in cross-cultural settings.

(2) *Community at Present:* The pupil conducts a study of the local community through the use of social survey methods.

(3) *Community in the Future:* The unit examines some of the local amenities and facilities that can promote a better social life in a residential community in the future. The emphasis is on planning, decision-making and conflict resolution.

Unit 3B Community

The unit will examine work and school as communities; the problems of minorities in the community, and pay attention to communities undergoing conflict.

Year 4 ALL KINDS OF HOMES

Unit 4A Minorities and their Problems

This unit is divided into two sections. The first section looks at Gypsies and other travelling people, treating the problems associated with cultural differences. Prejudice and discrimination, particularly in relation to Irish travellers is explored. Section two deals with the North American Indians as a culturally deprived minority group.

Unit 4B Substitute Homes

The unit concentrates on two models of substitute homes:

(1) the Workhouse, and (2) Orphanages and homes for children in care. The aim is to focus attention on alternative types of homes for the homeless.

Unit 4C International Conflicts.

In this unit a study of conflict is made in two cross-cultural settings: (1) The Middle East, and (2) Viet Nam. Tension, conflict and inter-group relations are explored. A study of prejudices and competing political ideologies helps to prepare the pupil conceptually to undertake analysis and discussion of controversial problems related to Northern Ireland society.

Year 5 ULSTER

Unit 5A Ulster: A Divided Society?

The unit is presented in the form of a case study of Londonderry in two parts:

(1) Londonderry (Pre-1968). The city is examined in relation to the rest of Northern Ireland and the United Kingdom;

(2) Londonderry: One Community or Two? This section addresses itself to the internal character of Derry itself.

In both sections, pupils test hypotheses related to the problems which are manifest in 'the troubles' today

Unit 5B Ballymillis

This unit examines life in a 'fictional' village — Ballymillis, in rural Northern Ireland. Pupils can examine a number of real-life situations characteristic of Ulster society e.g. problems of mixed marriages, letting of houses, unfair dismissal from employment etc. The aim is to foster understanding of contrasting points of view and to develop problem-solving skills necessary for coping with important social situations and controversial issues.

Unit 5C Ulster: An Analysis of Conflict

The purpose of this final unit is to provide pupils with experience in discussing, analysing and understanding controversial issues related to Northern Ireland society. The unit is made up of packs of 'evidence' related to two themes 'Violence' and 'Loyalty'. It is felt that the most appropriate teaching strategy for such work would have *discussion* rather than instruction as its mode of enquiry.

Values Education: Towards A Common Teacher Strategy

A few words are in order about the strategies that teachers use to help pupils to clarify personal values. The social studies course pays particular attention to value issues in the classroom. To this end, participating teachers have developed (and are continuing to develop) a number of teaching strategies specifically designed to give pupils experience in the *process of valuing,* rather than telling pupils *what to value.* Valuing (1) in this sense has to do with seven sub-processes:
Choosing:
(1) Choosing freely; (2) Choosing from alternatives; (3) Choosing after consideration of the consequences.
Prizing:
(4) Prizing and cherishing; (5) Affirming publicly.
Acting:
(6) Acting; and (7) Acting repeatedly.

In order to help pupils clarify values, teachers are developing strategies that give pupils experience in each of the seven sub-processes of valuing. The seven sub-processes are the skills that will when used collectively, aid pupils in forging their own value systems in a thoughtful and reflective way.

Current Work

Twenty-six second-level schools, both Catholic, and Maintained (State) schools are participating in the project. During 1977-78, over 6,000 units of study are in schools, and this number will increase within the near future. The social studies course has been recognised for the Certificate of Secondary Education with a Mode III examination scheme.

In addition to the workshops already mentioned, the project has also established a group of *inter-school cells,* that is, meetings of groups of teachers using project materials, who are unable to attend workshops. The teachers meet informally, three or four times a term, in order to discuss trial materials, and to float ideas and make suggestions for revisions.

The principals of the participating schools have agreed to meet up to three days a year. The principals analyse the nature and function of their role in furthering cultural renewal in Northern Ireland and have facilitated the introduction of cultural studies within their respective schools.

The Project is being disseminated throughout the Province by means of short teacher's courses, conferences, publications, induction-days, pre-and-inservice teacher education programmes, and through a 'network' of concerned teachers, who believe that curriculum development ought to belong to the classroom teacher.

References

1. See Raths, L., Harmin, M., and Simon, S. *Values and Teaching.* Columbus, Ohio: Charles Merrill Inc. 1966. The authors propose a series of teaching strategies that focus on the valuing process. See also: Simon, S., Howe, L., and Kirschenbaum, H., *Values Clarification: A Handbook of Practical Strategies for Teachers and Students.* New York: Hart Publishing Co., 1972.

SOURCE: McKernan, J., *The Secondary Teacher*, Journal of the Association of Secondary Teachers in Ireland, Autumn 1977.

11 Postscript

Teaching about minorities cannot be a marginal issue. Minority groups are not merely interesting, often exotic, topics of study peripheral to the realities of everyday life. Because the whole minority experience is contingent upon the behaviour of a dominant group it is more appropriate to talk about majority/minority issues. That being so, the focus of interest shifts equally to the social structures, culture and values of the majority. Since most societies in today's world are pluralist, majority/minority relationships are central to everyday life and therefore must have an important bearing on education. This holds true whether or not members of a particular society are confronted with pluralism in their daily lives.

This resource book has attempted to map some of the main issues in this field, to understand the minority experience and to examine the background to such situations. In addition to offering some guidelines for thinking about majority/minority issues it has also explored some of the ways in which such issues might contribute to the curriculum. One may identify several further areas that need critical investigation:

(a) The study of minorities needs to be lifted out of the realms of primary school exotica and accepted as a serious area for concern.

(b) New teaching materials are needed that look at particular majority/minority issues in depth and with particular groups of students in mind.

(c) Such materials could range from school-based resources developed from files of cuttings on particular minority groups and leaflets such as the one on South Africa produced by Christian Aid to teaching packs to accompany all Minority Rights Group reports and a series of textbooks on majority/minority issues in the 1980s.

(d) The position of minority groups in society should form one of the threads of development education. This should not be restricted to minorities in the 'Third World' since all oppressed minorities suffer from underdevelopment.

(e) Multi-ethnic education could profit from a global dimension which considered majority/minority issues in a variety of societies.

(f) Different subject areas need to consider what their particular contribution to a multi-ethnic curriculum might be. For example what is the difference between geography as it is at present commonly taught and a multi-ethnic geography?

(g) The relationship between multi-ethnic education and development education needs to be explored further with particular reference to classroom materials and approaches.

(h) The importance of a multi-ethnic curriculum in all-white areas of the country needs to be stressed and an analysis made of what the specific requirements are here.

(i) Whatever materials are available they need to be assessed for ethnocentric bias and racism – this needs to be done by subject specialists as well as librarians and those involved with children's books. In Appendix 2 details will be found of a project on this theme run by the Minority Rights Group. It was called 'Multicultural Britain in an Interdependent World'.

Appendix 1

Aims, work and reports of the Minority Rights Group

Discrimination against ethnic, religious and cultural minorities (or majorities) underlies some of the gravest and most widespread problems facing the world today. Human beings may form a vulnerable group in a community through numbers, or status, or both. Their ill-treatment can not only involve suffering and disability on a massive scale, but has often led to communal violence and bloodshed. The systematic persecution of Jews in Central Europe and, more recently, racial disorders in the United States of America and the quasi-religious conflict in Northern Ireland show that these problems occur as readily in developed as in less developed countries. Throughout the world there are minority situations, involving a waste of human resources besides the denial of human rights, which represent threats to peace as well as a challenge to the conscience of man. Hence – particularly because minorities as yet have no forum at the United Nations – the need for an independent, international and non-governmental body to work in this difficult but vital field.

To meet this need an international specialized research and information unit called the Minority Rights Group has been founded by a number of concerned individuals connected with public life, the press, the academic world, religions and the law. It has been recognized and registered as an educational charitable Trust in London, where it has its headquarters, but its field is worldwide. *La Stampa* said in December 1973: 'Since most minorities have no means of expression at the centre of political power, it will bring some relief to our consciences to know that there is an organization, politically independent, with a high reputation internationally, devoted to these problems.' John Papworth wrote in *Resurgence* in February 1977: 'The work of the group puts us all in its debt.'

The founders of MRG included David Astor, the former Editor of *The Observer;* Sir Robert Birley, previously Head of the City University's Department of Social Science and Humanities; George Cadbury; Erwin D. Canham, Editor-in-chief of the *Christian Science Monitor;* and the Rt Hon Jo Grimond. The first Director of MRG was Laurence Gander, previously Editor-in-chief of the *Rand Daily Mail.* In May 1971 he was succeeded by the present Director, Ben Whitaker, the author, who was formerly a barrister, MP for Hampstead and the Junior Minister in Britain's Ministry of Overseas Development. Since 1975 he has been a member of the UN Human Rights Sub-Commission.

Objects

MRG has three principal aims:

● To secure justice for minority or majority groups suffering discrimination, by investigating their situation and publicizing the facts as widely as possible, to educate and alert public opinion throughout the world.

● To help prevent, through publicity about violations of human rights, such problems from developing into dangerous and destructive conflicts which, when polarized, are very difficult to resolve.

● To foster, by its research findings, international understanding of the factors which create prejudiced treatment and group tensions, thus helping to promote the growth of a world conscience regarding human rights.

The aims of MRG are remedial, preventive, and educative.

Methods

The main methods which MRG employs are:
1. MRG maintains a continual survey of current events throughout the world to monitor devel-

opments in minority situations. It selects specific problems on which to focus attention, on the basis of criteria such as the severity of the persecution or discrimination to which the victims of group prejudice are being subjected, the extent to which it is possible to obtain reliable information, and the prospect of securing an improvement in the treatment of the people concerned by making known the facts of their situation. In choosing priorities MRG aims to maintain an international balance, to remain politically impartial, and to include some of the lesser known instances of discrimination as well as the more publicized cases.

2. It conducts detailed research into the selected situations, usually by commissioning suitable experts to prepare impartial reports on them in depth. This often involves their conducting first-hand investigations in the countries concerned. MRG then submits these reports to verification by different authorities on the subject. Ascertaining the correct facts is an essential pre-requisite for any remedial action: MRG believes in the intrinsic value of making the truth known in the many cases where accurate publicity leading to an informed public opinion is the best hope of redress.

The future

Ghandi said that civilization is to be judged by the treatment that is shown to minorities. Given the necessary support, MRG can make a valuable contribution by providing reliable and impartial information, and by building up knowledge and experience about victims of group prejudice – thus helping to secure greater respect for human rights everywhere.

Reports

The Reports already published by the Minority Rights Group are as follows:

- No. 1 *Religious Minorities in the Soviet Union*
- No. 2 *The Two Irelands: the Double Minority – a Study of Inter-group Tensions*
- No. 3 *Japan's Minorities: Burakumin, Koreans and Ainu*
- No. 4 *The Asian Minorities of East and Central Africa*
- No. 5 *Eritrea and the Southern Sudan: Aspects of Wider African Problems*
- No. 6 *The Crimean Tatars, Volga Germans and Meskhetians: Soviet Treatment of Some National Minorities*
- No. 7 *The Position of Blacks in Brazilian Society*
- No. 8 *The Africans' Predicament in Rhodesia*
- No. 9 *The Basques and Catalans*
- No. 10 *The Chinese in Indonesia, the Philippines and Malaysia*
- No. 11 *The Biharis in Bangladesh*
- No. 12 *Israel's Oriental Immigrants and Druzes*
- No. 13 *East Indians of Trinidad and Guyana*
- No. 14 *The Roma: The Gypsies of Europe*
- No. 15 *What Future for the Amerindians of South America?*
- No. 16 *The New Position of East Africa's Asians*
- No. 17 *India and the Nagas*
- No. 18 *The Montagnards of South Vietnam*
- No. 19 *The Namibians of South-West Africa*
- No. 20 *Selective Genocide in Burundi*
- No. 21 *Canada's Indians*
- No. 22 *Race and Law in Britain and the United States*
- No. 23 *The Kurds*
- No. 24 *The Palestinians*
- No. 25 *The Tamils of Sri Lanka*
- No. 26 *The Untouchables of India*
- No. 27 *Arab Women*
- No. 28 *Western Europe's Migrant Workers*
- No. 29 *Jehovah's Witnesses in Central Africa*
- No. 30 *Cyprus*
- No. 31 *The Original Americans: U.S. Indians*
- No. 32 *The Armenians*
- No. 33 *Nomads of the Sahel*
- No. 34 *Indian South Africans*
- No. 35 *Australia's Policy towards Aborigines 1967–1977*
- No. 36 *Constitutional Law and Minorities*
- No. 37 *The Hungarians of Rumania*
- No. 38 *The Social Psychology of Minorities*
- No. 39 *Mexican-Americans in the U.S.*
- No. 40 *The Sahrawis of Western Sahara*
- No. 41 *The International Protection of Minorities*
- No. 42 *Indonesia, West Irian and East Timor*
- No. 43 *The Refugee Dilemma: International Recognition and Acceptance*
- No. 44 *French Canada in Crisis: A New Society in the Making?*
- No. 45 *Women in Asia*
- No. 46 *Flemings and Walloons in Belgium*
- No. 47 *Female circumcision, excision and infibulation: facts and proposal for change*
- No. 48 *The Baluchis and Pathans*
- No. 49 *The Tibetans*

Appendix 2

Ethnocentrism in UK teaching resources–
An MRG project

Introduction

The Minority Rights Group publishes reports on discrimination against ethnic, religious and cultural minorities (or majorities) in all parts of the world. Up to now educational activities have focused on the compilation of a handbook for teachers on majority/minority issues.

The project on ethnocentrism (1978–80) arose out of the latter, which explored the minority experience and the stereotyping of minorities in teaching materials. As the title suggests, it represents a broadening of concern to explore the 'images' found in teaching materials of (a) multi-ethnic Britain, and (b) the 'Third World'. The emphasis will be on resources for Geography at secondary level. The project is funded by a grant from the Development Education Fund of the Overseas Development Administration.

Background

Every textbook that deals with minority groups or the 'Third World' embodies a set of attitudes and assumptions, whether conscious or unconscious, explicit or implicit, about its subject matter. Ethnocentrism in textbooks is in large part a legacy of colonialism,[1] as are ideas commonly held by the public about world development and minority groups.[2] Perhaps this should not be surprising as traditional 'western' concepts, values and institutional structures may well support various forms of group oppression including racism and sexism.[3] The damaging effects of such attitudes on student self-image has been often noted.[4]

Support for these concerns comes from a variety of sources. The UNESCO Recommendation on International Education calls for 'appropriate measures to ensure that educational aids, especially textbooks, are free from elements liable to give rise to misunderstanding, mistrust, racialist reactions, contempt or hatred with regard to other groups or peoples'.[5] Galtung, the eminent peace researcher, has argued that 'one would *expect* school textbooks to reflect thinking about social affairs outmoded by, say, at least fifty but perhaps not as much as 100 years'.[6] The Schools Council Project on Multiracial Education pointed out that 'An insular curriculum, preoccupied with Britain and British values, is unjustifiable in the final quarter of the twentieth century. The curriculum needs to be both international in its choice of content and global in its perspective ... People from British minority groups and from other cultures overseas should be presented as individuals with every variety of human quality and attribute. Stereotypes of minority groups in Britain and of cultures overseas, whether expressed in terms of human characteristics, life-styles, social roles or occupational status, are unacceptable and likely to be damaging'.[7]

The interaction between the reader and the printed word is a complex one which relatively few researchers have looked at, and then generally in an American context.[8] The American experience in the 60s led to a detailed re-evaluation of the portrayal of minority groups and other cultures in teaching materials.[9] Thus guidelines are available for both teachers and publishers on countering stereotyping, racism and sexism, as well as comprehensive studies of texts from different subject areas.[10,11]

Very little of this has gained a foothold in the UK in any coherent form as sources are scattered. Important work has been done however by organizations such as the National Association for Multiracial Education,[12] the Children's Rights Workshop,[13] and the National Committee on Racism in Children's Books.[14] Concern comes mostly from teachers and librarians working in multi-ethnic areas.[15, 16, 17]

Subjects such as Geography are still lacking in any serious analysis of ethnocentric bias at school level. The need has been pointed out by geographers working in race relations,[18] and those teaching about the 'Third World',[19] whilst concern over how young children perceive other nationalities has been expressed for some time.[20] What is needed now is a major assessment of the hidden images conveyed by Geography.

Possible outcomes of the project

(a) An exploration of the nature of ethnocentrism and the ethnocentric curriculum, with particular reference to images of the 'Third World' and multi-ethnic Britain, as well as the relationships between development education and multi-ethnic education.

(b) A review of the current literature on bias in teaching materials from North America and Europe, and a comparison with the situation pertaining in the UK.

(c) A review of existing schemes and checklists for detecting various types of bias in textbooks and teaching materials.

(d) In conjunction with groups of teachers developing relevant tools for analysis e.g. relating to images of minority groups, images of development, images of interdependence, and to evidence of racism.

(e) A survey of Geography books available, and in use, that deal with the 'Third World' and Britain, together with an analysis of the forms of bias found.

(f) Consultation with educational publishers in the light of feedback from discussion with teachers and students.

(g) A series of guidelines for publishers, authors and book users in the UK, similar perhaps to some of those in use in the USA.

(h) Groups of teachers, students, curriculum developers, and educational publishers with some experience in using such guidelines and checklists.

(i) A report to the Department of Education and Science, and to the Standing Committee on Education for International Understanding, on the project's activities and findings, as MRG's contribution to the implementation of the UNESCO Recommendation.

(j) Publication of a project report as a manual for teachers, curriculum leaders, educational administrators, advisors and publishers.

The results of this project are written up in two booklets from the Centre for Multicultural Education at the University of London Institute of Education. They are:

Hicks, D. W., *Images of the World: An Introduction to Bias in Teaching Materials*, Occasional Paper No. 2, 1980.

Hicks, D. W., *Bias in Geography Textbooks: Images of the Third World and Multi-ethnic Britain*, Working Paper No. 1, 1981.

References and Notes

Chapter 1

1. I have also briefly explored the reasons for inclusion of majority/minority issues in the curriculum in 'Minorities: A Marginal Interest', *The Social Science Teacher*, 8 (1), October 1978.
2. This matrix is excellently used in *Learning for Change in World Society* (World Studies Project, 1979).

Chapter 2

1. Wirth, L., 'The Problems of Minority Groups' in Linton, R. (ed.), *The Sciences of Man in World Crisis* (New York: Columbia University Press, 1945).
2. Wagley and Harris (1958), quoted in ref. 11 below.
3. See, for example, the reports published by the Minority Rights Group, 36 Craven Street, London WC2N 5NG. Further details can be found on page 108.
4. Wirth, L., op. cit.
5. Wilson, J., *The Original Americans: U.S. Indians*, Minority Rights Group Report No. 31, 1976. See also the case study in ch. 5 of this book, pages 42–7.
6. Smith, D. J., *Racial Disadvantage in Britain* (Pelican, 1977).
7. Wirth, L., op. cit.
8. Freire, P., *Pedagogy of the Oppressed* (Penguin Education, 1972).
9. Wren, B., *Education for Justice* (SCM Press, 1977), ch. 6, 'The Marks of Cultural Oppression'.
10. Tajfel, H., *The Social Psychology of Minorities*, Minority Rights Group Report No. 38, 1978.
11. Simpson, G. E. and Yinger, J. M., *Racial and Cultural Minorities* (Harper and Row, 4th ed., 1972).
12. Katznelson, I., *Black Men, White Cities* (Oxford University Press for the Institute of Race Relations, 1973).

Chapter 3

1. Simpson, G. E. and Yinger, J. M., *Racial and Cultural Minorities* (Harper and Row, 4th ed., 1972).
2. Short, M. and McDermott, A., *The Kurds*, Minority Rights Group Report No. 23, 3rd ed., 1977.
3. Mercer, J., *The Sahrawis of Western Sahara*, Minority Rights Group Report No. 40, 1979.

4. Milner, D., *Children and Race* (Penguin Education, 1975).
5. LeVine, R. A. and Campbell, D. T., *Ethnocentrism: Theories of Conflict, Ethnic Attitudes and Group Behaviour* (New York: Wiley, 1977).
6. Hodge, J. J., Struckmann, D. K. and Trost, L. D., *Cultural Bases of Racism and Group Oppression* (Berkeley, Calif.: Two Riders Press, 1975).
7. ibid.
8. Parsons, M., 'When the Europeans Came', in Roberts, J., Parsons, M. and Russell, B. (eds.), *The Mapoon Story According to the Invaders* (Victoria, Aust.: International Development Action, 1975).
9. Husband, C. (ed.), *White Media and Black Britain* (Arrow Books, 1975).

Chapter 4

1. See Richardson, Robin, *Learning for Change in World Society: Reflections, Activities, Resources* (World Studies Project, rev. ed. 1979), Introduction.
2. See, for example, Palley, C. *Constitutional Law and Minorities*, MRG Report No. 36, 1978.
3. Wirth, L. 'The Problems of Minority Groups', in Linton, R. (ed.), *The Sciences of Man in World Crisis* (Columbia University Press, 1945).
4. Steiner, S., *The Mexican Americans*, MRG Report No. 39, 1979; also Ludwig, E. and Santibanez, J. (eds.), *The Chicanso: Mexican American Voices* (Pelican, 1971).
5. Power, J. and Hardman, A., *Western Europe's Migrant Workers*, MRG Report No. 28, 1976.
6. De Vos, G. and Wetherall, W., *Japan's Minorities: Burakumin, Koreans and Ainu*, MRG Report No. 3, 1974.
7. Hiro, D., *The Untouchables of India*, MRG Report No. 26, 1975.
8. For example see Medhurst, K., *The Basques and Catalans*, MRG Report No. 9, 1977; Smith, C. and Andrews, J., *The Palestinians*, MRG Report No. 24, 1977; and Schwarz, W., *The Tamils of Sri Lanka*, MRG Report No. 25, 1975.
9. Lemarchand, R. and Martin, D. *Selective Genocide in Burundi*, MRG Report No. 20, 1974.

10. Makielski, S. J., *Beleaguered Minorities: Cultural Politics in America,* (San Francisco: W. H. Freeman, 1973).
11. Wenner, M. W., 'The Politics of Equality among European Linguistic Minorities', in Claude, R. P. (ed.), *Comparative Human Rights* (Johns Hopkins Press, 1976), ch. 7.
12. *Report on the Supplementary School,* North Lewisham Project, 206 Evelyn Street, Deptford, London SE8 5RZ.

Chapter 6

1. Richardson, R., Flood, M. and Fisher, S., *Debate and Decision: Schools in a World of Change* (World Studies Project, 1979).
2. ibid.
3. Bowles, T. S., *Survey of Attitudes Towards Overseas Development* (HMSO, 1978).
4. Worrall, M., 'Multiracial Britain and the Third World: Tensions and Approaches in the Classroom', *The New Era,* 59 (2), March 1978, also 'New Approaches in Multiracial Education', *New Era,* 6 (3), Summer 1978.
5. Hicks, David W., 'Two Sides of the Same Coin: An Exploration of the Links Between Multicultural Education and Development Education', *The New Era,* 60 (2), March/April 1979, also *New Approaches in Multiracial Education,* 7 (2), Spring 1979.
6. National Association for Multiracial Education, General Secretary: Madeleine Blakeley, 86 Station Road, Mickleover, Derby DE3 5FP.
7. Afro-Caribbean Education Resource Project, 275 Kennington Lane, London SE11 5QZ.
8. Jeffcoate, R., *Positive Image: Towards a Multiracial Curriculum* (Chameleon Books, Writers' and Readers' Publishing Co-operative, 1979).
9. *Joint UN Plan of Support and Action for Development Education Activities, 1975–80* (Rome: Action for Development/Food and Agricultural Organization, 1975).
10. *Recommendation Concerning Education for International Understanding, Co-operation and Peace and Education Relating to Human Rights and Fundamental Freedoms* (Paris: UNESCO General Conference 18th Session, 1974).
11. Centre for World Development Education, 128 Buckingham Palace Road, London SW1V 1JS.
12. Crick, B. and Heater, D., *Essays on Political Education* (Falmer Press, 1977).
13. See, for example, 'The Trouble with Multi-culch', *Teacher's Action,* No. 9, and Dhondy, F., 'Teaching Young Blacks', *Race Today,* May/June 1978.

14. Montagu, A., *Man's Most Dangerous Myth: The Fallacy of Race* (New York: Meridian Books, World Publishing, 1964).
15. Rose, S. and Richardson, K., *Race, Education and Intelligence* (National Union of Teachers, September 1978).

Chapter 9

1. Dorothy Kuya, 'The Unacceptable Face of Publishing', *Times Educational Supplement,* 22 July 1977.
2. Recommendation Concerning Education for International Understanding (UNESCO, 1974).

Appendix 2

1. Kiernan, V. G., *The Lords of Human Kind: European Attitudes to the Outside World in the Imperial Age* (Penguin, 1972).
2. Bowles, T. S., *Survey of Attitudes Towards Overseas Development* (HMSO, 1978).
3. Hodge, J. L., Struckmann, D. K. and Trost, L. D., *Cultural Bases of Racism and Group Oppression* (Berkeley, Calif.: Two Riders Press, 1975).
4. Milner, D., *Children and Race* (Penguin, 1975).
5. *Recommendation Concerning Education for International Understanding, Co-operation and Peace and Education Relating to Human Rights and Fundamental Freedoms,* (Paris: UNESCO, 1974).
6. Galtung, J., 'Peace Research: Future Possibilities and Necessities', in *Peace: Research–Education–Action* (Copenhagen: Christian Ejlers, 1975).
7. Hadi, S., Jeffcoate, R., Street-Porter, R. and Worrall, M., *Multiracial Education: Curriculum and Context 5 to 13* (Schools Council, still to be published).
8. Zimet, S. G., *Print and Prejudice* (Hodder and Stoughton, 1976).
9. See for example the *Bulletin* of the Council on Interracial Books for Children, (CIBC, 1841 Broadway, New York, NY 10023, USA).
10. *Asia in American Textbooks* (New York: Asia Society Inc., 1976).
11. See also McDiarmid, G. and Pratt, D., *Teaching Prejudice: A Content Analysis of Social Studies Textbooks Authorised for Use in Ontario* (Toronto: Ontario Institute for Studies in Education, 1971).
12. See, for example, their portable exhibition on 'Bias in Books'; details about hire from Ann Hedge, 150 Weston Park, London N8.
13. The Children's Rights Workshop, 4 Aldebert Terrace, London SW8, has edited *Racist and Sexist Images in Children's Books* (Writers and Readers Publishing Co-operative, 1975).

14. Enquiries to the Chairperson, National Committee on Racism in Children's Books, The Methodist Church, Lancaster Road, London W10.

15. Klein, G. and Jones, C., *Practical Guidelines for Assessing Children's Books for a Multi-ethnic Society* (Centre for Urban Educational Studies, 34 Aberdeen Park, London N5, 1979).

16. Dixon, B., *Catching Them Young, 1: Sex, Race and Class in Children's Fiction* (Pluto Press, 1977).

17. Proctor, C., *Racist Textbooks* (National Union of Students Publications, 3 Endsleigh Street, London WC1 0DU, 1975).

18. Leach, B., 'The Social Geographer and Black People: can Geography Contribute to Race Relations?', *Race,* 15 (2), October 1973.

19. Marsden, W. E., 'Stereotyping and Third World Geography', *Teaching Geography,* 1 (5), July 1976.

20. Carnie, J., 'The Development of National Concepts in Junior School Children'. in Bale, J., Graves, N., and Walford, R. (eds), *Perspectives in Geographical Education* (Edinburgh: Oliver and Boyd, 1973).

Bibliography

This is an attempt to bring together a cross-section of the resources that are available for teaching about majority/minority issues. It is therefore a sample and is not, could not be, fully comprehensive. It will nevertheless provide a good start for teachers in search of resources. It offers a variety of starting points. The headings used are broad ones and obviously there is overlap between them, for example, minorities and race relations. References are placed under these headings according to their main emphasis. It is important that all the points made in chapter 9 about evaluating resources are borne in mind when considering the usefulness of particular items. This applies particularly to materials for use by students which should always be looked at critically by both teacher and students.

When looking through this chapter it will quickly become apparent that there are many gaps – there may be no, or few, resources on a particular minority situation that one wants to study. It is easiest, of course, to locate teacher resources: all MRG reports contain select bibliographies, and one can also fairly quickly build up a file of newspaper cuttings on any situation that is in the news. Good student resources still often remain to be written and the need for these has been referred to in the last chapter.

References are listed under the following headings:

1. Minorities: General
2. Minority groups (including UK)
3. Multi-ethnic education
4. Race relations
5. Attitudes, prejudice, racism
6. Resource evaluation
7. Development education
8. Political education
9. Other guides and handbooks
10. Organizations

(T): indicates for teachers' reference or sixth-form use.
(U): suitable for upper forms (14–16 years old).
(L): suitable for lower forms (10–13 years old).

1. Minorities: General

Blalock, H. M., *Towards a Theory of Minority Group Relations* (New York: Wiley, 1967). (T) One of the few books to attempt a series of generalizations and hypotheses about majority/minority issues derived from empirical data in a variety of situations.

Clay, R., *Focus on Europe: Minorities* (Harrap, 1976). (U) Suitable for sixth-form students; covers definitions and origins of minorities, results of prejudice, Cyprus, Ulster, Basques, Rom and migrant workers.

Kurokawa, M., *Minority Responses: Comparative Views of Reactions to Subordination* (New York: Random House, 1970). (T) A wide-ranging collection of papers on minority themes drawing together some of the key literature of the past thirty years.

Makielski, S. J., *Beleaguered Minorities: Cultural Politics in America* (San Francisco: W. H. Freeman, 1973). (T) Set in the particular context of the USA, but one of the best and most readable introductions to majority/minority issues.

Marland, M. and Ray, S., *The Minority Experience: A Documentary Collection* (Imprint Books, Longman, 1978). (U) Devised initially for use in conjunction with 'The English Programme' produced by Thames Television for ITV. An anthology for older secondary pupils; readings relate to gypsies, Native Americans, minorities in Britain and also to the old and disabled.

Omar, B., *Minorities,* World Topics series (Macdonald Educational Colour Units, 1978). (U) For average ability upper secondary pupils; looks at different minority groups and their place in society today.

Simpson, G. E. and Yinger, J. M., *Racial and Cultural Minorities: An Analysis of Prejudice and Discrimination* (Harper and Row, 4th ed., 1974). (T) The classic work on majority/minority issues that provides extensive coverage on a wide range of situations as well as detailed studies on the nature of prejudice, etc.

2. Minority Groups

(a) *General*

Ashworth, G. (ed.), *World Minorities 1* and *World Minorities 2* (Quartermaine House 1977 and 1978, available from MRG). (T) Each volume contains some fifty brief essays on minorities not yet covered by MRG reports, giving global coverage to majority/minority issues.

New Internationalist, 'The Last Frontier', No. 46, December 1976. (T) Special issue on native peoples' fight for survival: Aborigines, Amerindians, Sahel nomads, Inuit, Adivasis, etc.

Palley, C., *Constitutional Law and Minorities,* MRG Report No. 36, April 1978. (T) Examines a whole range of minority situations in terms of the legal measures used to alleviate, or in some cases to aggravate, them.

Zwerin, M., *A Case for the Balkanisation of Practically Everyone: The New Nationalism* (Wildwood House, 1976). (T) An interesting book on separatism in Europe from the Basques, Bretons and Occitans to the Same (Lapps), Welsh and Scots. Haphazard style but prophetic?

(b) *Native American*

Brown, D., *Bury My Heart at Wounded Knee: An Indian History of the American West* (Picador, 1971). (T/U) The definitive myth-destroyer on the American West describing what it felt like to be on the receiving end of internal colonialism. A children's version is also available.

Califf, J., 'Sensitising 9-year-olds to Native American Stereotypes', *Interracial Books for Children (IBC) Bulletin,* vol. 8 (1), 1977, pp. 3–7. (T)

Davis, C., *A Closer Look at Plains Indians* (Hamish Hamilton, 1977). (L) Attractively illustrated description of traditional nineteenth-century life suitable for top junior/lower secondary. Only one page touches on life today.

Dockstader, F. J., *Great North American Indians: Profiles in Life and Leadership* (Van Nostrand Reinhold, 1977). (T/U) Suitable for library references section; details of the life and achievements of 300 Indian leaders active between 1600 and 1977.

Frideres, J. S., *Canada's Indians: Contemporary Conflicts* (Prentice-Hall of Canada, 1974). (T) An excellent study of contemporary Indian problems by an Indian professor of sociology.

Heinrich, J. S., *Native Americans: What Not to Teach IBC Bulletin,* vol. 8 (4/5), 1977, pp. 26–7. (T)

Humphris, F., *Battle of the Little Big Horn* (Ladybird, 1976). (L) An unbiased and factual account of this controversial battle.

——, *The Story of the Indians of the Western Plains* (Ladybird, 1973). (L) Suitable for upper junior/lower secondary. A straightforward, well-illustrated account of the history of the Plains Indians.

Johansen, B. and Maestas, R., *Wasi'chu: The Continuing Indian Wars* (New York: Monthly Review Press, 1979).

Josephy, A. M., *The Indian Heritage of America* (Pelican, 1968). (T) A comprehensive account of Indian origins, history and cultural diversity. Extremely thorough coverage from prehistory to the present day.

Luling, V., *Indians of the North American Plains* (Macdonald Educational, 1978). (L) See review on page 93.

Makielski, S. J., 'The American Indian' (T) chapter 6 in Makielski, S. J., *Beleaguered Minorities: Cultural Politics in America* (San Francisco: W. H. Freeman, 1973).

Schools Council History 13–16 Project, *The American West: 1840–95* (Holmes McDougall, 1977). (U) An in-depth enquiry into certain aspects of this period which includes the life and culture of the Plains Indians.

United Society for the Propagation of the Gospel, *Testimony-Chief Seattle* (USPG, 15 Tufton Street, London WS1 3QQ; n.d.). (U) Resource pack including filmstrip and tape.

Wilson, J., *Canada's Indians,* MRG Report No. 21; new ed. March 1977. (T)

——, *The Original Americans: U.S. Indians,* MRG Report No. 31, October 1976. (T)

(c) *Inuit (Eskimo)*

Brody, H., *The People's Land: Eskimos and Whites in the Eastern Arctic* (Pelican, 1975). (T) An excellent account of the predicament of the Canadian Eskimo arising out of the insensitive impact of white culture. An antidote to all Inuit stereotypes.

Bugler, J., 'Which Comes First: the Whale or the Eskimo?' *The Observer* Colour Supplement, 25 June 1978. (T/U) Good photographs for wall display. Conservationist's moves to protect whales in turn threaten the livelihood of Point Hope in Alaska.

Hughes, J., *A Closer Look at Eskimos* (Hamish Hamilton, 1977). See review on page 92. (L)

The Inuit (Eskimos), Theatre Centre Ltd., 349 West End Lane, London NW6, 1981. (T)

d) Aborigine

Bennet, G., *Aboriginal Rights in International Law* (Royal Anthropological Institute in conjunction with Survival International, tel. 01 839 3267). (T)

Black Alternatives in Australia, August 1981 issue of *Social Alternatives*, from the University of Queensland. (T)

Coombs, H. C., *Australia's Policy Towards Aborigines: 1967–77*, MRG Report No. 35, March 1978. Note Aborigine comments, however. (T)

Gibbs, R. M., *The Aborigines* (Longman Australia, 1974). (T/U)

Hardy, F., *The Unlucky Australians* (Pan, 1978). (T)

Luling, V., *Aborigines*, Macdonald Surviving Peoples (Macdonald Educational, 1980). (L/U)

New Internationalist, 'Australia's Shame: The undermining of the Aborigines' No. 77, July 1979, special issue. (T) Articles on land rights, multinational mining companies, maps, facts etc.

Roberts, J., *From Massacres to Mining: The Colonisation of Aboriginal Australia* (War on Want/CIMRA, 1978). (T) The title speaks for itself; an excellent study of the Aboriginal struggle for rights.

—— (ed.), *The Mapoon Story by the Mapoon People* (Victoria, Aust.: International Development Action, 1975). See chapter 5. (T/U)

—— and McLean, D., *The Cape York Aluminium Companies and Native Peoples* (Victoria, Aust.: International Development Action, 1976). See chapter 5. (T/U)

——, Parsons, M. and Russell, B. (eds.), *The Mapoon Story According to the Invaders: Church Mission, Queensland Government and Mining Company* (Victoria, Aust.: International Development Action, 1975). See chapter 5. (T/U)

e) Migrant workers

Berger, J. and Mohr, J., *A Seventh Man: The Story of a Migrant Worker in Europe* (Penguin, 1975). (T/U) A moving series of photographs and extracts about the experiences of migrant workers from Mediterranean countries in Western Europe.

Montvalon, R. de, *The Aspirations of Young Migrant Workers in Western Europe*, Educational Studies and Documents No. 21, UNESCO, 1976. (T) An extremely useful study of the reasons for, and responses to, migration.

Padrun, R. and Guyot, J. *Migrant Women Speak* (Search Press and World Council of Churches, 1978). (T)

Power, J. and Hardman, A., *Western Europe's Migrant Workers*, MRG Report No. 28, rev. ed. 1978. (T)

SGS Associates, *Immigrants in Europe*, European Studies Unit 3, (Longman, 1974). (U) Articles and extracts for upper secondary and sixth-form pupils to work from.

f) Amerindians

CIMRA (see page 121 for address), *Natural People's News*. A newsletter packed with information and newspaper articles from all over the world on indigenous peoples. Very useful resource material for the classroom. (T)

——, *The Integration of the Indigenous Peoples of Roraima, Brazil* and *The Massacre at Panzos* (Guatemalan military kill protesting Indians). (T) Both produced by the International Workgroup for Indigenous Affairs and available from Colonialism and Indigenous Minorities Research and Action.

Hemming, J., *Red Gold: the Conquest of the Brazilian Indians* (Macmillan, 1978). (T) A detailed examination of the impact of European culture on an indigenous people, with a deep understanding of Indian values, customs and attitudes.

Moynahan, B., 'The Last Frontier: Brazil', *Sunday Times* Colour Supplement, 18 June 1978. Good photographs for display; the destruction of Indians and Indian culture as Whites move into Amazonia bringing 'progress' and 'development'. (T/U)

O'Shaughnessy, H. and Corry, S., *What Future for the Amerindians of South America?*, MRG Report No. 15, rev. ed. July 1977. (T)

Wachtel, N., *The Vision of the Vanquished: the Spanish Conquest of Peru through Indian Eyes* (Harvester Press, 1977). (T) An Indian view of the Spanish conquest of Mexico and Peru rather than the conquerors' view which has dominated historical writing.

g) Namibia

Counter Information Services (CIS) Anti-Reports, *The Rio Tinto Zinc Corporation Ltd.* (CIS, 9 Poland Street, London W1, 1972). (T) A revealing examination of the operations of RTZ in Namibia and other countries.

Fraenkel, P., *The Namibians of South West Africa*, MRG Report No. 19, rev. ed. 1978. (T)

(h) South Africa

Bernstein, H., *Steve Biko* (IDAF, 1978). (T) The life and death of this major figure in the black consciousness movement, the forty-sixth person to die in security police detention.

Christian Aid, *Family Life and Migrant Labour in South Africa* (London, 1979). An eight-page illustrated topic sheet for use in the classroom discussing the effect of apartheid on family life. (U)

Counter Information Services, *Black South Africa Explodes* (CIS, 1977). A detailed, dramatically illustrated, account of the uprisings of 1976. (T/U)

——, *Buying Time in South Africa* (CIS, 1978). (T) The role of western governments and investors in supporting apartheid.

Herbstein, D., *White Man, We Want to Talk to You* (Pelican, 1978). (T) A detailed background to, and description of, the uprisings in Soweto.

Sikakane, J., *A Window on Soweto* (IDAF, 1977). (T/U) A personal account of living in South Africa's largest township and the historical and social background to this experience.

Troup, F., *Forbidden Pastures* (London: International Defence and Aid Fund (IDAF) for South Africa, 1976). (T) Essential reading for any teacher dealing with South Africa in the classroom.

'Southern Africa: the Imprisoned Society' (portable exhibition of photographs), 80 photos, map and comprehensive display text. 'A powerful account of the systematic degradation of a people', *Times Educational Supplement*. IDAF. (U)

This is Apartheid: a Pictorial Introduction (IDAF, 1978). (U) Produced for International Anti-Apartheid Year (1978–79) at an especially low price (20p) to encourage widest possible use in colleges and schools.

Woods, D. *Biko* (Penguin, 1979). (T)

(i) Zimbabwe

International Defence and Aid Fund (IDAF), *Zimbabwe: the Facts About Rhodesia* (IDAF, 1977). (T) A clear and concise account of the history, government, economy of, and resistance to, white minority rule.

——, *Zimbabwe In Struggle* (an exhibition of 80 photographs). (U) (IDAF, 1978). An excellent portable exhibition in the form of twelve posters which include text.

(j) Sahara

Gretton, J., *Western Sahara: the Right for Self-determination*. (T) (London: Anti-Slavery Society for the Protection of Human Rights, 1976). Description of the struggle of the peoples of the Western Sahara against Morocco and Mauritania.

Marnham, P., *Nomads of the Sahel*, MRG Report No 33, July 1977. (T)

Mercer, J., *The Sahrawis of Western Sahara*, MRG Report No. 40, 1979. (T)

Oxby, C., *Pastoral Nomads and Development* (London International African Institute, 1975). (T)

(k) Chicanos

Interracial Books for Children (IBC), *Chicano Culture in children's books*. (T) Special issue of *IBC Bulletin*, vol. 5 (7/8), 1975.

Ludwig, E. and Santibanez, J., *The Chicanos: Mexican-American Voices* (Penguin, 1971). (T) A unique and striking anthology by and about Mexican Americans.

Steele, J., 'Mexamerica', *Guardian* Weekend report, Saturday November 11th 1978. (T) An up to the minute account of the problems faced by the original inhabitants of the South-west, an area taken from Mexico a century ago.

Steiner, S., *The Mexican Americans*, MRG Report No. 39, 1979. (T)

(l) United Kingdom

Bethnal Green and Stepney Trades Council, *Blood on the Streets: A Report on Racial Attacks in East London* (Bethnal Green and Stepney Trades Council, 58 Watney Street, London E1, 1978). (T)

Blakeley, M., *Nahda's Family* (A. and C. Black, 1977). (L) Factual and informative account of a Muslim family living in the north of England.

Commission for Racial Equality, *Ethnic Minorities in Britain: statistical data* (Community Relations Commission, (now CRE), 1976). (T)

Community Service Volunteers, *Greenham Gypsy Site: A Simulation Game* (CSV, 237 Pentonville Road, London N1 9NJ, 1975). (U) For upper secondary pupils; on problems faced by gypsies and the provisions local councils can and should make.

The Crossfield Family, *Seven of Us* (A. and C. Black, 1978). (L) The Crossfields live in London, the parents from Jamaica and the children born in Britain.

Krausz, E., *Ethnic Minorities in Britain* (Paladin, 1971). (T) The cultural background of the main ethnic minority groups, their reasons for migration, and their housing and employment situations.

Lyle, S., *Pavan is a Sikh* (A. and C. Black, 1977). (L) Beautifully illustrated and sensitive account of a Sikh family in London.

Mackinnon, K., *The Phoenix Bird Chinese Take-Away* (A. and C. Black, 1978). (L) An account of the Lee family in Glasgow and about Hong Kong where they came from.

ryce, K., *Endless Pressure* (Penguin Education, 1979). (T) A first-hand account of West Indian life-styles in a provincial British city.

unnymede Trust, *Ethnic Minorities in Britain: A Select Bibliography* (Runnymede Trust, 1977). (T)

——, *Ethnic Minorities in Society* (Community Relations Unit of the British Council of Churches, 1976). (T) A reference guide to patterns of immigration into the UK.

Waterson, M., *Gypsy Family* (A. and C. Black, 1978). (L) Description of a travelling gypsy family, their traditions and culture.

Watson, J. L. (ed.), *Between Two Cultures: Migrants and Minorities in Britain* (Blackwell, 1977). (T) Summarizes the research of twelve anthropologists on Pakistanis, Sikhs, Montserratians, Jamaicans, West Africans, Chinese, Poles, Italians, Greek and Turkish Cypriots.

Wilson, A., *Finding a Voice: Asian Women in Britain* (Virago, 1978). (T) The experiences of Asian women in Britain recorded for the first time in their own words.

8. Multi-ethnic education

Afro-Caribbean Educational Resource (ACER), *Images and Reflections: Education and the Afro-Caribbean Child* (ACER Project, Centre for Learning Resources, 275 Kennington Lane, London SE11 5QZ, 1981).

Bagley, C., *A Comparative Perspective on the Education of Black Children in Britain* (Manchester: Centre for Educational Disadvantage, 1978). (T)

Barrett, L., *The Rastafarians* (Heinemann, 1977). (T)

——, *The Sun and the Drum: African Roots in Jamaican Folk Tradition* (Heinemann, 1977). (T)

Bourdieu, P., 'The School as a Conservative Force: Scholastic and Cultural Inequalities' ch. 12 in Dale, R., Esland, G. and MacDonald, M. (eds.), *Schooling and Capitalism* (Routledge, 1976). (T)

Brennan, D. F. (ed.), *Calender of Religious Festivals* (R.E. Centre, West London Institute of Higher Education, Borough Road, Isleworth, Middlesex TW7 5DU). (T/U)

Coard, B., *How the West Indian Child is Made Educationally Sub-normal in the British School System* (New Beacon, 1971). (T)

Commission for Racial Equality (CRE), *Schools and Ethnic Minorities: Comments on 'Education in Schools: a Consultative Document' Issued by the DES* (CRE, February 1978). A memorandum from the CRE. (T)

——, *Education of Ethnic Minorities: Comments on the Consultative Document Issued by the DES on the Report on the West Indian Community issued by the Select Committee on Race Relations and Immigration* A memorandum from the CRE, October 1977. (T)

Community Relations Commission (CRC), *The Education of Ethnic Minority Children: From the Perspectives of Parents, Teachers and Education authorities* (CRC (now the CRE), 1977). (T)

Dhondy, F., 'Teaching Young Blacks', *Race Today*, May/June 1978. (T) See also replies to Dhondy's article in *Race Today*, Sept./Oct. 1978.

Dumont, R. V. and Wax, M. L., 'Cherokee School Society and the Intercultural Classroom', ch. 10 in *School and Society: A Sociological Reader*, Cosin, B. R., Dale, I. R., Esland, G. M., Mackinnon, D. and Swift, D. F. (eds.), (Routledge, 1971). (T)

Edwards, V., *West Indian Language: Attitudes and the School* (National Association for Multiracial Education, 1977). (T)

—— and Sutcliffe, D., 'Broadly Speaking', *Times Educational Supplement*, 13 October 1978, p. 19. On Creole in the classroom. (T)

Fisher, G., 'Learning Strategies in the Multi-ethnic Context', *Multiracial School*, vol. 5 (3), Summer 1977. (T)

Haringey, London Borough of, *Racialist Activities in Schools* (Haringey Education Service, Somerset Rd., Tottenham, London N17 9EH, July 1978). (T) Guidelines produced by the Council at the request of recognized teachers' associations.

ILEA Learning Materials Service, *Lifestyles of Cyprus; Caribbean Lifestyles;* and *Some Lifestyles of Chinese People from Hong Kong and Singapore*. Booklets for teachers. (T)

James, A., 'The Core Curriculum and Multiracial Schools', *Multiracial School*, vol. 6 (1), Winter 1977. (T)

James, A., and Jeffcoate, R. (eds.), *The School in the Multicultural Society* (Harper and Row, 1981).

Jeffcoate, R., *Positive Image: Towards a Multiracial Curriculum* (Chameleon Books, Writers' and Readers' Publishing Co-operative, 1979). (T) A useful contribution to some of the main issues in multi-ethnic education.

Keddie, N. (ed.), *Tinker, tailor ... the Myth of Cultural Deprivation* (Penguin, 1973). (T)

Khan, V. S., *Bilingualism and Linguistic Minorities in Britain* (Runnymede Trust, 1977). (T)

Little, A., *Educational Policies for Multiracial Areas* (University of London, Goldsmith's College, 1978). (T)

Milner, D., *Children and Race* (Penguin Education, 1975). (T) Extremely useful account of how racial prejudice develops in children, the effects of this on black children, and ways to combat prejudice.

National Association for Multiracial Education, *New Approaches in Multiracial Education* — the official journal of NAME comes out termly and contains a wide variety of articles on multicultural issues in education. (T) *Issues in Race and Education* — a twice-termly paper produced by members of the London NAME branch, available from 11 Carleton Gardens, Brecknock Road, London N19 5AQ. (T)

National Union of Teachers, *All Our Children* (NUT, Jan. 1978). (T) NUT views and initiatives on multi-ethnic education.

——, *Race, Education, Intelligence: A Teacher's Guide to the Facts and the Issues* (NUT, Sept. 1978). (T)

Rai, U., 'Enthusiasm and discipline give hope to the children who lag behind', *Times Educational Supplement*, 10 November 1978, p. 10. (T) Short article on supplementary schools.

Reiss, C., *Education of Travelling Children*, Schools Council Research Studies (Macmillan, 1975). (T)

Searle, C., *The Forsaken Lover: White Words and Black People* (Penguin, 1973). (T) Illustrates through children's writing the crisis of identity that can face black children using a language that devalues their culture.

——, *The World in a Classroom* (London: Writers' and Readers' Publishing Co-operative, 1977). (T/U) The writings of students in an East London secondary school about racism, the minority experience and their local area.

Sikes, P. J. (ed.), *Teaching About Race Relations*, National Association for Race Relations Teaching (University of East Anglia, 1979).

Snyder, P. A. and Stone, F. A., *Minority Education in Global Perspective*, Proceedings of the World Education Workshop (University of Connecticut School of Education, 1972). (T) Wide-ranging selection of papers on the education of minority group children in various parts of the world.

Stone, M., *The Education of the Black Child in Britain* (Fontana, 1981).

Street-Porter, R., *Race, Children and Cities* (Open University, E361, Block V, 1978).

Tankits, *1. The Nazis and British Racism; 2. Multicultural Rhymes and Stories for the 5–8s; 3. Women and the Nazis; 4. 'John Bull'; 5. The Roots of British Racism Show* (Tankits, PO Box 151, London WC2, 1978). (U) Five separate packs of material aimed at showing how to combat racism.

Teachers' Action, 'Issue on Multi-ethnic Education', No. 9. Distributed by Publications Distribution Co-operative, 27 Clerkenwell Close, London EC1. (T)

Teaching London Kids, Issue on teaching Black students No. 11, 1978. 79 Ronald Road, London N5. (T)

Taylor, F., *Race, School and Community: A Survey of Research and Literature on Education in Multiracial Britain* (NFER, 1974). (T)

Twitchen, J., *Multicultural Education* (BBC, 1981).

Union of Muslim Organizations, *Guidelines and Syllabus on Islamic Education* (Union of Muslim Organizations of the UK and Ireland, 1976). (T)

Verma, G., 'Teaching Styles and Race Relations: Some Effects on White Teenagers', *New Era*, vol. 59 (2), March/April 1978. (T)

—— and Bagley, C. (eds.), *Race and Education Across Cultures* (Heinemann, 1975). (T)

Walvin, J., 'Much More than a Side Show' *Times Educational Supplement*, 6 October 1978, p. 36. (T) Teaching about minorities and British black history.

4. Race relations

Baxter, P. and Sansom, P., *Race and Social Difference* (Penguin, 1972). (T)

Bowker, G. and Carrier, J. (eds.), *Race and Ethnic Relations: Sociological Readings* (Hutchinson, 1976) (T)

Community Relations Commission, *Five Views of Multi-racial Britain* (CRC (now CRE), 1978). Full texts of talks on race relations broadcast on BBC TV by Professor John Rex, Dr Stuart Hall, Dr Bhikhu Parekh, Professor Alan Little and Bishop Trevor Huddleston. (T)

——, *Race Relations in Britain: A Select Bibliography* (CRC (now CRE), 1976). (T)

Deakin, N., *Colour, Citizenship and British Society* Modern Society (Panther, 1970). (T)

Dummett, A., *A Portrait of English Racism* (Penguin 1973). (T)

Fanon, F., *Black Skin White Masks* (Paladin, 1970). (T)

Husband, C. (ed.), *White Media and Black Britain: A Critical Look at the Role of the Media in Race Relations Today* (Arrow, 1975). (T)

Khan, N., *The Arts Britain Ignores: The Arts of Ethnic Minorities in Britain* (Gulbenkian Foundation and CRC (now CRE), 1976). (T) A report to the Arts Council of Great Britain.

Miles, R. and Phizacklea, A., *Racism and Political Action in Britain* (Routledge, 1979). (T)

Morrison, L., *As They See It: A Race Relations Study of Three Areas from a Black Viewpoint* (CRC (now CRE), 1976). (T)

Rex, J. and Tomlinson, S., *Colonial Immigrants in a British City* (Routledge and Kegan Paul, 1979).

mith, D. J., *Racial Disadvantage in Britain* (Penguin, 1977). (T) One of the most recent and thorough documentations of the extent of racial discrimination in education, housing and employment.

. Attitudes, prejudice, racism

anton, M., *The Idea of Race* (Tavistock, 1977). (T)

arnie, J., 'Children's attitudes to other nationalities ...' in *The Development Puzzle: A Sourcebook for Teaching about World Development* (Centre for World Development Education, 1978). (T)

dgar, D., *Racism, Facism and the Politics of the National Front* (Institute of Race Relations, 1977). (T)

hrlich, H. J., *The Social Psychology of Prejudice* (Wiley, 1973), (T) A systematic review of everything published in the English language up to 1973.

lodge, J. L., Struckmann, D. K. and Trost, D. L., *Cultural Bases of Racism and Group Oppression: An Examination of Traditional 'Western' concepts, values and institutional structures which support Racism, Sexism and Elitism* (Two Riders Press, P.O. Box 4129, Berkeley, California 94704, USA, 1975). (T) The title speaks for itself. An important book for understanding the consequences of a Western perspective throughout history and today.

looper, F., *The Language of Prejudice*, Connections Series (Penguin, 1969). (U) Suitable for upper secondary pupils.

Jurman, A., *As Others See Us*, Network Social Studies (Edward Arnold, 1977). (U) On attitudes and prejudice.

Kiernan, V. G., *The Lords of Human Kind: European Attitudes to the Outside World in the Imperial Age* (Penguin, 1972). (T)

Killingray, D., *A Plague of Europeans: Westerners in Africa Since the Fifteenth Century*, Topics in History (Penguin Education, 1973). (U)

Littlewood, R. and Lipsedge, M., *Aliens and Alienists: Ethnic Minorities and Psychiatry* (Pelican, 1982).

New Internationalist 'The Colours of Injustice' Special issue on race, no. 59, January 1978 (T)

Race Today, the Voice of the Black Community in Britain, 74 Shakespeare Rd., London SE24 (T)

Tinker, H. *Race, Conflict and the International Order: From Empire to United Nations* (Macmillan, 1977). (T)

Walker, M. *The National Front* (Fontana/Collins, 1977). (T)

6. Resource evaluation

Children's Rights Workshop, *Children's Book Bulletin*. On non-racist books and resources. (T)

——, *Racist and Sexist Images in Children's Books* (Writers' and Readers' Publishing Co-operative, 1975). (T) A collection of ten articles which in various ways examine racist and sexist bias in children's literature.

Council on Interracial Books for Children (CIBC) *Bulletin* and other resources on non-racist approaches to education (CIBC, 1841 Broadway, New York, N.Y. 10023.)

Dixon, Bob, *Catching Them Young, I: Sex, Race and Class in Children's Fiction* (Pluto Press, 1977). (T) A survey of the ruling attitudes of children's fiction: sexism, racism and middle-class bias towards social divisions.

Hicks, D. W., *Images of the World: An Introduction to Bias in Teaching Materials*, Occasional Paper No. 2, Centre for Multicultural Education, University of London Institute of Education, 1980.

——, *Bias in Geography Textbooks: Images of the Third World and Multi-ethnic Britain*, Working Paper No. 1, Centre for Multicultural Education, University of London Institute of Education, 1981.

Hoyles, Martin (ed.), *The Politics of Literacy* (Writers' and Readers' Publishing Co-operative, 1977). (T) Includes sections on sexism and racism as well as on class and culture and the meaning of literacy.

Kuya, Dorothy, 'The unacceptable face of publishing'. *Times Educational Supplement*, 22 July 1977. (T)

Marsden, W. E., 'Stereotyping and Third World Geography', *Teaching Geography*', vol. I, no. 5, July 1976. (T)

National Committee on Racism in Childrens Books (NCRCB), *The Dragon's Teeth*, Bulletin of NCRCB. Available from The Methodist Church, 240 Lancaster Rd., London W11. (T)

Prieswerk, R. (ed.) *The Slant of the Pen: Racism in Children's Books* (Geneva: World Council of Churches, 1980).

Worrall, Mary, 'Roots and Change in Children's Literature', *New Era*, vol. 58, no. 2, March/April 1977. (T) A review of a number of children's books, mainly fiction and poetry, about or from the Caribbean and South Asia.

Zimet, Sara Goodman, *Print and Prejudice* (Hodder and Stoughton, 1976). (T) A study of the influence of the printed media on the reader with particular reference to minority groups, racism and sexism.

7. World studies

Reference was made in chapter 6 to the overlap between multi-ethnic education and development education. Other overlapping fields would also be International Education, World Studies, Peace Education, teaching about the Third

World. A few selected references are given below to signpost the way into these fields of study.

Buergenthal, T. and Torney, J. V., *International Human Rights and International Education* (US National Commission for UNESCO, Dept. of State, Washington, D.C. 20520; 1976). (T)

Haavelsrud, M. (ed.), *Education for Peace: Reflection and Action*, Proceedings of the First World Conference of the World Council for Curriculum and Instruction, University of Keele, 1974. (IPC Science and Technology Press, 1975). (T)

Hanvey, R. G., *An Attainable Global Perspective* (available from Center for War/Peace Studies, 218 East 18th Street, New York, N.Y. 10003; 1976). (T)

Hicks, D. W., 'Global Perspectives in the Curriculum: A Geographical Contribution', *Geography* 64 (2), April 1979. (T)

——, 'Racial Justice, Global Development or Peace: Which Shall We Choose in School?' *World Studies Journal* 2 (4), 1981.

——, and Townley, C. (eds.), *Teaching World Studies: An Introduction to Global Perspectives in the Curriculum* (Longman, 1982).

Jackson, R., 'Why teach about World Religions: A Review of Some of the Reasons', *New Era*, vol. 59 (2), March/April 1978. (T)

New Era, 'Internationalising the Curriculum', special issue, vol. 59 (4), July/August 1978; available from World Studies Project. (T) Also see other issues for articles on innovatory developments in this field.

New Internationalist, 'The Message of Islam', No. 67, September 1978. (T)

——, 'Answering Back: The Questions People Are Asking about World Poverty' no. 68, October 1978. (T/U)

Ministry of Overseas Development, *Development Education*, Overseas Development Paper No. 14; Report and Recommendations by Working Party of the Advisory Committee on Development Education, 1978. (T)

Rogers, E., *Thinking About Human Rights* (Lutterworth, 1978). (T)

Schools Council/Rowntree Project, *World Studies 8–13*, Interim Papers available from Simon Fisher, 12 Fairfield Road, Bedminster, Bristol BS3 1LG or Centre for Peace Studies, St. Martin's College, Lancaster LA1 3JD.

Worral, M., 'Multiracial Britain and the Third World: Tensions and Approaches in the Classroom', *New Era*, vol. 59 (2), March/April 1978. (T)

Wright, J. and Wright, D., *The Changing World in the Classroom* VCOAD (now Centre for World Development Education, 1974). (T)

Wright, D., 'Third World Teaching: Which Way Now?' *Times Educational Supplement*, supplement on Geography, 10 November 1978. (T)

8. Political education

Cobden Trust, *Rights, Responsibilities and the Law Introduction and Bibliography for Teachers*, 18 King's Cross Road, London WC1, (Cobden Trust 1978). (T)

Crick, B. and Heater, D., *Essays on Political Education* (Falmer Press, 1977). (T)

—— and Porter, A. (eds.), *Political Education and Political Literacy* (Longman, 1978). (T)

Hutchinson, A., 'A note on the growth of a political perspective within teaching for international understanding', *Cambridge Journal of Education*, Vol. 8 (2/3), 1978. (T)

Hansard Society, *A Programme for Political Education: An explanatory paper* (Hansard Society, 12 Gower Street, London WC1E 6DP, 1974). (T)

Hansard Society, *A Programme for Political Education* (T)

Lister, I., *The Aims and Methods of Political Education in Schools*, (Political Education Research Unit University of York, 1976). (T)

9. Other Guides and Handbooks

Africa: A Teachers' Handbook, Killingray, M. (School of Oriental and African Studies, 1978).

Anthropology: Teachers' Resource Guide (Royal Anthropological Institute, 1976).

The Cartoon as an Instrument of Political Education IDAC Document No. 7 (Institute of Cultural Action 27 Chemin des Crets 1218, Grand Saconnex, Geneva)

Debate and Decision: Schools in a World of Change Richardson R., Flood, M. and Fisher, S. (World Studies Project, 1979).

The Development Puzzle: A Sourcebook for Teaching about World Development (Centre for World Development Education, 1978).

Development Studies: A Handbook for Teachers, Jones P., Morgan, R., Shipton-Smith, R. and Wright, D. (School of Oriental and African Studies, 1977).

Education for Justice, Wren, B. (SCM Press, 1977).

Education: the Practice of Freedom, Freire, Paulo (Writers' and Readers' Publishing Co-operative, 1974).

An Experience-Centred Curriculum: Exercises in Perception, Communication and Action, Wolsk, D. (UNESCO, 1975).

The Friendly Classroom for a Small Planet: A Handbook on Creative Approaches to Living and Problem-Solving for Children, Prutzman, P. *et al.* (Wayne, N.J.: Avery Publishing Group, 1978).

Guide to Teaching Anthropology in Schools and Colleges, Bulmer Joan (School of Oriental and African Studies, 1977).

Gronks and Friends: the Social Labelling and Group Identity Game (Cockpit Arts Workshop, Gateforth Street, Marylebone, London NW8 8EH, 1976).

Introducing World History (School of Oriental and African Studies, 1978).

Learning for Change in World Society: Reflections, Activities, Resources, compiled by Robin Richardson (World Studies Project, 1976; revised 1979).

A Manual on Non-violence and Children, Judson, S. (ed.) (Non-violence and Children Program, Friends Peace Committee, 1515 Cherry Street, Philadelphia PA19102).

Perspectives on World Religions: A Handbook for Teachers, Jackson, R. (ed.), (School of Oriental and African Studies, 1978).

Race in the Curriculum, reprints from *Education and Community Relations*, 1977 (Commission for Racial Equality).

Seeing and Perceiving: Films in a World of Change, Taylor, N. and Richardson, R. (Ikon Productions and Concord Films Council, 1979).

Teaching About Africa, reprints from *Education and Community Relations*, 1974/5 (Commission for Racial Equality).

Teaching About Islam, reprint from *Education and Community Relations*, May/June 1976 (Commission for Racial Equality).

Teaching in the Multiracial Primary School, reprints from *Education and Community Relations*, 1975 (Commission for Racial Equality).

White Student Black World: A Handbook for Action against Racism, Wilson, Maggie (Third World First, 1978).

The World of Islam: A Teachers' Handbook, Tames, Richard (School of Oriental and African Studies, 1977).

World Religions: A Handbook for Teachers, Cole, Owen (ed.), (Commission for Racial Equality in conjunction with SHAP Working Party on World Religions in Education, 1976).

World Studies: Resource Guide (Council for Education in World Citizenship, 1980).

Film Catalogue: Community and Race Relations (Commission for Racial Equality, 1978).

Catalogue of 16mm Films 1978–9 (Concord Films Council, 201 Felixstowe Road, Ipswich, Suffolk IP3 9BJ, tel.: 0473 76012).

10. Organizations

Afro-Caribbean Educational Resource Project, Centre for Learning Resources, 275 Kennington Lane, London SE11 5QF. (01-582-2771)

Aklowa: Centre for Traditional African Drumming and Dancing, Takeley House, Brewers End, Takeley, Essex CM22 6QJ. (0279 871062)

All London Teachers Against Racism and Facism (ALTARF), c/o Lambeth Teachers' Centre, Santley Street, London SW4.

American-Indian Movement (AIM), UK Committee, 6 Woodland Road, Birmingham 31. (021-476-7003)

Amnesty International, Tower House, 8-14 Southampton Street, London WC2E 7HF.

Anti-Nazi League/Teachers Against the Nazis, 12 Little Newport Street, London WC2. (01-734-5456)

Anti-Slavery Society for the Protection of Human Rights, 60 Weymouth Street, London W1N 4DX. (01-935-6498)

Bogle L'Ouverture Publications, 5a Chigwell Place, Ealing, London W13. For Afro-Caribbean materials.

Books from India, 69 Great Russell Street, London WC1.

Centre for Human Rights and Responsibilities, 16 Ponsonby Street, London SW1. (01-834-2457)

Centre for Peace Studies, St. Martin's College, Lancaster LA1 3JD.

Centre for Urban Educational Studies, 34 Aberdeen Park, London N5. (01-226-5437)

Centre for World Development Education, 128 Buckingham Palace Road, London SW1V 1JS. (01-730-8332/3)

Children's Rights Workshop, 4 Aldebert Terrace, London SW8 1BH. (01-582 4483)

Christian Aid, Education Dept., PO Box 1, London SW9. (01-733-5500)

Churches Commission for Participation in Development, PO Box No. 66, 150 Route de Ferney, 1211 Geneva 20.

Cockpit Theatre in Education, Gateforth Street, Marylebone, London NW8 8EH.

Collins Children's Books, 14 St James's Place, London SW1A 1PS. Awards for multi-ethnic books.

Colonialism and Indigenous Minorities Research and Action (CIMRA), 218 Liverpool Road, London N1.

Commission for Racial Equality, Education Officer, Elliot House, 10/12 Allington Street, London SW1E 5EH. (01-828-7022)

Commonwealth Institute, Kensington High Street, London W8 6NQ.

Council for Education in World Citizenship (CEWC), Cobham House, 26 Blackfriars Lane, London EC4V 6EB. (01-236 0348)

Half Moon Photography Workshop, Produce Camerawork, special issue No. 8 on Lewisham; 119/121 Roman Road, London E2.

ILEA Learning Materials Service, Highbury Station Road, London N1.

Institute of Race Relations, 247-9 Pentonville Road, London N1 4NG. (01-837-0041)

International Defence and Aid Fund for Southern Africa, 104-5 Newgate Street, London EC1A 7AP. (01-606-6123)

International Labour Organisation, Dolcis House, 87/91 New Bond Street, London W1Y 9LA.

International Workgroup for Indigenous Affairs, c/o Colonialism and Indigenous Minorities Research and Action (CIMRA), see above.

The Islamic Foundation, 223 London Road, Leicester LE2 1ZE. (0533 700725)

Minority Rights Group, 36 Craven Street, London WC2N 5NG. (01-930-6659)

Namibia Support Committee, 21–5 Tabernacle Street, London EC2.

National Association for Multiracial Education, General Secretary: Madeleine Blakeley, 86 Station Road, Mickleover, Derby DE3 5FP. (0283 702848) Termly journal: *New Approaches in Multiracial Education.* Exhibition on Racial Bias in Learning Materials.

National Association for Race Relations Teaching and Action Research (NARTAR), c/o Centre for Applied Research in Education, University of East Anglia, Norwich NR4 7TJ.

National Committee on Racism in Children's Books, The Methodist Church, 240 Lancaster Road, London W11.

National Council for Civil Liberties, 186 King's Cross Road, London WC1. (01-278-4575)

National Gypsy Council, 61 Blenheim Crescent, London W11 2EG. (01-727 2916)

New Beacon Books, 71 Stroud Green Road, London N14.

New Internationalist, Monthly; 62a High Street, Wallingford, Oxon OX10 0EE. (0491 37800)

Onaway Trust, 275 Main Street, Shadwell, Leeds, W. Yorks LS17 8LH. (0532-659611) Concerned with preserving native cultures, especially Native American.

Oxfam Education Department, 274 Banbury Road, Oxford OX2 7D2 (0865-56777)

Romenastan Publications, 119 Blenheim Crescent, London W11 2EQ. (01-727 2916) Materials on Gypsy issues.

Royal Anthropological Institute, 56 Queen Anne Street, London W1M 9LA.

Runnymede Trust, 62 Chandos Place, London WC2N 4HH. (01-836-3266) Reports on race relations.

Sahara Action Committee, 9 Poland St., London W1. Supports self-determination for Saharan peoples.

Schools Cultural Studies Project, The New University of Ulster, Coleraine BT52 1SA, N. Ireland. Materials from the SCSP are available from the Association of Teachers of Cultural and Social Studies, c/o the Coleraine Regional Teachers Centre, Coleraine, Co. Derry, Northern Ireland.

School Kids Against the Nazis (SKAN), 12 Little Newport Street, London WC2.

School of Oriental and African Studies, Extra-Mural Department, University of London, Malet Street, London WC1.

Survival International, 36 Craven Street, London WC2N 5NG. (01-839 3267) Concerned with threatened tribal peoples.

Third World First, 232 Cowley Road, Oxford OX4 1UH. (0865-45678)

Third World Publications, 151 Stratford Road, Birmingham B11 1RD. (021-773 6572)

Ujamaa Centre Loan Service, Multi-ethnic Development and Third World Studies Centre, Oxfam Education Dept.; 14 Brixton Rd., London SW9. (01-582 2068)

Union of Muslim Organisations of UK and Ireland, 30 Baker Street, London W1M 2DS. (01-229 0538)

War on Want, 467 Caledonian Road, London N7 9BE.

World Studies Project, c/o One World Trust, 24 Palace Chambers, Bridge Street, London SW1. (01-930-7661) Back copies of *New Era* available.

World Studies Teacher Education Network, c/o Westminster College, North Hinksey, Oxford OX2 9AT.

Index